IN HER PRIME

IN HER PRIME

A New View
of Middle-Aged Women

WITHDRAWI

JUDITH K. BROWN
VIRGINIA KERNS
AND CONTRIBUTORS

foreword by Beatrice Blyth Whiting

BERGIN & GARVEY PUBLISHERS, INC.
Massachusetts

Acknowledgments: Several people helped us turn a manuscript into a book. Our thanks to Alan Bayer who made it possible; to Shanti Jeyanayagam for her many hours of work and for grace under pressure; to Susan Hill Gross and Bradley Hertel who generously offered photographs; and to Linda Coffey for tying up the loose ends.

Photo credits: p. 22, Richard B. Lee; p. 36, Jacqueline S. Solway; p. 48, Dorothy Ayers Counts; p. 66, Michael Lambek; p. 86, Virginia Kerns; p. 100, Janice Boddy; p. 116, Karen P. Sinclair; p. 136, Bradley H. Hertel; p. 154, Douglas Raybeck; p. 172, Susan Hill Gross; p. 180, Maurice Brown.

Library of Congress Cataloging in Publication Data
Main entry under title:

In her prime.

Bibliography: end of chapters
Includes index.
1. Middle-aged women—Cross-cultural studies
I. Brown, Judith K.   II. Kerns, Virginia, 1948–
GN479.7.I5 1985   305.2'44   84-14671
ISBN 0-89789-056-6
ISBN 0-89789-059-0 (pbk.)

First published in 1985 by
Bergin & Garvey Publishers, Inc.
670 Amherst Road
South Hadley, Massachusetts 01075

Permission to reprint table on p. 176 granted by The Johns Hopkins University Press.

56780   987654321

Printed in the United States of America

CONTENTS

TABLES

FIGURES

CONTRIBUTORS

Aaron Antonovsky
Ben-Gurion University of the Negev, Israel
Janice Boddy, Department of Anthropology
University of Toronto, Canada
Judith K. Brown, Department of Sociology & Anthropology
Oakland University, USA
Dorothy Counts, Department of Anthropology
University of Waterloo, Canada
Nancy Datan, Department of Psychology
West Virginia University, USA
David Gutmann, Division of Clinical Psychology
Northwestern University Medical School, USA
Patricia Kaufert, Department of Social & Preventive Medicine
University of Manitoba, Canada
Virginia Kerns
New Delhi, India
Barbara King, Department of Anthropology
University of Oklahoma, USA
Michael Lambek, Department of Anthropology
University of Toronto, Canada
Jane Lancaster, Department of Anthropology
University of Oklahoma, USA
Richard Lee, Department of Anthropology
University of Toronto, Canada
Benjamin Maoz
Ben-Gurion University of the Negev, Israel
Douglas Raybeck, Department of Anthropology
Hamilton College, USA
Jacqueline Solway, Department of Anthropology
University of Toronto, Canada
Karen Sinclair, Department of Sociology & Anthropology
Eastern Michigan University, USA
Sylvia Vatuk, Department of Anthropology
University of Illinois at Chicago Circle, USA

FOREWORD

The descriptive data presented in this volume will enable social scientists to assess the similarities and differences in the experiences of middle-aged women in a variety of societies. Judith Brown and Virginia Kerns are to be complimented for stimulating cross-cultural research on the development of women. Kerns' pioneering studies of older women (1979, 1980, 1983) are well-known. Judith Brown's earlier research on rituals at menarche (1963, 1981) has stimulated detailed analyses of female transition ceremonies (e.g., Paige and Paige 1981). Her recent article in Current Anthropology (Brown 1982) was the impetus to the writing of the chapters collected in this volume. Tracing themes suggested in the article, they describe the status of women, their rights and privileges, and their daily routines during their middle years, a period of life that until recently has been neglected. In the popular media in the United States "middle age" has often been characterized as a period of depression and aimlessness, concerned with the loss of children, beauty and sexual pleasure. This volume presents a welcomed new perspective.

Anthropologists during the last decades have contributed greatly to our understanding of human development over the life course. The work of primatologists, biological and psychological anthropologists has broadened our perspective on the similarities and differences in the human experience across time and geographic areas. Without comparative data psychologists and other social scientists have no way of assessing the relative contribution of nature and culture to the cognitive, emotional and social behavior of individuals growing up in the United States or Western Europe. It is from populations in these countries that the majority of generalizations about human development are drawn. If we are to be sure that the generalizations will hold true they must be subjected to the widest possible spectrum of conditions.

There are promising indications that theories that hold across all societies can be developed. The recent research of anthropologists and cross-cultural psychologists indicates that universal and testable theories of human development are possible. Similarity has been found across a variety of cultures in the cognitive abilities of children as they mature during the first years of their lives. Piagetian theories of cognitive development during the preadolescent years have been tested in many parts of the world and, although the rate of development varies between societies, it progresses in a similar way (for review articles see Kagan 1981; Price-Williams 1971; Cole and Scribner 1974; Cole, Gay, Glick and Sharp 1971). Continuing research on the development of infants promises new insights into the relative impact of neurophysiology and socialization on infant growth and development (Chisholm 1983; Howrigan 1984; Kagan 1981; Super 1981; Super and Harkness 1982). Through collaboration among researchers the definition of the important variables has been agreed upon and viable techniques of measurement designed. As a result, comparable studies of infants have been made or are in progress in many parts of the world.

Progress in the development of a science of human development is only possible when researchers are willing to include the same variables in their studies and use techniques of measurement that produce comparable data. They must be willing to replicate studies, attempting to adapt the design to local cultural conditions to the best of their ability. Without this comparable data collected in a wide variety of societies, the progress toward a social and developmental science is impossible.

Anthropologists collect the data on which comparative studies can be based. Very often, however, when researchers attempt to use ethnographies, they find that the data they need to test their theories are not available. This is inevitable. No ethnography can anticipate all the information that is required. Describing in detail all the aspects of the culture and social behavior of a society is a monumental task, one that few modern anthropologists would venture to try. The sense of emergency that motivated anthropologists in the early decades of the century to attempt to record the culture of isolated, unknown communities has been replaced by more focused problem-oriented studies. Collaborative research in societies allows for a variety of these detailed studies. The testing of social science theories depends on these types of study, especially those that are so designed and described as to make replication in other environments possible.

The problems selected for focused study change with the intellectual climate and the preoccupations of social scientists. Most recently, the feminist movement has instigated detailed studies of the lives of women. Anthropologists motivated by recurrent interest in the relative power of nature and culture to shape the development of men and women have focused on the lives of women in the non-western societies where they have studied.

One of the most important contributions of this volume is the documenting of the need for a transcultural definition of "middle age." It is clear that etic and emic definitions are required, the former based on identifiable physiological changes in a woman's body, the latter a sociocultural definition with its associated role specifications. In this volume Raybeck suggests a definition which is the most clearly of the first type: "by middle-age, I refer to the period that generally begins near the onset of menopause in the middle to late thirties and gradually ends with the decline of physical vigor around the mid-fifties" (p. 156). Each individual chapter gives the authors' judgments as to whether middle-age is identified as a discrete age grade in the societies they studied and how it is defined. The chapters describe the sociocultural environments which are associated with the emic definitions.

The descriptive material, assembled by Virginia Kerns and Judith Brown is drawn from societies in many parts of the world that vary in the complexity of their subsistence activities and in their ideologies as to the role of men and women. The focal interests of the authors and their research methods ensure that a wide variety of cultural conditions are described. The contribution of a primatologist, medical anthropologists and a developmental psychologist add breadth to the presentations. However, despite the variety of cultural niches, there is a commitment among the authors to comment on Judith Brown's conclusion in the Current Anthropology article that there are similar changes in the lives of women. They present their descriptive data with reference to the transcultural variables identified in her article thus enabling the authors and the readers of the volume to evaluate the possibility of developing a universal and coherent theory of the developmental changes in women's lives in the middle years and the way in which these changes are channeled by the physical and social environment.

I commend this volume as an example of how one should initiate cross-cultural studies; defining the problem to be explored, reviewing the data that are available for comparison, identifying cultural domains that need to be detailed, and developing and exploring the validity of hypotheses concerning the contextual conditions that may illuminate similarities and differences in the cultural patterns that are being explored. It is fortunate that *In Her Prime* is published and that a wider audience can benefit by the work of the authors to analyze the structure of women's lives in diverse cultural environments during the period that is defined by the universal physiological changes that occur at the beginning of the onset of menopause and end when women have perceptible physical deterioration.

Beatrice Blyth Whiting
Henry A. Murray
Research Center

REFERENCES

Brown, Judith K.
  1963 A Cross-Cultural Study of Female Initiation Rites. American Anthropologist 65: 837–853.
  1981 Cross-Cultural Perspectives on the Female Life Cycle. *In* Handbook of Cross-Cultural Human Development. R. H. Munroe, R. L. Munroe, and B. B. Whiting, eds., pp. 581–610. New York: Garland STPM Press.
  1982 Cross-cultural Perspectives on Middle-aged Women. Current Anthropology 23: 143–156.

Chisholm, J.
  1983 An Ethological Study of Child Development. New York: Aldine Press.

Cole, M., J. Gay, J. A. Glick, and D. W. Sharp
  1971 The Cultural Context of Learning and Thinking. New York: Basic Books.

Cole, M., and S. Scribner
  1974 Culture and Thought. New York: John Wiley.

Howrigan, G. A.
  1984 Making Mothers from Adolescents: Context and Experience in Maternal Behavior in Yucatan. Thesis presented to the Harvard Graduate School of Education.

Kagan, J.
  1981 Universals in Human Development. *In* Handbook of Cross-Cultural Human Development. R. H. Munroe, R. L. Munroe, and B. B. Whiting, eds., pp. 53–63. New York: Garland STPM Press.

Kerns, Virginia
  1979 Social Transition at Menopause. Paper presented at the Annual Meeting of the American Anthropological Association, Cincinnati.
  1980 Aging and Mutual Support Relations Among the Black Carib. *In* Aging in Culture and Society. Christine Fry ed., pp. 112–125. New York: Praeger/Bergin & Garvey.
  1983 Women and the Ancestors: Black Carib Kinship and Ritual. Urbana: University of Illinois Press.

Paige, K. E., and J. W. Paige
  1981 The Politics of Reproductive Ritual. Berkeley: University of California Press.

Price-Williams, D.
  1975 Explorations in Cross-Cultural Psychology. San Francisco: Chandler and Sharp Publishers.

Super, C. M.
  1981 Behavioral Development in Infancy. *In* Handbook of Cross-Cultural Human Development. R. H. Munroe, R. L. Munroe, and B. B. Whiting, eds., pp. 181–271. New York: Garland STPM Press.

Super, C. M., and S. Harkness
  1982 The Infant's Niche in Rural Kenya and Metropolitan America. *In* Cross-Cultural Research at Issue. L. L. Adler, ed., pp. 47–55. New York: Academic Press.

*To Pauline M. Kolenda — colleague,
mentor, and friend — whose
encouragement and support made this book possible.*

Introduction

Judith K. Brown

The subject of this book is unique: middle-aged women in developmental, cross-cultural and evolutionary perspective. It is the first book of its kind, resulting from two relatively new trends within anthropology. Only in the past decade has there been a strong interest in an anthropology of women. And the development of an anthropology of aging is still more recent. The chapters that follow combine these contemporary trends within anthropology, providing a new look at the worlds of middle-aged women.

There have been earlier studies of older women, but the pioneering cross-cultural research by Bart (1969), Griffen (1977), Kaufert (1979), and Kerns (1979, 1980) of necessity tended toward inclusiveness. Grandmotherhood, menopause, the status of the aged, and a whole variety of topics were considered, simply because *any* relevant data were difficult to find. For example, Bart surveyed information from the more than 700 societies in the Human Relations Area Files, but she found appropriate entries for a cross-cultural sample of only 30 societies. Today there is more information and the research has become more focused. An entire literature has developed on menopause including a special issue of *Maturitas*, edited by Flint in 1982, the book of readings *Changing Perspectives on Menopause* (Voda, Dinnerstein, and O'Donnell 1982), the ethnographic studies that

1

focus on Israel (Datan, Antonovsky, and Maoz 1981) and on a fishing village in Newfoundland (Davis 1983), and a great variety of articles (e.g., Flint 1975; Dougherty 1978; Wright 1979; and Burgess 1982). A cross-cultural literature on aging is represented by Fry (1980) and Amoss and Harrell (1981), among others. And there is literature on the evolutionary significance of aging and the sex differences in the aging process, which includes the work of Alexander (1974), Gaulin (1980) and Mayer (1982). The present volume is part of this trend toward greater specialization. It deals with middle-aged women, but not with aged women, grandmotherhood, and widowhood; nor does it deal with middle-aged men.[1]

I have devised the following definition: middle-aged women (matrons) are women who have adult offspring and who are not yet frail or dependent.   The lack of specificity about ages is appropriate for cross-cultural data, which are derived from many societies where the ages of adults are approximations because there are no birth records.   Furthermore, since there are societies in which the end of childbearing and rearing is negotiable by means of adoption and fosterage, the end of childbearing does not provide a definition that can be applied cross-culturally.   Middle age will be considered independently of menopause.   Menopause is typically unmarked by ritual and therefore often remains unreported by ethnographers.   Also the perimenopausal period in a woman's life tends to be briefer than middle age.   Finally, although most traditional ethnographies have not noted menopause, older women are not absent from these descriptive accounts.   The information about them is scattered under a variety of topics such as ritual, food distribution, and marriage arrangements.   And so a social rather than a physiological definition seems in order here.

Researchers who conducted the early cross-cultural studies of older women expected to find variable conditions-- some societies in which status improved with age and some in which it declined.   But this is curiously not the case.   The changes in a woman's life brought about by the onset of middle age appear to be somewhat positive in nonindustrialized societies.   What does vary is the degree of discontinuity in women's lives.   In some societies a younger woman is restricted and confined, and her life is one of subservience and toil, until she is middle-aged.   Then she moves into a position of authority and relative leisure.   In other societies, the life of young women is less onerous and does not differ so much from the life of matrons.

As women reach middle age in nonindustrialized societies, three kinds of changes take place in their lives.   First, they are often freed from cumbersome restrictions which they had to observe when younger. Second, they are expected to exert authority over specified younger kin. This may involve the right to extract labor or it may be the right to make important decisions for the younger person. Third, the changes may include eligibility for special statuses, and thus for recognition beyond the confines of the household. Each of these is more fully explained below.

THE REMOVAL OF RESTRICTIONS

In many societies, middle-aged women are freed from exhibiting the deferential and even demeaning behavior which they had previously been expected to display to the senior generation or to the husband. Although some aged persons may still require expressions of respect, at middle age women have become the active senior generation and now receive the deference they once had to display. Furthermore, menstrual customs no longer apply in those societies that regard menstruating women as dangerous and defiling. In societies that demand great propriety in younger women, in which their conduct is narrowly prescribed, many rules are lifted. Older women may interact informally with men who are non-relatives; they may be allowed to drink too much on ceremonial occasions; they may use foul language, dress immodestly, and even urinate in public.

One aspect of this major change is the greater geographic mobility that older women are often allowed. Child care has ceased or can be delegated, domestic chores are reduced, and so commercial opportunities, the hospitality of relatives living at a distance, and religious pilgrimages may provide an opportunity to venture forth from the village. In some societies, all younger women are restricted to the household because they are believed to be sexually voracious and in need of constant supervision. Here older women are the supervisors because they are believed to be beyond sexual escapades that would bring dishonor to the entire kinship group. In many societies in which the young bride must move into the household of her husband and his family, she is at first mistrusted. It is only as the mother of grown sons that she is viewed as assimilated into her kin group by marriage. She is finally considered above disloyalty. In societies where travel is dangerous and where young women need protection, older women may be granted a certain immunity and therefore some freedom of movement. Thus, once a woman is the mother of adult offspring, she is no longer encumbered with elaborate rules of conduct concerning menstrual custom, modesty, and display of respect; nor is she confined.

THE EXERCISE OF AUTHORITY

A second major change brought on by middle age is a woman's right to exert authority over specified younger kin. This authority is of two kinds. The first is the right to extract labor from younger family members. In matrilocal societies this pertains to daughters, married and unmarried, and to sons-in-law. In patrilocal societies, this pertains to unmarried daughters and daughters-in-law. In many societies, an older woman is expected to be leisured, and it reflects unfavorably on the entire family if she is not. The daughters and daughters-in-law will be reprimanded by the matron's sons and will be the object of disapprobation by the community.

The work of older women tends to be administrative: delegating subsistence activity tasks and making assignments to younger women (see Mary Jemison on the Iroquois [Seaver 1961], Richards [1956] on the Bemba, Murphy and Murphy [1974] on the Mundurucú). They administer the food production, processing, preparation, and preserving; and they oversee food distribution. Within the household the matron may have absolute control over who eats what and when. A recalcitrant daughter-in-law can be starved into submission or even poisoned. In traditional societies, hospitality and the authority to distribute food to nonhousehold members have significant political and ritual implications. By providing or withholding food, older women can influence the celebration of a ceremony or the meeting of a political council (Hahn 1919; Brown 1970).

The authority of older women also finds expression in shaping important decisions for certain members of the junior generation: what a grandchild is to be named, who is ready to be initiated, and who is eligible to marry whom. In some societies, older women have specific responsibilities in the material exchanges that solemnify a marriage. In the societies that maintain very separate worlds for men and women, older women are the go-betweens. The mother of the groom may be the only member of his kin group who actually sees the potential bride and converses with her before formal negotiations take place (see Mernissi 1975). The report of the older woman is crucial to the arrangements, although the groom's father is officially in charge.

Perhaps most significant are reports by many ethnographers concerning the tremendous influence that mothers exercise over and through grown sons. Often a man's relationship to his mother supersedes that with his wife. In some societies the husband is typically very much older than his wife. Early in the marriage, the age discrepancy favors the husband, but as he grows aged and feeble, his middle-aged wife gains in power. This power is further enhanced when combined with the allegiance of grown sons, the old man's successors.

ELIGIBILITY FOR SPECIAL STATUS

A third major change brought on by middle age is the eligibility that older women have for special statuses and the possibility these provide for recognition beyond the household. Societies vary in the number of special positions that their female members can occupy. In some, such opportunities are restricted and there is only the vocation of midwife. In other societies, there are a variety of special offices: curer, mistress of girls' initiation ceremonies, holy woman, guardian of the sacred hearth, matchmaker.[2] Such positions are typically not filled by younger women, sometimes because the exercise of spiritual power is considered harmful to a nursing child or to the baby a pregnant woman is carrying. Sometimes the incompatibility is the result of the great demands of child care and subsistence activities, which when undelegated, allow neither time nor energy for ritual roles. Further, in many societies the belief that menstruation is defiling, disgusting to the spirits, or dangerous makes women ineligible for dealing with sacred matters until later in life. Even a midwife evokes more confidence if she has given birth to many children and has attended at the births of many more.

THE AMERICAN MATRON

The circumstances of middle-aged women in industrial societies like our own differ from those suggested by the cross-cultural data. The "40-year-old jitters" (Henry 1977) and the "empty nest syndrome" may have exaggerated the unenviable aspects of the lives of American middle-aged women (see Neugarten 1970). Or perhaps these descriptions were accurate for the matrons of a previous generation. Nevertheless there are reasons why middle age does not bring as many positive changes into the lives of women in our own society as it does into the lives of women elsewhere. First, middle age does not usher in a life of fewer restrictions, because these are negligible in the first place. Second, although Philip Wylie's classic *Generation of Vipers* (1942) decried the power of "Mom" in an earlier generation, American middle-aged women have far less power over their younger kin than their matron counterparts in other societies. Adult offspring often live at great distances from their mothers, since the location of employment determines the place of residence. The support given by adult children, so central to the definition of middle-aged women cross-culturally and so crucial to their relatively privileged position, often consists merely of occasional telephone conversations, letters, and brief holiday visits. Younger kin may seek advice, or may be manipulated covertly. The latter is seen as unbecoming meddlesomeness and not as a maternal right. The control of food is also not the matron's prerogative. Caterers, vending machines, restaurants, and fast food emporiums have undermined the family meal, trivialized food, and reduced its political and religious implications. Third, our society does provide the possibility for recognition beyond the household, either through volunteer activities in the community or through a career,[3] but such opportunities are open to all women, regardless of age. Spiritual power, delivering babies, and curing are not associated with older women but with various specialists in our society, and the specialists are likely to be males. Although American middle-aged women are not as sinister or as pitiable as they have been portrayed, they do not share all the advantages enjoyed by matrons in nonindustrialized societies.

TOWARD A NEW VIEW

These generalizations[4] will be explored and augmented in the chapters that follow--a unique collection of ethnographic accounts focusing on the lives of middle-aged women. The opening chapter and the last chapter are interpretive. The others are arranged according to the society being described: from small-scale traditional to complex modern.[5]

The first chapter, by Lancaster and King, presents an evolutionary perspective on the postchildbearing years, stressing their adaptive value. Next, several accounts provide examples from small-scale traditional societies. Lee reports on the lives of older women among the hunter-gatherer !Kung. Solway examines the roles of older women among the Bakgalagadi herders of Botswana. And Counts describes the *Tamparonga* "big women" of Kaliai, horticulturalists of West New Britain Province, Papua New Guinea. The next group of accounts deals with middle-aged women among intermediate societies (a designation used by Simić [1978]).[6] Lambek reports on the Malagasy speakers of Mayotte, one of the Comoro Islands, located between the coast of east Africa and Madagascar. Kerns presents data on the Garífuna, or Black Carib villagers of Belize. Boddy describes varying strategies and their outcomes in the lives of middle-aged women of northern Sudan. And Sinclair examines the bewildering contrast between the traditional and postcolonial worlds confronting older Maori women. The third group of descriptions covers complex nonwestern societies. Vatuk provides data on older women in India, and Raybeck compares traditional Chinese women with women of Malaysia. The final examples are drawn from Israel and Canada. Datan, Antonovsky, and Maoz introduce data on older women in five Israeli subcultures, varying from traditional to modern. Kaufert's subjects are middle-aged women from Manitoba, participating in an ongoing research project. The concluding chapter, by Gutmann, urges greater interdisciplinary cooperation, and notes similarities in clinical and cross-cultural data on "post-parental" women.

The ethnographic examples are drawn from societies that differ not only in complexity, but in type of setting, in means of livelihood, and in gender ideology. In these widely varied contexts, there is a consistent, basic theme: women experience a relatively enhanced position, once middle-aged. The opening chapter notes that the evolutionary significance of this phenomenon is in dispute. The final chapter suggests an explanation based on developmental psychology.

There is no such thing as "the status of women" in any particular society. Age modifies the position of women, just as gender modifies the position of the aged. Nor does having adult offspring usher in immediate frailty and dependence. For women there appears to be a period of florescence later in life, and this has been noted by theorists as varied as Meillassoux and Jung. Thus Meillassoux writes:

> Marx is therefore right to believe that women probably constituted the first exploited class. All the same, it is still necessary to distinguish different categories of women in terms of the function they fulfill according to age by which they are not in the same relations of exploitaton and subordination.... After menopause, and even more so as a grandmother,...socially she comes into her own (1981:76,78).

And from a psychoanalytic perspective Jung remarks:

> There are many women who only awaken to social responsibility and to social consciousness after their fortieth year.... One can observe women...who have developed in the second half of life an uncommonly masculine tough-mindedness which thrusts the feelings and the heart aside.... Intelligent and cultivated people live their lives without even knowing of the possibility of such transformations. Wholly unprepared, they embark upon the second half of life (1960:398).

Fortunately the readers of this book will not chance "wholly unprepared" upon the phenomenon both authors describe. The chapters which follow provide full details of the "transformation" which Jung merely intimates. As Meillassoux notes, the matron is woman come into her own.

NOTES

[1] Gilligan (1981) presents the rationale for a "sex-segregated" study of adulthood.

[2] See Kerns (1983) for an unusually full description of ritual roles for older women among the Garífuna.

[3] Barnett and Baruch stress the importance of considering the conditions and the status of American women's work, as these "appear to have a profound effect upon women's experiences particularly in the second half of the life span" (1978:192).

[4] The foregoing generalizations are documented in detail in a previous article (Brown 1982).

[5] All but one of the chapters consist of papers presented in two symposia dealing with middle-aged women at the 1982 Meetings of the American Anthropological Association, held in Washington, D.C.

[6] Simić (1978) uses this classification in introducing a collection of studies of aging. "Intermediate societies" are those in which modernization is occurring, yet many elements of traditional life persist.

REFERENCES

Amoss, Pamela, and Stevan Harrell, eds.
    1981   Other Ways of Growing Old: Anthropological Perspectives.   Stanford, Calif.:   Stanford University Press.
Alexander, Richard
    1974   The Evolution of Social Behavior.   Annual Review of Ecology and Systematics 5:325-383.

Barnett, Rosalind C., and Grace K. Baruch
1978   Women in the Middle Years: A Critique of Research
and Theory.   Psychology of Women Quarterly 3:187-197.
Bart, Pauline
1969   Why Women's Status Changes in Middle Age: The
Turn of the Social Ferris Wheel.   Sociological Symposium
3:1-18.
Brown, Judith K.
1970   Economic Organization and the Position of Women
among the Iroquois.   Ethnohistory 17:151-167.
1982   Cross-cultural Perspectives on Middle-aged Women.
Current Anthropology 23:143-156.
Burgess, Carolyn
1982   A Cultural View of Menopause.   Paper presented at
the Women and Mental Health Conference and Proceedings.   Norman, Okla.
Datan, Nancy, Aaron Antonovsky, and Benjamin Maoz
1981   A Time to Reap: The Middle Age of Women in Five
Israeli Subcultures.   Baltimore: Johns Hopkins University
Press.
Davis, Dona
1983   Blood and Nerves: An Ethnographic Focus on Menopause.   St. John's: Memorial University of Newfoundland.
Dougherty, Molly
1978   An Anthropological Perspective on Aging and Women
in the Middle Years.   In The Anthropology of Health.
Eleanor E. Bauwens, ed. pp. 167-176.   St. Louis: C.
V. Mosby.
Flint, Marcha
1975   The Menopause: Reward or Punishment?   Psychoso-
matics 16:161-163.
Flint, Marcha, guest ed.
1982   Maturitas 4(3).
Fry, Christine L., ed.
1980   Aging in Culture and Society: Comparative View-
points and Strategies.   New York: Praeger/Bergin.
Gaulin, S. J. C.
1980   Sexual Dimorphism in the Human Post-reproductive
Life Span: Possible Causes.   Journal of Human Evolution
9:227-232.
Gilligan, Carol
1981   Adult Development and Women's Development:
Arrangements for a Marriage.   In Women in the Middle
Years: Current Knowledge and Directions for Research
and Policy.   J. Z. Giele, ed. pp. 89-114.   New York:
Wiley-Interscience.

Griffen, Joyce
  1977　A Cross-cultural Investigation of Behavioral Changes
  at Menopause.　Social Science Journal 14:49-55.
Hahn, Ida
  1919　Dauernahrung und Frauenarbeit.　Zeischrift fur Eth-
  nologie 51:243-259.
Henry, Jules
  1977　[1966]　Forty-Year-Old Jitters in Married Urban
  Women.　In Annual Editions:　Readings in Anthropology
  77/78.　David Rosen, et al., eds. pp. 262-268.　Guil-
  ford, Conn.: Dushkin.
Jung, C. G.
  1960　[1931]　The Structure and Dynamics of the Psyche.
  R. F. C. Hull, transl.　New York:　Pantheon Books/Bol-
  lingen Series 20.
Kaufert, Patricia
  1979　The Menopause as a Life Crisis Event.　Paper presented at the Annual Meeting of the Society for Applied
  Anthropology, Philadelphia.
Kerns, Virginia
  1979　Social Transition at Menopause.　Paper presented at
  the Annual Meeting of the American Anthropological Association, Cincinnati.
  1980　Menopause and the Post-reproductive Years.
  National Women's Anthropology Newsletter 4(2):15-16;
  4(3):26-27.
  1983　Women and the Ancestors:　Black Carib Kinship and
  Ritual.　Urbana:　University of Illinois Press.
Mayer, Peter J.
  1982　Evolutionary Advantage of the Menopause.　Human
  Ecology 10(4):477-494.
Meillassoux, Claude
  1981　Maidens, Meal and Money:　Capitalism and the
  Domestic Community.　Felicity Edholm, transl.　New
  York:　Cambridge University Press.
Mernissi, Fatima
  1975　Beyond the Veil:　Male-female Dynamics in a Modern
  Muslim Society.　Cambridge, Mass.: Schenkman.
Murphy, Yolanda, and Robert Murphy
  1974　Women of the Forest.　New York:　Columbia Univer-
  sity Press.
Neugarten, Bernice
  1970　Dynamics of Transition of Middle Age to Old Age:
  Adaptation and the Life Cycle.　Journal of Geriatric Psy-
  chiatry 4:71-87.
Richards, Audrey
  1956　Chisungu: A Girls' Initiation Ceremony among the
  Bemba of Northern Rhodesia.　New York:　Grove Press.

Seaver, James E.
   1961   [1824]   A Narrative of the Life of Mrs. Mary Jemison.   New York: Corinth Books.
Simić, Andrei
   1978   Introduction: Aging and the Aged in Cultural Per-
   spective.   *In* Life's Career--Aging: Cultural Variations on
   Growing Old.   Barbara Myerhoff and Andrei Simić, eds.
   pp. 9-22.   Beverly Hills: Sage.
Voda, Ann, Myra Dinnerstein, and Sheryl O'Donnell, eds.
   1982   Changing   Perspectives   on   Menopause.   Austin:
   University of Texas Press.
Wright, Anne
   1979   Roles   and   Cultural   Interpretation   of   Menopause.
   Paper   presented   at   the   Annual   Meeting of the American
   Anthropological Association, Cincinnati.
Wylie, Philip
   1942   Generation of Vipers.   New York: Farrar & Rine-
   hart.

1 An Evolutionary Perspective on Menopause

Jane B. Lancaster
Barbara J. King

An evolutionary perspective on the history of menopause in the human female life cycle has led recent theorists
to ask whether it represents an evolved pattern that actively
promotes a nonreproductive phase in the life cycle or
whether it is an accidental by-product of other processes
that selected for healthy adults during the reproductive
phase itself. Proponents of the position that menopause is
an evolved phenomenon all present some version of a parental
investment theory beginning with a "grandmother hypothesis," which suggests that a woman maximizes her reproduction if she ceases producing new children toward the middle
years and concentrates on giving her parental investment to
grandchildren and to her last born (Alexander 1974; Gaulin
1980; Mayer 1982; Trivers 1972). Another version of this
hypothesis suggests that senescence itself is actively selected
so that parents will remove themselves from competition with
their offspring (Williams 1957). In such an analysis menopause is only an early step along the way to a total withdrawal from competition.

Other evolutionary theorists reject menopause as an
evolved phenomenon and suggest that evolutionary selection
has favored long-lived, healthy, reproducing adults but not
a postreproductive phase in the life cycle (Washburn 1981;
Weiss 1981). They argue that during most of human history

life expectancy was too short and women rarely lived past menopause so that selection for a such a period of nonproduction would be impossible. They note that the current evidence indicates that the maximum human life span has been unchanged for the last 100,000 years but that many more of those born are now likely to reach maximum length of life. They see the fact that nonreproductive middle-aged women are now an important percentage of the human population as an artifact of recent improvements in the human condition.

HUMAN REPRODUCTIVE RESTRAINT

The relative merit of these perspectives can best be evaluated if certain relevant areas are explored. The first is the question of why human patterns of parental investment might select for reproductive restraint in the middle years so that the production of children is halted well before the development of other aspects of senescence, such as reduced physical capacity. Lancaster and Lancaster (1983) argue that the human pattern of parental investment represents a unique evolutionary adaptation that was both profound and critical in the evolution of the genus *Homo*. According to this hypothesis, the sexual division of labor and the feeding of juveniles by adults from the time of weaning until reproductive maturity distinguishes humans from other animal species. The Lancasters' survey of the literature for data on the demography of survivorship of juveniles among human hunter-gatherers and horticulturalists, and among populations of free-ranging primates that are self-feeding and others that are fed by humans, suggests that humans living in simple economies enjoy a survivorship to adulthood comparable to primate populations with no food limitation on population growth. Improved survivorship through the juvenile period based on the feeding of juveniles by adults may have given evolving humans two significant evolutionary advantages compared to their closest relatives, the great apes. The first was a more efficient production of offspring because of a lower rate of loss of juveniles to starvation and disease. Second, the freeing of human juveniles from the demands of the food quest provided them with leisure spent in the protected atmosphere of home base, where they could invest large segments of their time-energy budgets in play and the manipulation of objects. The improved feeding efficiency from the human division of labor between hunting and gathering, guided by human intelligence, permitted the nutritional dependency of multiple young of differing ages upon their parents. From this point of view the human species represents an extreme evolutionary development of two linked patterns of behavior: intelligence based on learning and high levels of parental investment from both sexes, par- ticularly during the juvenile period.

In order to test this theory, two major questions emerge: is menopause unique to the human species and did human females regularly survive menopause in time past?   A number of primatologists have reviewed the possibility of models for human menopause in nonhuman primates (Gould, Flint and Graham 1981; Graham, Kling, and Steiner 1979; Hodgen et al. 1977; Jones 1975).   These investigations reveal that there are physiological models for human menopause in the sense that the end of the life cycle of the female primate may be marked by irregular and lengthened menstrual cycles, reduced levels of estrogens, and in some species the cessation of ovulation altogether.   However, in all these cases the subfertile or postreproductive phase is at the very end of the life cycle (perhaps only one-tenth of the total life span) and associated with marked evidence of diminished physical capacity.   To date the only example of a relatively long postreproductive phase (one-third of the life span) comes from one strain of mouse and not from other primates (Jones 1975).   In fact data from great apes in the laboratory indicate menstrual cycling and even pregnancy just before death at an advanced age (Gould, Flint, and Graham 1981). At present it seems that among primates a long post-repro- ductive phase may be uniquely developed in humans.

An equally important question is whether women lived long enough in time past for a postreproductive phase to be selected.   To test this, biologically relevant parameters must first be established.   The first of these is to recognize that life expectancy at birth is an irrelevant, though often cited statistic.   Although humans are very successful in raising juveniles compared to other species, among humans living in simple economies such as hunting and gathering, only 50 percent of those born usually survive to reproduction.   Such a loss of immatures greatly lowers life expectancy at birth. The significant measure is not life expectancy at birth but life expectancy at the age of 15 or at the onset of reproduc- tive life.   The relevant statistic for establishing the end of the reproductive phase is not the end of menstrual cycling but the birth of the last child.   The mean age of the mother at the birth of the last child for noncontracepting, breast- feeding populations ranges from 35 to 40 years (Bongaarts 1980; Howell 1979). This fits well with other evidence taken from modern Western populations, which indicates that fertil- ity declines markedly and the frequency of fetal abnormalities abruptly increases after the age of 35 (Washburn 1981).

Using these two markers, life expectancy at 15 and last birth at 35, we can examine data drawn from life tables of 24 hunting-gathering and horticultural populations in the archaeological and ethnographic record. Pooling data from the ethnographic records on both hunter-gatherers and horticulturalists shows that of those women who survived to the age of 15 about half--53 percent--could expect to reach the age of 45. This means that a good proportion of reproducing women can expect to live long enough past the birth of the last child to see it through most of its juvenile years. If natural selection actively favored parental investment by mothers during their middle years into a last child and grandchildren, demographic restraints would not have prevented it.

RECENT HISTORIC CHANGE

Regardless of whether menopause and a postreproductive phase of the life cycle were favored by natural selection in the course of human history, an evolutionary historical perspective leads us to note that there have been major alterations in the life-cycle experiences of women caused by historic changes in activity patterns, diet, and health. These changes affect the actual timing of the event in the life cycle, as well as the way in which it is experienced by women. Although the data are controversial (Bongaarts 1980; Flint 1978; Frisch 1978, 1982; Short 1976), there is some evidence that the length of the reproductive phase of the life cycle has expanded and contracted during various periods of history. In general, when women are healthy, fat, and not extremely active physically, they enter reproduction early and remain late. Current values for modern Western women are menarche at the age of 12 and menopause at 50. Women who are less healthy, and/or lean and very active, may have their reproductive lives shortened by possibly as much as five years at both ends of the fertile period. Thus !Kung hunter-gatherer women are reported to have menarche at 17, first birth at 19, last birth at 35, and menopause at 40 (Howell 1979). Probably the norm for most of human history lay between these extremes, but it appears that recent developments have maximized the length of the reproductive period. In other words, menopausal women may be becoming progressively older and the secular trend in the age of menarche is probably paralleled by a secular trend in the age of menopause.

The actual experience of menopause in modern society may be very different from that in time past because of recent changes in child-care practices. As a number of anthropologists have noted, unpleasant physiological symptoms such as hot flashes, profuse sweating, and atrophic vaginitis are more frequent and more extreme in modern societies, with 10 percent of U.S. women experiencing major discomfort and another 74 percent reporting some problems (Flint 1982). Other symptoms, such as depression and irritability, are also frequently reported. Usually this variation between societies has been ascribed to cultural differences in the meaning of menopause. As Flint puts it, whether menopause is viewed as reward or punishment greatly affects its symptomatology. However, we would like to propose that other factors may also contribute to the unpleasant experiences of so many modern women. As Short (1976) has argued, lactational amenorrhea is the normal biological state for women once they begin their reproductive lives. He estimates that for most of human history women spent over 15 years in lactation and just under four each in pregnancy and menstrual cycling. In contrast, in the reproductive life history of the modern woman with fewer pregnancies and a longer reproductive period, the average woman will be pregnant and lactating for a total of only two years, whereas she will spend nearly 35 years in menstrual cycling. There is abundant but scattered literature from the ethnographic record that women in many tribal societies nurse their last child for a longer period than is typical for earlier-born children. Figures of 3-5 years are frequently mentioned and isolated cases of 8-10 years are reported for !Kung, native Americans and tribal India (Stephens 1963). This means that for many women in time past menopause occurred within the hormonal context of lactation. Unpleasant symptoms caused by abrupt fluctuations in circulating hormones may have been masked or regulated by the continuous presence of prolactin and oxytocin. As Howell (1979) notes, !Kung women may never actually experience menopause. They simply nurse their last infant for a long period and then find that they do not resume cycling when the child is weaned.

Thus, although the verdict is not yet in on whether menopause represents an actively evolved pattern in the life cycle of women to promote parental investment in their last child, it is clear that such a selected program cannot be ruled out on the basis of demography of the past. Regardless of the evolutionary origins of menopause, its experience in the modern world is very different from that of former times. Women may be older at menopause than they used to be and they experience it without the modulation that was once available from the hormones of lactation. An evolutionary and historical perspective on menopause may help us to appreciate some of the problems particular to modern women by virtue of major changes in their reproductive lives.

NOTES

This material has been excerpted from a manuscript being prepared by Jane Lancaster entitled *The Human Nature of Women: Evolutionary and Cross-Cultural Perspectives for Women of Today*.

REFERENCES

Alexander, Richard D.
   1974   The Evolution of Social Behavior.   Annual Review of Ecology and Systematics 5:325-383.
Bongaarts, J.
   1980   Does Malnutrition Affect Fecundity?   A Summary of Evidence.   Science 208:564-569.
Brown, Judith K.
   1982   Cross-cultural Perspectives on Middle-aged Women. Current Anthropology 23:143-156.
Flint, Marcha
   1978   Is There a Secular Trend in Age of Menopause? Maturitas 1:133-139.
   1982   Male and Female Menopause: A Cultural Put-On.   *In* Changing Perspectives on Menopause.   A. Voda, M. Dinnerstein, and S. O'Donnell, eds. pp. 363-378.   Austin: University of Texas Press.
Frisch, R. E.
   1978   Population, Food Intake, and Fertility.   Science 199:22-30.
   1982   Malnutrition and Fertility.   Science 215:1272-1273.
Gaulin, S. J. C.
   1980   Sexual Dimorphism in the Human Post-Reproductive Life-Span: Possible Causes.   Journal of Human Evolution 9:227-232.
Gould, K. G., M. Flint, and C. E. Graham
   1981   Chimpanzee Reproductive Senescence: A Possible Model for Evolution of Menopause. Maturitas 3:157-166.

Graham, C. E., O. R. Kling, and R. A. Steiner
1979 Reproductive Senescence in Female Nonhuman Primates. *In* Aging in Nonhuman Primates. D. Bowden, ed. pp. 183-202. New York: Van Nostrand Reinhold.

Hassan, F. A.
1981 Demographic Archaeology. New York: Academic Press.

Hodgen, G. D., et al.
1977 Menopause in Rhesus Monkeys: Model for Study of Disorders in the Human Climacteric. American Journal of Obstetrics and Gynecology 127:581-584.

Howell, Nancy
1979 Demography of the Dobe !Kung. New York: Academic Press.

Johnston, T. D.
1982 Selective Costs and Benefits in the Evolution of Learning. Advances in the Study of Behavior 12:65-106.

Jones, E. C.
1975 The Post-Reproductive Phase in Mammals. *In* Frontiers of Hormone Research 3:1-20, P. van Keep and C. Lauritzen, eds. Basel: Karger.

Lancaster, Jane B., and C. S. Lancaster
1983 Parental Investment: The Hominid Adaptation. *In* How Humans Adapt: A Biocultural Odyssey. D. Ortner, ed. pp. 33-65. Washington, D.C.: Smithsonian Institution, Government Printing Office.

Lee, Richard B.
1980 Lactation, Ovulation, Infanticide, and Women's Work. *In* Biosocial Mechanisms of Population Regulation. M. Cohen, R. Malpass, and H. G. Klein, eds. pp. 321-348. New Haven: Yale University Press.

Mayer, Peter J.
1982 Evolutionary Advantages of Menopause. Human Ecology 10:477-494.

Short, R. V.
1976 The Evolution of Human Reproduction. Proceedings, Royal Society, (London) Series B., Vol. 195:3-24.

Stephens, William
1963 The Family in Cross-Cultural Perspective. New York: Holt, Rinehart and Winston.

Trivers, R. L.
1972 Parental Investment and Sexual Selection. *In* Sexual Selection and the Descent of Man. B. Campbell, ed. pp. 136-179. Chicago: Aldine.

Washburn, S. L.
1981 Longevity in Primates. *In* Aging, Biology and Behavior. J. March and J. McGaugh, eds. pp. 11-29. New York: Academic Press.

Weiss, K. M.
  1981 Evolutionary Perspectives on Human Aging. *In* Other Ways of Growing Old. P. Amoss and S. Harrell, eds. pp. 25-58. Stanford, Calif.: Stanford University Press.
Williams, G. C.
  1957 Pleiotrophy, Natural Selection and the Evolution of Senescence. Evolution 11:398-411.

I SMALL-SCALE TRADITIONAL SOCIETIES

Although their settings and their subsistence activities differ, the !Kung, the Bakgalagadi and the Lusi are small-scale traditional societies, whose middle-aged women lead somewhat similar lives. The importance of "kin keeping" by older !Kung women is stressed by Lee. This specialized knowledge gives them considerable influence over the lives of their juniors, since kinship information provides the basis for marriage arrangements. A similar theme appears in Solway's data on the Bakgalagadi, and Counts reports that mothers are as involved as fathers in arranging marriages, although the Lusi claim it as a male prerogative.

Older women among the !Kung enjoy a relatively more leisured life, one which is physically less demanding than that of younger women. The Bakgalagadi matron delegates the labors she formerly performed to younger members of the household. In all three societies, older women become increasingly active in trade networks, because they have more time to devote to such activities, and they enjoy increased geographic mobility and greater control over resources.

Both Counts and Solway introduce the theme of responsibility. (Also see the chapter by Sinclair.) Mere longevity does not guarantee esteem for a foolish or improvident woman. Yet Lee notes a relaxation of inhibitions among older !Kung women. Although their sexuality is less inflammatory, !Kung matrons are neither expected nor compelled to withdraw from this aspect of life (as Vatuk reports for Indian women in a later chapter).

None of the accounts mentions a special status such as matchmaker or holy woman for individual middle-aged women. The absence of such statuses reflects the way of life of these small-scale traditional societies, and does not imply a lack of esteem for matrons. Middle-aged women enjoy the authority to contribute to important decisions, the right to extract labor from younger kin and exemption from restrictions which they had to observe earlier in life. It is particularly significant that a relatively enhanced position is reported for older women among the !Kung, a society with an egalitarian gender ideology. In other words, changes in the status of women at middle age are not restricted to those societies in which younger women are relegated to powerlessness and low status.

2 Work, Sexuality, and Aging Among !Kung Women

Richard B. Lee

In many societies of sub-Saharan Africa and other areas discussed in this volume, we find older women coming out of their homes and playing leading roles on the stage of life. The !Kung San, a former gathering and hunting people of northwestern Botswana, are a case in point. The status of !Kung women, generally high, increases with age and reaches a peak in the decades after the child-rearing tasks are completed. The post-menopausal !Kung woman is a mover and shaker in !Kung society and is one of the main agents and sources of sexual joking. The high status of !Kung women has been noted by a number of observers. What has received less attention is the way in which this status waxes and wanes through the life cycle among the !Kung and in other societies as well.

The purpose of this chapter, therefore, is threefold. First, I want to review some facts about the life of !Kung women in work and play, particularly in the contexts of food gathering, parenting, and sexuality. Second, I will document how women's status rises in the later years; and third, I will offer for discussion a tentative causal analysis of these changes. It will be argued that the sources of this transformation are to be sought in, first, the labor process and women's changing commitment of labor to the group, and second, in the changing self- and cultural evaluation of woman's sexuality.

The !Kung are a Khoisan people speaking a click language who live in Botswana and Namibia and number about 15,000. Botswana, where I did my field work from 1963 on, is an independent African nation, while Namibia is a neocolony illegally occupied by South Africa. Until the early 1960s about 20 percent of all !Kung continued to live as relatively isolated full-time gatherer-hunters without agriculture and without domestic animals. More recently the pace of change has accelerated; the Botswana !Kung have become involved in stock raising, agriculture and wage labor, while their Namibian neighbors have been settled on government stations for two decades. Since 1975 (unfortunately) a number of Namibia !Kung have been working full-time as trackers and soldiers for the South African occupation army. In this chapter, I will be referring to the !Kung in the Dobe area of Botswana during the period 1963-69, the time of my main field work.

The !Kung San are one of the best documented gatherer-hunter peoples in the world. Detailed studies of many aspects of !Kung life have been published (see Lee and DeVore 1976; Marshall 1976; Lee 1979; Howell 1979; Yellen 1977; Katz 1982). !Kung studies are particularly fortunate to have a rich corpus of data on !Kung women to draw upon. At least six anthropologists have worked on this topic since 1950. The work of Lorna Marshall (1976) is well known; Pat Draper has written about sex roles (1975) and gender aspects of child rearing (1976); Nancy Howell has done studies of !Kung demography (1979); Marjorie Shostak has collected life history materials (1981); Megan Biesele has worked on folklore (1976; in press) and Pauline Wiessner on trade relations (1982), and others have also contributed. In particular, in addition to my own field data, I will be drawing on two important recent papers on !Kung aging, one by Biesele and Howell entitled "The Old People Give You Life" (1981) and the other by Shostak called "Being of Age among the !Kung San" (1980).

DEMOGRAPHICS AND FOOD GATHERING

First we need to ask the question how many older !Kung there are. What proportion of the !Kung live to the ripe age of 60? According to popular belief, which characterizes foraging peoples like the !Kung as being worn out by the struggle to survive, the answer would be "not very many." The literature on foragers is full of impressionistic statements to the effect that men and women are old at 30 and dead at 45. Thus it may come as a surprise that a considerable proportion of !Kung--about 10 percent--are over the age of 60, a proportion comparable to that of the North American population around the turn of the 20th century. Infant mortality is high among the !Kung--about 400 per 1,000 live births (Howell 1979)--but those who do survive to age 15 have a reasonable expectation of reaching 60, and not a few !Kung live to be 70 or even 80.

In the older age groups women heavily outnumber men. Table 1 shows the proportion of men and women in three age groups in three different censuses (1964, 1968, and 1973). This preponderance of older women has important consequences for rates of widowhood and remarriage.

Table 1. Age-sex composition of Dobe population.

Age	Males No.	%	Females No.	%	Total No.	%
1964						
Old	14	8.1	23	11.2	37	9.8
Adult	112	64.7	123	59.7	235	62.0
Young	47	27.2	60	29.1	107	28.2
Total	173	100.0	206	100.0	379	100.0
1968						
Old	17	7.8	23	9.5	40	8.7
Adult	141	65.3	145	60.2	286	62.6
Young	58	26.9	73	30.3	131	28.7
Total	216	100.0	241	100.0	457	100.0
1973						
Old	19	9.1	30	12.1	49	10.7
Adult	125	60.1	140	56.2	265	58.0
Young	64	30.8	79	31.7	143	31.3
Total	208	100.0	249	100.0	457	100.0

Note: Old = 60+; Adult = 15-59; Young = 0-14 years.

Let us now look at women's work in the foraging context. Gathering of wild plant foods provides between 60 and 80 percent of the diet by weight and women play a very important role in providing food for the group. Young women don't really start to gather seriously until the age of 15. But then for the bulk of their adult lives, the women produce the major proportion of all the food brought into camp, about 55 percent of the total. Men produce the other 45 percent, including almost all of the meat that is eaten (about 30 percent of the total diet), and about 15-20 percent of the gathered food.

Women's economic importance is underscored by the fact that women produce more food than men but actually work shorter hours to do it: one study showed a 2.4-day work week for women and a 3.0-day work week for men (Lee 1979: 260).   If one breaks down women's work effort by age, a rather interesting point emerges: the highest work effort is among women in the age group 20-39, i.e., women who are raising young children.   Not only are they producing more of the food and working longer hours, but they are also carrying their babies around on their backs.   After age 40, a !Kung woman's work effort drops considerably, a point we will return to below.

WOMEN AND CHILD CARE

Now let us look at women's work in parenting. Menarche is late in the !Kung woman.   According to Howell, it occurs at age 16.5, and age at first birth is even later-- about 19.5 years (1976: 144-45).   Adolescent sterility is common, so if there are premarital affairs, they don't normally lead to pregnancies.   Fertility is overall very low for the !Kung--Howell's data indicate 4.6 live births or 4.6 completed family size for post-menopausal women, a very low value for a noncontracepting population.   There is a tremendous investment of labor in each individual child; the !Kung have few children, but their quality of child care is quite high.   Birth spacing is three or four years and breast-feeding continues for two or three years.   The !Kung must be among the world's most prodigious lactaters: 24-hour breast-feeding on demand continues into the child's third year of life.   Evidence now indicates that until recently lactation suppressed ovulation amongst the !Kung for at least the first 24 months of the child's life (cf. Lee 1979,1980; Konner and Worthman 1980).   !Kung women also carry the child on their back for the first 24 months of the child's life, and although overall work effort among the !Kung is moderate, a rather high proportion of that work effort falls on the parents with young children.   With the growth of the children to maturity, of course, this high level of work effort declines.

SEXUALITY

Like her counterparts in other foraging societies, the !Kung child becomes familiar with sexuality early in life. The youngest children sleep under the same blankets with their parents and are under the blankets during their parents' lovemaking.   From the age of 8 or 10, children engage in sex play, which may include intercourse.   Shos-

tak, in her insightful biography of a !Kung woman, quotes
N≠isa as saying,

> At night, when a child lies beside her mother, in
> front, and her father lies down behind and her
> mother and father make love, the child watches....
>
> Perhaps this is the way the child eventually
> learns, because as she gets older, she begins to
> understand that her mother and father are making
> love. At first she thinks, "So that's another thing
> people do with their genitals." Then if the child is a
> little boy, he'll take the little girl, or perhaps his
> sister, and do the same thing to her, he'll teach him-
> self. He'll make believe he's having sex with her as
> he saw his mother and father do. And once he's
> learned it, he'll try to play that way with everyone.
> . . .
>
> That's what an older child does. He waits until
> he is with a little girl and lies down with her. He
> takes some saliva, rubs it on her genitals, gets on
> top and pokes around with his semi-erection, as
> though he were actually having intercourse, but he is
> not. Because even though young boys can get hard,
> they don't really enter little girls. Nor do they yet
> know about ejaculation. Only when a boy is almost a
> young man does he start to have sex like an adult.
>
> At first, girls refuse that kind of play--they
> say all that poking around hurts. But when they are
> a little older, they agree to it and eventually, even
> like it (1981: 111-112).

It will be clear from the above that the !Kung have no
notion of virginity. I have never been able to come up with
a concept or a sense of a word that would correspond to our
word "virgin." Given the early sex play, I will hazard a
guess that there are few !Kung virgins, male or female, at
puberty. (Puberty for girls is marked by a dramatic ritual
which is still performed. In the Eland Dance, the menstruating girl is secluded for several days and nights while the
women of the village dance naked before her. Men are
excluded from the Eland Dance.)

As puberty approaches, however, a girl's sexuality,
once a trifling matter, becomes an explosive issue for the
!Kung. The existence of an unattached sexually attractive
young woman in a group draws male suitors like moths to a
flame, and many fights, some fatal, have broken out amongst
rival suitors (Lee 1979: Ch. 13). Therefore, the goal of
parents is to betroth their daughters as young as possible
and to marry them off early to minimize the chance of potential conflict. Before 1960, most !Kung girls were married

between the ages of 12 and 15, well before reaching menarche. This eagerness to marry girls off at a young age sometimes reached absurd lengths. Concerning the Nyae Nyae !Kung, for example, people in other regions have a saying: "the girls of Nyae Nyae go from their mother's breast to their husband's bed on one day." In some of Lorna Marshall's photographs of brides, they look like they are nine or ten years old, and N!ai, the subject of a television documentary (John Marshall 1980) was married at the age of eight. Thus the saying about the girls of Nyae Nyae, though not literally true, does have an element of truth in it.

Because the girls are so young, the first years of marriage are usually spent uxorilocally, with the wife's family. Husbands are usually 7 to 15 years older than wives at first marriage. Once married, a woman's sexual development, or we should say further sexual development, may be delayed, and a further stormy period follows as she adjusts to life with a much older man in an arranged marriage. We have a number of accounts of !Kung marriages being consummated only two or three years after the actual ceremony. About half of these arranged first marriages fail, and the divorce is almost always initiated by the wife. The woman may then take a series of lovers before settling down in a second match that usually lasts for many years.

Adult sexuality is an area about which we have a lot of fragments of information but no systematic study. Summing up observers' impressions, we can say the following. By western standards, the !Kung have good sex lives. Sexuality is a topic of light, easy banter among groups of men and groups of women. It is regarded as a natural and positive area of life. There are few cases of reported sexual dysfunction. Women experience orgasm and have spoken about it at length with observers (e.g., Shostak 1981). The term *tain*, which is used for orgasm, is the same as the term describing the sublime sweetness of wild honey. A rather nice metaphor.

Do married !Kung have affairs? Some married people are generally acknowledged by the community to be strictly monogamous. For others, extramarital love affairs seem to play an important role in their lives. As Shostak's interviews revealed, love affairs, while not very frequent among the !Kung, do loom large in women's consciousness. But love affairs, while exciting, are also risky. Privacy is at a premium among the !Kung, and no matter how discreet they are, lovers are from time to to time discovered and exposed. Aggrieved spouses, both male and female, will frequently attack their spouse or rival, and other family members will get drawn in. Arguments, brawls, and even poison arrow fights have occurred over the question of adultery. I recorded about a dozen such fights without weapons during three years of fieldwork, and when I collected histories of homicide in the past, adultery was time and again mentioned as one of the precipitating causes. It is interesting to note, however, that the person who gets killed is often not a principal in the original conflict, but a bystander or third party who got drawn in.

The possibility of serious conflict over extramarital sex puts a certain damper on the activity. !Kung women in the active child-bearing years, 20 to 40, go to great lengths not to flaunt their sexuality in a provocative way. The preferred behavior in public for a woman in this age group is a shy sweetness--they are supposed to cover their mouths when they laugh and they are supposed always to take care to smooth the pubic apron over the genitals when they seat themselves. There is a great deal of arranging of skirts and tucking in and fidgeting when a woman sits down; this is considered modest decorous behavior. If women in this age group do have affairs, they do so with the utmost discretion.

LIFE AFTER FORTY

After the age of 40, however, major changes occur in !Kung women's behavior, body language, dress code, and demeanor. They become more open about sexuality, more playful, more outspoken at public events, and more politically central. What is the basis for this change and how is it manifested? I will document this transition by reference to several areas.

First, the older !Kung women become central nodes in kinship networks. Kinship play, the manipulation of kin terms and behavior for fun, is a central theme of !Kung kinship. In their complex kin system, it is by no means clear what term of address is to be used in any given case. Older women are the experts who decide what is the appropriate kin term. They are referred to on a daily basis about how this or that person should be addressed. In a very real sense, they are in charge of kinship classification for the society.

Second, older women gain power and responsibility from their role in arranging marriages and gift exchange. The !Kung traditional *hxaro* network involves men and women with dozens of exchange partners throughout the Dobe area and beyond (Wiessner 1982). People in the 40 to 55 age group have the peak number of *hxaro* partners, and also are the age group with offspring of marriageable age.

Perhaps most striking are the changes in sexual behavior. An older woman may take a younger man as a lover and do this more openly. The reasons are not clear to me. There seems to be less danger attached to it, since husbands are often away for long periods or perhaps are less jealous. In a number of recorded cases, after divorce or widowhood a woman has married a man younger than herself, in some instances 10 or 20 years younger. I know of one case in which a woman married a man 30 years younger than herself. At the /Xai/xai water hole, about 20 percent of all marriages are of older women and younger men.

The freedom of older women is graphically illustrated by changing dress codes. The height at which !Kung women wear their pubic apron on their abdomens is a very important marker in their presentation of self; it communicates something about status, marital situation, and age. The higher the position of the apron above the navel, the more chaste and modest is the woman's demeanor, while the lower positions, which can get very low indeed, can mean several different interesting things.

First of all it can refer to informality. When the !Kung are living in small groups in the bush instead of living in large groups at the permanent water holes, the women lower their pubic aprons two or three inches and wear them just above the public bone. The lowering of the apron is an index of familial intimacy; in a small camp with a dozen people who know each other well or are all related, the aprons indicate ease and familiarity but not sexual intimacy.

If the lowered pubic apron is worn in a larger group, however, it *can* indicate a sexual message. If a woman's husband is away, she may be communicating something about her sexual availability. On the other hand, women who are fighting with their husbands may wear the apron lower as a way of indicating their anger.

The lowering of the apron also seems to correlate with age. The apron gets lower and lower as the woman goes from 50 to 60, and it continues to get even lower as the woman goes from 60 to 70. One can actually see daylight between the apron and the pubes of some 65-year-old women, a manner of dress that would be unthinkable for a younger woman. Thus what appears to be an inviolable dress code *is* violable; a 60- or 70-year-old woman feels no compunction about letting her genitals be partially displayed.

The !Kung use of the pubic apron as a marker of age or sexual status reminds me of Murphy's famous study of the Tuareg entitled "Social Distance and the Veil" (1964). Murphy described how the veil goes up in Tuareg men to cover the face in front of strangers and how it goes down in more intimate situations. On the whole question of the pubic apron and the exposure of the female genitals, I would refer the reader to Olson's fascinating discussion of the Northwest Coast, "Some Trading Customs of the Chilkat" (1936). Olson relates how Bella Coola women traders would move inland, marry Carrier Indian men, and take them as trading partners in order to provide goods for the burgeoning Bella Coola potlatches. In some sense, one could talk of these women as being in a Big Woman's system. As the Bella Coola potlatches increased in scale and the demand for goods became greater and greater, the women used all sorts of tricks in their trading relations with the inland peoples. They would have enormous success during gambling sessions, for example, by lifting their genital apron while seated in the middle of a tense game. The men's concentration would be broken, and the women could win every hand and walk away with the whole pot.

The contemporary !Kung don't gamble, but the women do engage in provocative public displays that parallel the Chilkat practices. With male joking partners, for example, older women may engage in bawdy horseplay including grabbing the men's genitals and playfully mounting the man and pretending to have intercourse. We see this kind of grabbing as well among men, and also among women of the appropriate joking categories, but only women over 50 will engage in this kind of horseplay with the opposite sex. I well remember the day that five !Kung women aged 50 to 65 jumped a male co-worker, Richard Katz, and myself, with shouts of hilarity and tried to force us to have intercourse with them. However, our virtue was preserved by the timely intervention of a Herero neighbor and by the fact that we were all laughing too hard to continue. (Howell also tells a story of how she came into camp once and saw five females jumping rope, four girls from the age of 10 to 15 and one 65-year-old woman, who was not only having a good time but was also very good at it.)

DISCUSSION

The boldness and ease of public presentation of self coupled with the prominent social and economic role played by older !Kung women deserves some explanation. We know that menopause is a time of transition for women in all societies. Why among the !Kung--in common with other Third World women--do the women undergo a blossoming rather than a shrinking or contraction? Let us review three areas of explanation suggested earlier. First of all, there is the major drop in the work demands upon these older women. Their children are grown and doing their own foraging, and the flow of food from parents to children may reverse. Mothers who had fed children for years and years may now become net receivers, getting more food from their adult off-spring than they are giving.   Also, the labor of carrying children is no longer required.   Clearly, one aspect of the "coming out" of older !Kung women has to do with taking a vacation from the world of work.

The second area of explanation focuses on the social and political centrality of the generations of people in the 45-65 age group.   These are the people, male and female, who are at the peak of their political powers.   Collectively, they are the parents, the older siblings, or parents-in-law of the 75-90 percent of the population who are younger than they are.   In !Kung kinship, age is a crucially important factor and all kin terms have an older/younger designation built in.   To be the older member of a kinship dyad carries with it important prerogatives of respect and deference.   Kin terms are assigned according to a complex set of rules derived from personal names.   One of the mysteries of !Kung kinship is that from the point of view of the younger person the kinship term used for an older person often doesn't fit. The reason is that it is the older persons who generate the kin term and they decide what term to use according to their lights, whether or not it makes sense to the younger person (cf. Lee 1984:   Ch. 5).   Yet once imposed, the kin term chosen by the older person begins to develop a logic of its own as it becomes transmitted in turn by the younger people to others even younger than they.   In a real sense, there-fore, the elders are legislating the classification structure of society.

One could argue that by the criterion of age it must be the very oldest people, those in their seventies and eighties, who are the most respected, because they have in effect classified all the people younger than themselves.   But the eldest of the elders, the "old-dead" in !Kung terms, are well past their physical prime and they play an increasingly marginal role in !Kung society.

Rose (1968) took these same biological and social facts about age, political centrality, and power and applied them to the Australian Aborigines.   He argued that these facts generated in Australia a gerontocracy in which elder males controlled the lives of women and younger males.   A similar model has been developed for West African agricultural socie-ties by Meillassoux (1964) and Dupré and Rey (1973), to mention just two studies.   Among the !Kung, however, both women and men take the central roles, though the power of either sex is severely circumscribed by the strongly egalita-rian social arrangements of the !Kung.   (Woodburn has writ-ten a useful overview of the nature of egalitarian societies [1981].   See also Silberbauer 1982.)

To the factors of easing of work demands and socio-political centrality must be added a third, which may turn out to be the most important: the changing evaluation of women's sexuality. From the age of 15 to 40 women's (and men's) sexuality was a potentially explosive issue, probably the most explosive issue the !Kung had to deal with. After a woman's menopause, however, the emotional level of this tension falls precipitously.

People rarely fought in the past over land or property, but we have over a dozen cases of men fighting over contested betrothals or adultery. Sexual matters were the main causes of fatal fighting among the !Kung (Lee 1979: Ch. 13). One of the paradoxes of !Kung life is that despite the low development of property concepts, there is a high level of sexual jealousy: both men and women express a great deal of it and will attempt to hurt or kill a spouse or rival if they discover an act of adultery.

After a certain age, however, this situation changes dramatically. The angry jealous sexuality of the young gives way to a much more relaxed attitude. Affairs become more open and tolerated; although fights may still occur, they are less intense and less likely to escalate into bloody battles. A woman's (and a man's) sexuality can now be expressed without unleashing disruptive, destructive social forces.

To conclude, then, the !Kung San have been regarded as a society exhibiting one of the world's highest levels of sexual egalitarianism. We have seen how !Kung women behave as actors on the stage of their society's history and not just as spectators. The aging process enhances women's power instead of weakening it. For the older !Kung women the long-term cycles of work effort and family responsibility and rising social centrality converge to make the period of middle age a time of unparalleled influence in the affairs of the community. And it is also the period in which a woman's sexuality, which until now was a strictly private affair, becomes a subject for public display and celebration.

NOTE

This study, originally presented at the Annual Meetings of the Canadian Ethnology Society/Société Canadienne d'Éthnologie, Ottawa, in March 1981, has been substantially revised for this volume.

REFERENCES

Biesele, Megan
    1976   Aspects of !Kung Folklore. *In* Kalahari Hunter-
    Gatherers.   R. B. Lee and I. DeVore, eds. pp. 302-324.
    Cambridge, Mass.: Harvard University Press.
    In press Women Like Meat: Aspects of Folklore among the
    !Kung San. Cambridge, Mass.:   Harvard University
    Press.
Biesele, Megan, and Nancy Howell
    1981   "The Old People Give You Life": Aging among
    !Kung Hunter-Gatherers. *In* Other Ways of Growing
    Old: Anthropological Perspectives. P. Amoss and S.
    Harrell, eds. pp. 77-98.   Stanford, Calif.:   Stanford
    University Press.
Draper, Patricia
    1975   !Kung Women: Contrasts in Sexual Egalitarianism in
    the Foraging and Sedentary Contexts. *In* Toward an
    Anthropology of Women.   R. Reiter, ed. pp. 77-109.
    New York: Monthly Review Press.
    1976   Social and Economic Constraints on Child Life among
    the !Kung. *In* Kalahari Hunter-Gatherers.   R. B. Lee
    and I. DeVore, eds. pp. 199-217. Cambridge, Mass.:
    Harvard University Press.
Dupré, G., and P. Rey
    1973   Reflections on the Relevance of a Theory of the His-
    tory of Exchange. Economy and Society 2:131-163.
Howell, Nancy
    1976   The Population of the Dobe Area !Kung. *In* Kalahari
    Hunter-Gatherers.   R. B. Lee and I. DeVore, eds. pp.
    152-165. Cambridge, Mass.: Harvard University Press.
    1979   Demography of the Dobe Area !Kung. New York:
    Academic Press.
Katz, Richard
    1982   Boiling Energy: Healing among the Kalahari !Kung.
    Cambridge, Mass.: Harvard University Press.
Konner, M., and C. Worthman
    1980   Nursing Frequency, Gonadal Function, and Birth
    Spacing among !Kung Hunter-Gatherers.   Science
    207:788-791.
Lee, Richard B.
    1979   The !Kung San: Men, Women, and Work in a Forag-
    ing Society. New York: Cambridge University Press.
    1980   Lactation, Ovulation, Infanticide and Women's Work:
    A Study of Hunter-Gatherer Population Regulation. *In*
    Biosocial Mechanisms of Population Regulation. M.
    Cohen, R. Malpass, and H. Klein, eds. pp. 321-348.
    New Haven, Conn.: Yale University Press.

1984 The Dobe !Kung. New York: Holt Rinehart and Winston, Case Studies in Anthropology.

Lee, Richard B., and Irven DeVore, eds.
1976 Kalahari Hunter-Gatherers: Studies of the !Kung San and Their Neighbors. Cambridge, Mass.: Harvard University Press.

Marshall, John
1980 N!ai: The Story of a !Kung Woman. Watertown, Mass.: Center for Documentary Resources. (Film)

Marshall, Lorna
1976 The !Kung of Nyae Nyae. Cambridge, Mass.: Harvard University Press.

Meillassoux, Claude
1964 Anthropologie Economique des Gouro de Côte d'Ivoire. Paris: Mouton.

Murphy, Robert
1964 Social Distance and the Veil. American Anthropologist 66(6):1257-1274.

Olson, R. L.
1936 Some Trading Customs of the Chilkat Tlingit. In Essays in Anthropology Presented to A. L. Kroeber, pp. 211-214. Berkeley: University of California Press.

Rose, Frederick G. G.
1968 Australian Marriage, Land-Owning Groups, and Initiations. In Man the Hunter. R. B. Lee and I. DeVore, eds. pp.200-208. Chicago: Aldine.

Shostak, Marjorie
1980 Being of Age among the !Kung San: Adulthood and Aging in a Gathering-Hunting Society. Paper presented at the Conference on Cultural Phenomenology of Adulthood and Aging, Harvard University.
1981 Nisa: The Life and Words of a !Kung Woman. Cambridge, Mass.: Harvard University Press.

Silberbauer, G. B.
1982 Political Process in G/wi Bands. In Politics and History in Band Societies. E. Leacock and R. B. Lee, eds. pp. 23-36. New York: Cambridge University Press.

Wiessner, Pauline
1982 Risk, Reciprocity and Social Influences on !Kung San Economics. In Politics and History in Band Societies. E. Leacock and R. B. Lee, eds. pp. 61-84. New York: Cambridge University Press.

Woodburn, James
1981 Egalitarian Societies. Man (n.s.) 17:431-451.

Yellen, John E.
1977 Archaeological Approaches to the Present: Models for Reconstructing the Past. New York: Academic Press.

3 Middle-Aged Women in Bakgalagadi Society (Botswana)

Jacqueline S. Solway

Much of the anthropology of women has focused on women's status as compared to men's, and it has generally been found that women occupy a lower status than do men in most societies. Although arguments claiming that male dominance is necessarily universal or inevitable are unconvincing, the fact remains that some degree of male dominance strikes us as a cross-cultural reality in the contemporary world (Ortner 1974; Rosaldo and Lamphere 1974; Leacock 1981).

However, only posing questions evaluating the relative status of men and women probably obscures relevant issues instead of elucidating them. Status is not a unidimensional feature; rather, categories of people may have high status in one domain of social life but lower status in other domains (cf. Tiffany 1979; Quinn 1977; Whyte 1978). The determinants of status vary cross-culturally. And in any particular society, the individual's rights and obligations in relation to other sex-age groups will vary with progress through the life course.

Status is used here to indicate the general position of a member or a category of members in society. Among the Bakgalagadi high status is achieved when individuals attain greater degrees of autonomy in determining the course of their lives. No individual as a member of society is ever

completely   autonomous.   However,   given   the   constraints
imposed by the values, norms, and rules of any society,
autonomy relates to an individual's ability to make decisions
about his or her activities, the use of his or her labor and
the fruits of this labor.   It relates to an individual's capacity to make decisions concerning the activities of others, the
respect with which these decisions and opinions are greeted
by the community, and the general degree of deference the
individual is afforded.

ETHNOGRAPHIC BACKGROUND

The Bakgalagadi are a Sotho-speaking people in the
Kalahari desert.   They are similar to the neighboring Bat-
swana studied by Schapera (1950,1967) but are less politically centralized and live in smaller, less concentrated, and
more isolated villages.   The economy is based on pastoralism
supplemented by agriculture, and the Bakgalagadi are
dependent on earnings derived from migrant labor to the
South African mines (Solway 1979a, 1979b).
The kinship system is largely patrilineal in that the
majority of property is inherited patrilineally, political office
is inherited patrilineally (and based on the principle of pri-
mogeniture), and the individual is identified with and comes
under the jural authority of the patrilineage.   However, like
other Sotho-speaking peoples, the Bakgalagadi permit cousin
marriages of all kinds, therefore allowing lineage endogamy.
This element complicates the principle of unilineality by
creating ambiguous and overlapping links (Schapera 1950:
149-165; Comaroff 1980:639; Kuper 1970:468), thus weakening
the patriline and lending a cognatic element to the system.
Postmarital residence is initially patrilocal, and ideally local
residential groups are formed by lineage segments.   However, in practice less than two-thirds of local households
reside according to the ideal of lineal-based local groups,
and matrilateral links and other cooperative relations frequently influence residential decisions.
Among the Bakgalagadi local ideology recognizes men as
being more important: their work is more highly valued,[1]
they are considered to have greater skills at making and
enforcing decisions about most matters, their opinions are
taken more seriously, and at most stages of the life cycle,
they have greater autonomy.   In addition, deference behavior is more often displayed toward men.   However, this is a
very general view and does not account for the fact that
status is a dynamic phenomenon, changing with age for both
men and women.   Also, the spheres of activity, the domains
of social life in which people attain prestige and position, are

different for men and women in Bakgalagadi society and are not necessarily comparable in all respects. Toward middle age there tends to be a blurring of sex-role distinctions, and for women in particular, there are more avenues open for the achievement of high status.

Middle age is not an age-category marked or recognized as a particular phase of life, nor are middle-aged people recognized as a unit. Perhaps before the 1930s, when initiations and the associated age-regiments were common and had more importance, certain regiments were "middle-aged." However, several age-regiments (*mephato*) would fall simultaneously into the middle-aged category, and it is unlikely that the middle-aged regiments formed a coherent unit.

Thus "middle age" is a designation I impose upon a clustering of features that tend to occur simultaneously in a Bakgalagadi woman's life. The most important are becoming mistress of the compound and the attainment of young adult status by her elder children, a status usually indicated by marriage or employment. Unlike younger women, a middle-aged woman has greater control over her productive and reproductive powers, greater authority over junior relatives, and within the larger community, greater opportunity to participate in social life.

A similar pattern emerges from an examination of the position of Bakgalagadi women in the context of the three phases of the domestic cycle identified by Fortes (1958): expansion, dispersion, and replacement. A married woman's status reaches its highest point at the overlap of the expansion and dispersion stages (Solway 1981). This is when her children marry, and her mother-in-law loses control over the domestic sphere in the extended family household.

SEX ROLES

For most of their lives, men and women participate in different domains of social life. Women's domain is the domestic sphere and agriculture. Men's domain lies outside the domestic sphere in herding (the activity from which the major means of publicly recognized exchange is produced), in the public political arena, and for a period of their lives, in wage labor employment outside the village. Only on ritual occasions are the domains kept rigidly distinct. The separateness of the sexes' domains is most clearly expressed in funeral practices.[2] On a day-to-day basis however, distinctions are less strict and some overlap in activities occurs. The extent to which sex-role boundaries are crossed depends largely on an individual's place in the life cycle. Middle-aged women, particularly widows, are least tied to their traditional female domains and most able to participate in a full complement of social activities.

In a previous study (Solway 1981), I described the transformations in women's status that culminate in middle age. To summarize, a young adult unmarried woman enjoys a short period of relatively high status. She resides in her parents' compound, where younger siblings and sisters-in-law assume many household responsibilities. She has some autonomy over her activities, and is often afforded luxuries, such as education, by her parents. Upon marriage and assumption of patrilocal residence, a woman's status declines significantly. A young wife is under the constant scrutiny of her affines, particularly her mother-in-law, and the young wife is expected to work hard and to produce children. In fact, one of her few times of relief occurs when she returns to her mother's compound to give birth. She spends two months in postnatal seclusion, during which female relatives indulge her. A young wife has few rights in her affines' compound, and she has little autonomy.

As a woman approaches middle age her status improves. She is no longer under the tutelage of her mother-in-law and is normally mistress of her compound. She has adult children to support and assist her. As mistress of her compound, she can delegate chores and responsibilities to daughters and to daughters-in-law who have assumed residence in her household, thus allowing the middle-aged woman greater participation in activities outside the domestic sphere. All Bakgalagadi women participate in exchange networks throughout their lives. However, a middle-aged woman, by virtue of her control over agricultural harvests, participates more substantially in public exchanges through both gift giving and sales of agricultural produce.

In addition, as grandmothers--a role that begins in middle age and extends through old age--women exert some control over kinship networks (cf. Lee 1981; also see Lee this volume). In the field, I asked people why they applied specific kinship terms to others. Often they explained the kinship relationship that indicated a particular term. However, in many cases people did not know their precise relationship to others and they explained that they used the term because their grandmothers had told them to do so. Grandmothers thus influence future generations' social relations by contributing to their grandchildren's socialization into the kinship system.

In Bakgalagadi society status improves for both men and women as they advance through the life cycle. While women become mistresses of their compounds and managers of agricultural activities, men become heads of households, herd managers, and active participants in the *kgotla* (central village meeting place and court). Women also participate in the *kgotla* but rarely to the extent that men do. Although multiple factors interact to improve the position of both sexes, an important factor for both is parenthood and the associated statuses of husband and wife. The Bakgalagadi have a proverb which translates "An impala without a baby impala is stupid. Cleverness of the impala comes from its young one." It is believed that the responsibilities of parenthood make one wise. While parenthood is clearly important for all Bakgalagadi, women's status is more dependent on the roles of wife and mother than the status of men is on the roles of father and husband. Status (here identified with levels of autonomy and decision-making power) increases not only with age, but with the respect acquired when rights and obligations are fulfilled responsibly. Women more than men fulfill their obligations through others.

Responsible behavior (also see Counts this volume) must be demonstrated in a variety of ways, including participation in culturally prescribed exchanges and public participation in community matters at the *kgotla*. In both activities, men take a more visible and active role. *Kgotla* participation is expected of adult males, particularly household heads, as they reach middle age. While the role of household head occurs at a similar stage in the life cycle and contains parallels to the role of compound mistress, the former involves publicly representing the household in extra-domestic matters and the disposal of household resources other than food, and normally includes ultimate decison-making powers over household members' extradomestic activities (although all adult household members confer about most decisions). The role of compound mistress revolves around managing agricultural and domestic activities and the distribution of agricultural produce. In terms of production, the household head is responsible for herd production while the compound mistress is responsible for agricultural production. However, agricultural production depends upon herd production in that plow animals must be available for agricultural activities to commence.

Household headship is normally a male role, but the position is occupied by a female if the household lacks a man of the appropriate age or level of responsibility. Those women who assume household headship do so when they are middle-aged or approaching middle age and are single as a result of divorce or widowhood, or as a result of never marrying--an increasingly common option in Botswana (cf. Gulbrandsen 1982).[3] *Kgotla* participation is not limited to household heads but is open to all adults. Yet middle-aged people are most active because they have reached the stage of life when they are freed somewhat from routine activities. They are also considered wiser. However, all Bakgalagadi households should be represented, and household heads have the strongest voice. Thus women, while ideally able to participate in the *kgotla*, do so less than men, and are never listed by the court clerk as officially making up the court. Women are most welcome in the *kgotla* when they represent their households.

EXCHANGE RELATIONSHIPS

Mother's brother (*malome*) is an important position in Bakgalagadi society. Many rights and obligations accrue to mother's brother, and if carried out responsibly, they contribute to a person's elevated status. Women can never participate on the senior side of the mother's brother-sister's child relationship. There is a specific kinship position for father's sister (*rakgadi*). However, it does not carry equivalent status, place the individual in a similar exchange network, or carry many of the rights and obligations inherent in the mother's brother position.

The mother's brother-sister's child relationship is marked by exchanges that occur throughout life. However, a particular linked set of exchanges is a fundamental part of the relationship. Sister's child initiates the exchange relationship by giving mother's brother a male animal, usually a bull, and the first item of importance acquired by sister's child. In the past this was usually the first animal successfully hunted. Today an individual's first paycheck often replaces or is given in addition to the first animal. Innovations occur in this category of gift, e.g., a child's mother's brother was presented a comb won in a Botswana Independence Day running race. Subsequent gifts include parts of animals hunted or slaughtered, small gifts of cash or other material items, and general types of assistance and support. Mother's brother is meant to return to sister's child a cow, thus contributing to herd accumulation on the part of the sister's child. In addition, mother's brother offers sister's child general aid and support.

On the junior side of the relationship, the kinship term for sister's child (*motgogolo*) is not sex specific. Thus ideally both sexes could participate equally. However, the socioeconomic circumstances of young men and women are different, a fact which is reflected in their differential participation in the exchange. Women rarely have the resources to allow them to independently give their mother's brother an appropriate gift. Men and women both inherit livestock but they do so at different stages of the life cycle. Men inherit as small boys; thus by the time they are young adults they have small herds from which an animal can be selected to give to mother's brother. Women inherit as young adults and thus have a reduced ability to accumulate a herd. In addition a woman's livestock are often turned over to her husband by her father, or they are secretly kept for her by her father or brother. Since they are the woman's secret security base, public exchanges are not made from them.

Employment opportunities for young women are extremely rare compared to those for men. Women can find employment as domestics, teachers, nurses, etc. Most of these options require education, and positions are limited in number. Young men work as herdboys, teachers, civil servants, etc., and virtually all able-bodied young men can find employment at the South African mines. Over 90 percent of the men, but fewer than 10 percent of the women I interviewed had held wage employment outside the village. Wage employment inside the village is virtually nonexistent. Thus women are less likely to have a first paycheck to give to their mother's brother, and since women do not hunt, they cannot present their mother's brother with a hunted animal.

Women are said to have their obligations to their mother's brother fulfilled by their husbands upon marriage. A young man must give his wife's mother's brother an ox when he marries. This exchange is different and independent of bridewealth and is said to meet the obligations of the woman to her mother's brother. Women thus often depend on their husbands in fulfilling their obligations and mother's brother is not under the same obligation to return a gift of a cow to sister's daughter when her obligation has been fulfilled by her husband. Women usually also are excluded from bridewealth, which is perhaps the most significant exchange in Bakgalagadi society. Although collected from a number of sources, bridewealth is given by a man, representing himself and his close agnatic kin, to his wife's father or brother. Rarely will a woman receive the bridewealth payment, and if she does so, it is in lieu of her son or some male relative who is either absent or too young to accept the bridewealth. The delivery of bridewealth cattle is a public event announced to the village by the ululating of the wife's relatives. Bridewealth exchange is marked by long and elaborate festivities sponsored by the wife's family. Payment of bridewealth occurs some years after the marriage has taken place, usually when the husband is approaching middle age. Providing much prestige to the parties paying, it is an avenue for status achievement virtually confined to men.[4]

Although women are restricted from participating in certain exchange relationships, they take part in others for which livestock are the medium of exchange. Middle-aged women are most likely to take part in these activities. A young wife has an insecure relationship to the means of production. In the household in which she is producing (her affines') she has little control over resources and produce. In addition, she is supposed to be home, helping her mother-in-law and producing children. The longer she is married, the more secure her position in her affines' home becomes. Once a woman's bridewealth has been paid, her children are legitimate members of their father's patrilineage, and thus the children are owners of property. This clarifies and substantiates the woman's claim to her affines' resources and her own produce. Thus it is in large part through her children's secure position in their lineage that a woman's position in her affines' lineage is strengthened.

Middle-aged women may sell agricultural produce, and it is common for women to send buckets or bags of grain as gifts. Women are more likely to be involved in livestock exchange during middle age than at any other stage of their life cycle. In fact, some of the larger livestock owners in the village are widows. Upon reaching middle age, the women become increasingly autonomous from their brothers-in-law and brothers and take part in selling and exchange of livestock like any head of household.

Thus, as the preceding discussion illustrates, women generally achieve high status in the domestic sphere and in agriculture. But, in middle age a blurring of sex-role distinctions occurs, and women participate in a wider variety of activities. Nonetheless, women have fewer opportunities open to them for achieving high status, and unlike men, they are more dependent on their children and spouses for fulfilling obligations and gaining security. In Bakgalagadi society, status improves for both sexes with increasing age, yet the transformations of middle age are more marked for women. No longer controlled by and dependent on their affines, they manage their own compounds and gain the autonomy associated with being mistress of the compound. Middle-aged women manage the domestic sphere and agriculture, and control agricultural produce. They can delegate chores and responsibilities, thus gaining greater freedom of movement to visit, travel, and actively engage in village and extra-village political affairs.

NOTES

My fieldwork in Botswana was carried out from October 1977 through July 1979 with the assistance of a University of Toronto Open Fellowship and an Ontario Graduate Scholarship. I would like to thank Michael Lambek and Judith K. Brown for their support and comments. In addition, I am indebted to the Bakgalagadi for their patience and help when I was in the field.

[1] Contributing to social reproduction by rearing children and participating in subsistence activities is certainly important. However, other activities are important as well, such as those discussed in the chapter.

[2] Women are buried in the compound whereas men are buried in the kraal. During the days of mourning following a funeral, other restrictions are applied to the sexes. For example, men and women eat different parts of the ritually sacrificed animals, and in the evenings men and women separate. Men meet and sleep at the kraal, women in the compound.

[3] Women who assume household headship achieve high status, and indeed some women household heads are among the most influential and respected people in the village. However, the position often has negative aspects as well, as the combined responsibilities of household head and compound mistress can be quite formidable.

[4] There are odd cases where a woman could pay bridewealth. While woman-woman marriage is not practiced among the Bakgalagadi with whom I worked, a woman could conceivably pay her widowed mother's bridewealth or pay for her deceased brother's wife. In such cases a woman would be paying bridewealth in the name of a deceased male relative.

REFERENCES

Comaroff, Jean
  1980 Healing and the Cultural Order: The Case of the Barolong Boo Ratshidi of Southern Africa. American Ethnologist 7:637-657.
Fortes, Meyer
  1958 Introduction. *In* The Developmental Cycle in Domestic Groups. J. Goody, ed. pp. 1-14. Cambridge: Cambridge University Press.

Gulbrandsen, ∅.
   1982   To Marry--or not to Marry.   Department of Anthropology, University of Bergen, Norway.   Unpublished
   manuscript.
Kuper, A.
   1970   The Kgalagari and the Jural Consequences of Marriage.   Man 5:466-482.
Leacock, Eleanor
   1981   Myths of Male Dominance.   New York: Monthly
   Review Press.
Lee, Richard B.
   1981   Social Transformation: The Lives of !Kung Women.
   Paper presented at the Annual Meeting of the Canadian
   Ethnology Society. Ottawa, Canada.
Ortner, Sherry
   1974   Is Female to Male as Nature Is to Culture?   In
   Woman, Culture and Society. M. Z. Rosaldo and L. Lam-
   phere, eds.   pp. 67-87.   Stanford, Calif.:   Stanford
   University Press.
Quinn, Naomi
   1977   Anthropological Studies on Women's Status.   In
   Annual Review of Anthropology 6. B. Siegel, A. Beals,
   and S. Tyler eds.   pp. 181-225.   Palo Alto, Calif.:
   Annual Reviews.
Rosaldo, Michelle Z., and Louise Lamphere
   1974   Introduction.   In Woman, Culture and Society. M.
   Z. Rosaldo and L. Lamphere eds. pp. 1-15.   Stanford,
   Calif.: Stanford University Press.
Schapera, Isaac
   1950   Kinship and Marriage among the Tswana. In African
   Systems of Kinship and Marriage. A. R. Radcliffe-Brown
   and D. Forde, eds. pp. 140-165. London: Oxford
   University Press.
   1967   The Political Organization of the Ngwato of Bechua-
   naland Protectorate. In African Political Systems. M.
   Fortes and E. E. Evans-Pritchard, eds. pp. 56-82. London: Oxford University Press.
Solway, Jacqueline
   1979a   People, Cattle and Drought.   Gaborone, Botswana:
   Ministry of Agriculture.
   1979b   Socio-Economic Effects of Labour Migration in Western Kweneng.   Gaborone, Botswana: Central Statistics
   Office.
   1981   Women, Marriage and the Domestic Cycle in Bakgalagadi Society. Paper presented at the Annual Meetings of
   the Canadian Ethnology Society. Ottawa, Canada.
Tiffany, Sharon
   1979   Introduction.   In Women and Society. S. Tiffany,
   ed. pp. 1-35. Montreal: Eden Press.

Whyte, Martin
    1978   The Status of Women in Preindustrial Societies.
    Princeton, N.J.: Princeton University Press.

4 Tamparonga:

"The Big Women" of Kaliai (Papua New Guinea)

Dorothy Ayers Counts

For women in many societies, middle age and the end of childbearing bring about a radical change in their lives. Women whose activities and options were limited when they were young and who were denied the opportunities and privileges enjoyed by their male peers (Ortner 1974; Friedl 1975; Reiter 1975; Kessler 1976), often find that their lives improve dramatically after menopause. They enjoy more opportunity for achievement and recognition, fewer restrictions, and more authority, sometimes even over their aging husbands and certainly over younger people of both sexes (Keith 1980; Brown 1982).

Various explanations for this phenomenon are discussed by Brown (1982), including the following:

1. Explanations that stress the importance of menopause and the end of a woman's reproductive life.

2. Explanations that, while stressing menopause, focus on the end of a woman's ability to contaminate men by her menstrual blood.

3. Explanations assuming that physical changes ending female reproductive capacity also end responsible parenthood--the care of dependent children.

4. Hypotheses emphasizing the domestic, political, and economic authority that accrue to a woman in her middle and later years.

Based on my research with the Lusi women of Kaliai, West New Britain Province, Papua New Guinea, I argue that attention should be focused on a component that is implicit but not emphasized in many of these explanations: the notion of responsibility (also see Solway this volume). The increased prestige, authority, and autonomy of the Lusi *tamparonga* "big woman," or more accurately, "elder," does not represent a radical departure from her way of life as a younger woman. Neither can it be explained as being a result of biological or social changes associated with menopause--changes such as asexuality, declining ability to contaminate, or an end to active mothering of small children. Instead, as I argue, the changes associated with elder status occur because, with the maturity of her children and the decline of her parents, a woman becomes *responsible*: responsible for herself, for her younger kin and affines, for the care of her dependent parents, and for the maintenance of society.

The Lusi are an Austronesian-speaking people numbering about 1,000 who live in five villages located along the coast of the Kaliai area. They are primarily swidden horticulturalists whose major cash income is from the sale of copra. They maintain an active traditional life that includes ceremonial celebrations of the initiation of children, marriage, and death. These ceremonies involve feasting and the distribution of shell money, pandanas mats, pigs, and other wealth items. The Lusi are also actively involved in a trading system that links New Britain's northwest coast with the Kaliai interior, the Vitu and Siassi Islands, and the New Guinea mainland. Socially, the Lusi are normatively patrilineal and virilocal. Married people reside together in single family dwellings that include separate houses for sleeping and cooking. It is common for a couple to have residing with them, usually sleeping in the cook house, an elderly woman whom one of them calls "mother."

Nevertheless, Lusi women who are in their late childbearing or postreproductive years enjoy considerable autonomy. Some neutralization of gender roles occurs for both Lusi men and women in extreme old age (Gutmann 1969, 1975; Counts and Counts 1982). This does not, however, significantly affect everyday life, and it is not a primary factor in the independence of Lusi women who are in their middle years. Instead, these women are very like younger Lusi women, only more so: in middle age the cultural themes that provide a counterpoint to the idea of male dominance reach culmination. There is a multiplicity of rules, to which both women and men subscribe. Some of these rules oppose or contradict one another. People must choose among alternatives when they formulate a course of action to explain behavior, and their choice is almost always contextually determined. For example, Lusi women are forbidden to enter the men's house, to see or touch certain sacred masks, or to remain in the village when especially dangerous spirits are released at a ceremonial climax. When I asked if these restrictions were ever lifted for old women, my consultants insisted that they were not. Later, during another discussion on a different topic, one of these same consultants recounted that when he was a boy an old woman was permitted to remain in the village when the spirits left the men's house. When he asked his father for an explanation, the older man had replied, "It's all right. She's an old woman. Her hair is white and she will die before long. She is just like us men. *Aia mali mao* (she has no contaminating essence). She can stay." This remark led other people present to elucidate the circumstances and contexts under which specific old women might enter the men's house, handle sacred items, and remain in the village when dangerous spirits are abroad. The general rule then, is that as a category, old women must behave as do other women, but in specifically defined contexts, certain old women follow a different set of rules. I shall return to this point.

THE NORMS OF MALE DOMINANCE

I have enumerated elsewhere (Counts 1980b: 338-340) the ways in which male dominance is expressed in Lusi society. To sum up briefly,

1. Political leaders, both traditional and modern, are male. There is no female equivalent of the male term *maroni* (*bikman*), leader or "bigman," a title that must be earned and applies only to some men.

2. A woman derives her status from the older men with whom she is associated, especially her father and husband.

3. Men claim the right to control the sexuality of their female kin. Fathers, and to a lesser extent older brothers, arrange the marriages of their daughters and sisters, and husbands have exclusive rights over the sexuality of their wives.

4. Husbands have authority over wives, authority that is occasionally enforced by violence. Wife beating is not an everyday occurrence,[1] but it is not uncommon and falls within the boundaries of normal marital behavior.

TAMPARONGA

There is no Lusi term for middle age, but there are terms that translate as female and male elder. The terms of address *tamparonga*, "female elder," and *taparonga*, "male elder," are terms of respect used by younger to older persons. Women become elders (*tamparonga*) when they have grandchildren and when their own parents are either dependent or deceased. Although most are near the end of their childbearing years,[2] there is no special term for menopause and no special significance attached to it. Lusi women do not retire to menstrual huts, nor do they avoid cooking for their families or eating particular foods. Menstrual blood is considered to be *mali* ("contaminating"), and a menstruating woman must be careful not to get even a trace of it in food or water lest she or someone else become ill. Menstrual blood poisoning (also called *mali*) is the only form of poisoning that Lusi women are thought to do. Most fertile women, however, do not spend much of their lives in a state where their contaminating potential is a problem. As Lancaster and King (this volume) observe, women such as the Lusi-Kaliai, who lack effective birth control methods and who customarily nurse their children for two years or longer, spend a relatively small portion of their reproductive years menstruating as compared with women in industrialized countries. If menopause is seen in this context, it is reasonable that a postmenopausal Lusi woman enjoys no special privileges and suffers no particular disadvantages not shared by younger women simply because she is no longer menstruating. The only change in their lives that older women note is the end of fertility, and the *tamparonga* who were my consultants said that women generally welcomed the end of pregnancy and childbearing. They attributed to menopause none of the symptoms of illness--depression, hot flashes, emotional instability--that are stereotypically associated with it by North Americans.

Sexuality

The end of the reproductive ability does not bring an end to either sexual activity or the responsibilities of parenthood. My consultants considered sexual behavior to be a private and personal matter, and opined that some people remain sexually active until very old age. As one consultant said, "Some old people 'itch for sex.' Others don't."

Because the Lusi consider the effluvia and odors of sexual intercourse to be contaminating (*mali*) and dangerous to newborns, ritually incised children, and the very ill (people who are in a liminal state), sexually active but postmenopausal women continue to have the potential to endanger others and are, therefore, still required to control their sexual essences.

Adults of both sexes and all ages are intensely interested in sexual activity, and adulterous affairs are common, even until midlife. Grandmothers are expected to be discreet in their adulterous affairs, however, and to choose partners who are near their own age. There was, in one village in 1981, a woman whose sexual appetite was considered to be insatiable and who continued having affairs with younger men even after she had several grandchildren. Her behavior was the subject of scandalized gossip, and she was nicknamed "The Frog" because she hopped from man to man. Both women and men were offended particularly by the fact that some of her partners were men who were younger than her own sons. Obviously, her husband did not effectively control her sexuality, and their neighbors speculated that he had given up trying.

Arranged Marriage

There are a number of factors that modify the ideal right of Lusi men to control the sexuality of their female kin.

1. Quinn makes a valid point when she observes that in societies where women are exchanged in marriage, both young people--the groom as well as the bride--lose their autonomy in selecting a mate (1977:209).

2. A right is only as effective as the holder's ability to enforce it. The Frog's husband could not enforce his rights over her sexuality, and fathers frequently have difficulty exercising their rights over the sexuality of their daughters. Young Lusi women regularly refuse to marry the husband selected for them and choose their own lovers. Many a disgruntled father is left to collect bridewealth for a marriage that became an accomplished fact without his consultation. Personal histories demonstrate that this has been going on for years--at least since the present great-grandparental generation was young--frequently with the collusion of one or both mothers.

3. In spite of the official line that marriages are transacted between fathers, it seems that those marriages that are successfully arranged according to the ideal are the product of negotiation between both sets of parents--mothers as well as fathers--at the request of at least one of the young people involved. If everyone is agreeable, or at least acquiescent, the proceedings go forward. A successful arrangement is not one that is imposed on anyone.

Affinal Relationships

    In some societies, the mother-in-law/daughter-in-law
relationship is marked by the authority and control of the
older woman over a young wife (see Brown 1982:145 for discussion and examples). This characterization does not
describe the interaction between Lusi mothers- and daughters-in-law.   Lusi affines avoid one another, but avoidance
rules are relaxed between affines of the same sex.   Ideally,
the relationship between mother-in-law and daughter-in-law
is one of friendly cooperation, courtesy, and mutual respect.
A young wife is expected to be respectful and obedient to
her husband's mother because she is a senior affine.   This
does not necessarily impose a burden on the daughter-in-law
because often the two women are fond of each other and
enjoy each other's company--especially if the two mothers
were involved in arranging the marriage.   A woman is
expected to give her daughter-in-law help and direction.
Cordial relations are especially important between the two
women if the young wife has settled virilocally and is living
far from her own kin.   In this case, the older woman should
not take advantage of her vulnerable daughter-in-law.
Instead, she should treat the younger woman with respect
and courtesy.   The Kaliai myth of Akro and Gagandewa contains an object lesson in the potential disaster that awaits
the woman, and society as well, should she abuse her son's
wife.
    In the myth, the wife, who is a foreigner, commits
suicide as a result of verbal abuse by her husband's mother.
Consequently, the older woman is murdered by her grieving
son, and war is declared on the husband's village by the
offended wife's kin (see Dorothy Counts 1980a for a detailed
analysis of the myth).
    This rule is normally followed in everyday life, and
Lusi mothers-in-law are urged to behave with restraint, even
when provoked.   One of my consultants told me of a crisis
that had occurred when her son, Peter, and his wife had
quarreled, and the wife had ambushed Peter outside his
mother's house, knocking him unconscious with a club.   For
a few minutes Peter's family believed him to be dead, and his
mother turned on the wife and began cursing her in Lusi.
The wife, who was an outsider, asked people standing by
what her mother-in-law was saying as she could not understand the local language.   "Nothing," she was told.   "She's
just upset because she thinks her son is dead."   At the
same time the distraught mother's friends were urging her to
be quiet and not say anything in Tok Pisin, which the wife

did understand. "They told me," she said, "that his wife was an outsider here, and that if she understood what I was saying she might be ashamed and kill herself. I really did want to kill her, but I couldn't even say what I thought."

A woman does become an elder when her children marry, but clearly she does not derive any significant degree of power from having a daughter-in-law at her mercy.

Motherhood

The end of a Lusi woman's childbearing ability does not necessarily mean the end of motherhood because parenthood, especially motherhood, is based on nurturance rather than biology, and people continue to nurture and adopt young children until late in life. Elders seek to adopt young kin for several reasons. First, the presence of children is said to give meaning to adult life. A number of older consultants have remarked to me that if they did not have youngsters to care for, their houses and lives would be empty and without meaning. A second important consideration is that children are the primary source of social security in Kaliai. Young people are expected to provide assistance to their elderly kin as they become increasingly feeble and dependent. Elderly people, especially widows, adopt children because they need help in gardening and in collecting firewood and water, but they are not yet ready to become totally dependent and a burden on others. Menopause does not usually mean an "empty nest" for a Lusi woman. Clearly, the reason why postmenopausal Lusi women do not suffer from the "empty nest syndrome" is that they do not permit the nest to stay empty. (Also see Kaufert this volume.)

Seniority

Birth order and relative age are at least as significant as gender in structuring the content of interpersonal relations. Firstborn children are the most important issue of a marriage, and older sisters, for example, have authority over younger brothers. By the same token, younger people are expected to respect and defer to their elders, who are responsible for the behavior of their juniors. The elder years are the prime of life, but they are also the years when physical ability begins to decline. This is compensated by the rule that no younger person should sit by and allow an elder to carry a heavy burden or do truly strenuous work.

Of course, Lusi women differ in character, and no one expects a lazy, foolish, slovenly young woman to become responsible, wise, and careful just because she becomes an elder. However, a *tamparonga* who aggressively participates in the cycle of ceremonial exchanges and trade that gives excitement and color to Lusi life will be esteemed and obeyed, especially if she is married to a village leader. In order to clarify this point, I must explain the role women play in the socioeconomic system of Kaliai.

Ceremony, Trade, and Exchange

Lusi men organize, manage, and receive the credit for the ceremonial exchanges that are the focus of Lusi social and economic life. A man who successfully controls and manipulates the system of ceremonial exchanges achieves renown and becomes a *maroni*, a leader. As noted above, there is no equivalent status for a Lusi woman. Nevertheless, women and the things they produce are critical to the functioning of the system, and women have economic autonomy.

A woman owns and controls her own sources of wealth and cash. An unmarried woman owns the coconut palms that she plants; furthermore, those trees and the money she earns from the copra she produces from them are hers, even after she marries. Married women consider themselves to own, in common with their husbands, the gardens, pigs, and coconut palms they have acquired during their marriage. Although the husband ultimately controls this property, he is expected to consult his wife before committing its use. A woman has autonomous control over the money she earns selling garden produce in the local market. She also owns the pandanas trees that she plants and the sleeping mats she makes from their leaves. Women's activities are, therefore, of considerable importance to Lusi economic life, especially because pandanas mats are the chief item of women's wealth and the primary export of the people of Kaliai.

The Lusi are deeply involved in a two-faceted system of exchange that structures and expresses both internal and external relations. Internally, ceremonial exchange celebrating rites of passage structures social relations within Lusi society. Externally, there is a system of trade that links the people of northwest New Britain with those of the Vitu Islands, the Siassi Islands, and the Rai Coast of New Guinea (Harding 1967; David Counts 1979, 1981). Two items, both produced by women, are essential in integrating this system. These items are *vula* ("shell money"), which is also produced by the Kove to the east, and pandanas sleeping mats. In

Kaliai, *vula* is the standard of value against which all other items are measured: when Lusi recount the amounts given in bridewealth or distributed to honor the dead, they recall the pigs that were killed and the fathoms of shell money that were given away (Counts and Counts 1970). Women are the primary makers of *vula,* but it is usually owned by, given by, and exchanged between men. Women who invest shell money in a distribution are usually acting as agents for male relatives; however, there is nothing to preclude a woman from owning it, and she may give and receive it in her own name.

In contrast, pandanas mats are entirely woman's wealth and are not distributed by men. Although their value is never recounted when men discuss the wealth that was distributed in ceremonies they sponsored, mats are critical to all exchanges. They are always part of the total given in internal distributions, and they are the unique item that the people of Kaliai contribute to the external trading system. They have practical utility, for they are used as sitting and sleeping mats, as raincoats, and as shrouds for the dead. They also express hospitality and establish social relationships. They are brought out for the comfort of honored and important guests, and when they are ceremonially given--as when they are thrown down before a child on the event of its first public dance performance--they establish a sharing relation between the child and the woman who has honored him. Pandanas mats are the stuff by which social ties are established and expressed. Their social importance is not limited to the Kaliai area, for Kaliai mats are prized throughout the area where they are traded.

The internal distribution system, in which women are most active, works in the following way. A couple routinely incurs numerous economic obligations during the course of its married life. The first of these, the one used here as an example, is usually the presentation of its firstborn child. The husband is responsible for sponsoring this expensive ceremony, and he is usually assisted and advised by the oldest ranking male of his kin group, probably a man he calls "father" or "older brother." The wife has obligations that parallel those of her husband. She must collect, for distribution, a supply of mats equivalent to the shell money accumulated by her husband. She is also responsible for preparing and distributing huge amounts of feast food. All guests (there may be several hundred) must be well fed during their visit, and there should be enough food for visitors to carry some home after everyone has eaten. The young wife is assisted in organizing this formidable task by the senior woman of her kin group, usually a woman she calls "mother" or "older sister." As a woman ages, she becomes more experienced in ceremonial procedure and she builds a network of women whom she has helped and who will reciprocate when she needs mats and cooked foods. As the women who were her advisers die or become dependent and withdraw from active life, her daughters marry and call on her to help them meet their responsibilities.

As a woman ages she has fewer older kin to whom she must defer and more younger kin for whom she is responsible and who owe her respect. If her husband is a *maroni*, she is increasingly obliged to provide the female wealth items and foods that he requires if he is to pursue his career successfully. Consequently, although she cannot make a name for herself as female equivalent of a *maroni*, an elder woman may direct and organize economic exchange activity, both in her own right as a senior female and as the wife of an important man.

Marital Violence

As I mentioned earlier, the relationship between husband and wife may be marked by violence, and wife beating is not uncommon. Several points should be noted here.

First, the violence is not always one-way. Wives also attack their husbands, sometimes with the intent to maim or kill. I know of three such instances, all precipitated by the husband's adulterous affairs or by his plans to marry a second wife.

Second, the reaction of others to domestic violence varies with the cause of the conflict. Generally, it is not unreasonable for a man to beat his wife if she neglects their children or draws blood while punishing one of them. Conversely, others--especially women--express sympathy with the violent response of a wife who has found her husband with another woman. There are community controls that contain domestic violence. For example, a person who publicly attacks her or his spouse may be subject to sanctions carried out by supernatural beings. Also, because men and women from the same village often marry, the relatives of an abused spouse are likely to witness the attack. I know of no case in which the kin of an attacked husband intervened. But men who beat their wives excessively or unjustly are subject to physical attack by her co-resident kin, supernatural sanctions invoked by her relatives, and ultimately the possibility that an abused and shamed woman will permanently leave her husband or kill herself. I know of examples of the invocation of all of these sanctions by abused wives or their kin (Dorothy Counts 1980b).

Finally, the relationship between spouses mellows as people reach middle age. This is true even in relationships that are characterized by violence. Why does this mellowing occur? Van Arsdale notes that whereas among the Asmat young women are sometimes beaten to death, grandmothers are not struck. This is, he says,

> not so much out of deference to their age or infirmity as out of fear of the public uproar they could create. Some were so vociferous and eloquent that their husbands would not even argue with them, let alone beat them. These women reprimanded their spouses at the top of their lungs before a rapt audience of fellow villagers, young and old, who took delight in hearing an imaginative catalogue of the unfortunate husband's sexual inadequacies (1981:115).

Van Arsdale's reasoning does not explain Lusi behavior. I am not sure why it is that the old Asmat women are permitted to publicly berate their husbands without fear of reprisal, while young women are not. Young Lusi women certainly have mouths, and although it is uncommon for a young wife to take a quarrel into the public arena, it does happen. Furthermore, if her cause is just, if for instance she finds her husband copulating with another woman in her own house, she may well have community sympathy and support.

An alternative explanation is suggested by Quinn, who argues that wife beating reflects the intimacy and tensions that exist within the marital relationship (1977:190). By the time they become elders, a Lusi couple whose marriage has survived the first turbulent 20 years are likely to have resolved most of the sources of tension, or at least have learned to contain those tensions at a relatively nonviolent level. In addition they have acquired common interests, which consume their energies. They are concerned with the proper presentation and marriage of their children; with the prosperity of their common property; with the maintenance of peaceful reciprocal relations with both sets of affines; with the establishment of a "name" for the husband, whose prestige devolves onto the wife; and with the duty of elders to organize and direct the activity of their children and followers. While it is not approved behavior, it is not unexpected for an angry young husband to beat his wife or for a mistreated young woman to run away with a lover, to threaten to kill her husband if he tries to take a second wife, or even to commit suicide. Such behavior however, is not appropriate for responsible elders, and perhaps for this reason, it is uncommon behavior.

SUMMARY

Lusi women are, in a sense, silent partners. Their participation in and contribution to Kaliai life are critical to the maintenance of society; yet this participation seldom receives public acknowledgement. For example,
1. Children are said to have physical and essential ties to their fathers but not their mothers. They are considered to belong to their father's patrikin group. A mother must forge her ties to her children through nurturance.
2. The contribution women make to economic life is not publicly proclaimed, yet ceremonial exchange and trade would not exist in their present form without the female production of mats and shell money.
3. The contribution that women make to the successful enterprise of their male kin is publicly acknowledged only in folk tales, where the mother who socializes her fatherless son in the esoteric knowledge reserved to males is a common theme.[3] The character and ambition of successful women is attributed to the influence of fathers, not mothers, and their activities directly enhance the prestige of husbands and sons, not themselves.
This generalization does not change significantly as women reach elder status. The independence that a *tamparonga* enjoys is not the result of a fundamental change in the way of life she knew as a young woman. A postmenopausal woman continues to do the same sorts of things she did when she was younger, except that as she becomes a senior female, she assumes increasing responsibility for the behavior of her juniors, and she assists her younger female kin to meet their obligations.
The key here is responsibility. The factors suggested by other scholars, and discussed at the beginning of this chapter, do not seem to affect significantly the life of a Lusi *tamparonga*.
1. Menopause brings no radical changes. A woman no longer produces menstrual blood, but a postreproductive woman is not perceived as being less feminine than a fertile one. As long as she is sexually active, she continues to produce odors and substances that are contaminating and dangerous to vulnerable people. There is, however, some neutralization of gender in the very young and the very old. Consequently, an old woman may be invited by her male kin to remain in the village when the spirits are abroad, and she may, in an emergency, enter the men's house and handle the sacred paraphernalia stored there. Conversely, an old man may baby-sit young children and even sweep the plaza in front of his men's house, a task usually done by women. These are, however, exceptional circumstances that do not

significantly affect everyday life, nor do they affect the rights and obligations of the elderly.

2. The end of a woman's fertility does not signal an end to responsible parenthood. Older couples and individuals, including widows, adopt and care for young children until they themselves become dependent.

3. A postmenopausal woman holds no new offices or positions and inherits no rights in land or property that she did not enjoy as a young woman.

4. A woman becomes a *tamparonga* when she has adult children who marry and bear children. Because the rules of residence are normatively virilocal, a woman is more likely to have co-resident adult sons than married daughters. She derives no significant degree of power from her role as mother-in-law, however. Young wives are not helpless, and a woman's authority over her son's wife is limited by the same sorts of considerations that limit the power of a bigman over his followers. Both have authority and receive respect in proportion to the responsibility they are prepared to undertake. An adept, responsible woman who is the wife of a bigman will be known as the "bone (or support) of the village." But a Lusi must delicately balance the exercise of power and authority. One must "use it or lose it," but it is also possible to "abuse it and lose it."

In closing, I should note that the permission that an old woman may receive to be present during the climax of male ceremonies is not evidence of any increase in authority or esteem. Women do not seem to resent their exclusion from male secrets, nor do they necessarily consider the invitation to witness these secrets an honor. In 1981 one of my friends, who is now in her sixties and blind, was invited to remain in the village while the spirits were released. She proudly refused and left with the other women as she had always done, to join them in feasting and making lewd fun of the men's "secrets."

NOTES

This study was written for a symposium on middle-aged women organized by Dr. Judith K. Brown for the 1982 American Anthropological Association Meetings, December 9, 1982. I wish to thank Dr. Brown for her helpful comments on earlier drafts of this chapter.

Research for this chapter was conducted in West New Britain Province, Papua New Guinea, in 1966-67, supported by the U.S. National Science Foundation; in 1971, supported by the Wenner-Gren Foundation and the University of Waterloo; in 1975-76 supported by the Canada Council and University of Waterloo sabbatical leave; and in 1981, supported by the Social Sciences and Humanities Research Council of Canada and sabbatical leave from the University of Waterloo.

[1] In 24 months of field research in West New Britain, I have witnessed no more than four instances of wife beating, although I have been told of many more. Some men are reputed to beat their wives frequently (although not when I was around), while others never do.

[2] The data which support my statement were supplied to me by the Kaliai clinic. They were collected by the missionaries when the clinic was run by the Kaliai Roman Catholic Mission and include chronological ages of local people that were estimated by the European mission personnel. According to these data, the average age at which the women of Kandoka (a Lusi-Kaliai village and the site of most of my field research) bear their last child is 44.58 years.

[3] In a number of Kaliai tales, widows teach their sons how to train hunting dogs, how to manufacture and use spears and shields, and other esoterica. These stories probably reflect cultural truth, for it is clear from my discussions with women that many of them know male secrets (one elderly woman corrected her husband when he made a mistake in telling a secret story describing the origin of masked ancestor figures) and that men know that they know.

REFERENCES

Brown, Judith K.
   1982   Cross-cultural Pespectives on Middle-aged Women. Current Anthropology 23(2):143-156.
Counts, David R.
   1979   Adam Smith in the Garden: Supply, Demand and Art Production in New Britain. *In* Exploring the Visual Art of Oceania. Sidney M. Mead, ed. pp. 334-341. Honolulu: University of Hawaii Press.
   1981   Taming the Tiger: Change and Exchange in West New Britain. *In* Persistence and Exchange. Roland W. Force and Brenda Bishop, eds. pp. 51-58. Honolulu: Pacific Science Association.

Counts, David R., and Dorothy Ayers Counts
1970 The Vula of Kaliai: A Primitive Currency with Commercial Use. Oceania 41:90-105.

Counts, Dorothy Ayers
1980a Akro and Gagandewa: A Melanesian Myth. Journal of the Polynesian Society 89:33-65.
1980b Fighting Back Is Not the Way: Suicide and the Women of Kaliai. American Ethnologist 7:332-351.
1982 The Tales of Laupu. Port Moresby: Institute of Papua New Guinea Studies.

Counts, Dorothy Ayers, and David R. Counts
1982 "I'm not dead...yet!" Aging, Death and the Dead: Process and Experience in Kaliai. Paper delivered at the Annual Meetings of the Association for Social Anthropology in Oceania. Hilton Head Island, S.C.

Friedl, Ernestine
1975 Women and Men: An Anthropologist's View. New York: Holt, Rinehart and Winston.

Gutmann, David
1969 The Country of Old Men: Cross-Cultural Studies in the Psychology of Later Life. Occasional Papers in Gerontology 5. Ann Arbor: University of Michigan and Wayne State, Institute of Gerontology.
1975 Parenthood: A Key to the Comparative Psychology of the Life Cycle. In Life-Span Development Psychology. Nancy Datan and L. Ginsberg, eds. pp. 167-184. New York: Academic Press.

Harding, Thomas
1967 Voyagers of the Vitiaz Strait: A Study of a New Guinea Trading System. American Ethnological Society Monograph 44. Seattle: University of Washington Press.

Keith, Jennie
1980 The Best Is Yet to Be: Toward an Anthropology of Age. In Annual Review of Anthropology, 9. Bernard Siegel, Alan Beals, Stephen Tyler, eds. pp. 339-366. Palo Alto, Calif.: Annual Reviews Inc.

Kessler, E. S.
1976 Women: An Anthropological View. New York: Holt, Rinehart and Winston.

Ortner, Sherry
1974 Is Female to Male as Nature Is to Culture? In Woman, Culture and Society. M. Rosaldo and L. Lamphere, eds. pp. 67-88. Stanford, Calif.: Stanford University Press.

Quinn, Naomi
1977 Anthropological Studies on Women's Status. In Annual Review of Anthropology, 6. Bernard Siegel, Alan Beals, and Stephen Tyler, eds. pp. 181-225. Palo Alto, Calif.: Annual Reviews Inc.

Reiter, R. R., ed.
  1975   Toward an Anthropology of Women.   New York:
  Monthly Review Press.
Van Arsdale, Peter
  1981   The Elderly Asmat of New Guinea.   *In* Other Ways of
  Growing Old.   Pamela Amoss and Stevan Harrell, eds.
  pp. 111-124.   Stanford, Calif.:   Stanford University
  Press.

II   INTERMEDIATE SOCIETIES

This group of societies is perhaps best defined by what they are not. They are not small-scale traditional societies, neither are they complex or industrialized, but elements of all these are present. Although subsistence depends upon cultivation, wage work is also available. Nominally Christian or Islamic, their religions nevertheless have a distinctive local character.

Unlike the traditional societies of the previous section, these societies reserve special statuses for older women. Some matrons participate in national politics among the Maori (as described by Sinclair) and among the Malagasi speakers of Mayotte (as described by Lambek). The status of the middle-aged women of Mayotte and of Sudan (as described by Boddy) is influenced by personal circumstances such as inheritance. For some older Maori women, Sinclair reports considerable public visibility, when in charge of religious festivals. Yet they must maneuver with care in a confusing post-colonial world. The middle-aged women of Sudan can aspire to a privileged position, but they need luck and perspicacity, or they face dismaying alternatives.

Kerns notes that women among the Garifuna enjoy greater freedom at middle age than during their childbearing years. Yet as their freedom increases, so does their insistence that younger women abide by the restrictions they themselves observed earlier in life. Influence over their juniors takes a somewhat different form among the Maori and among the women of Mayotte. Gradually their position becomes enhanced due to the growth of a network of supportive kin and due to increasing numbers of individuals who stand in obligation to them for a variety of past services and favors. These matrons are in a position to collect on the good will and influence they have built up over the years.

5 Motherhood and Other Careers in Mayotte (Comoro Islands)

Michael Lambek

The anthropological literature frequently presents a static picture of sex roles. Although it is now commonly argued that women have a good deal of informal power, even where they lack formal authority, women are viewed as using the power to respond to particular situations, usually those constructed by men. In this chapter I suggest that the women of Mayotte, Comoro Islands, Western Indian Ocean, develop long-term strategies of action. My point is not to show conscious, instrumental manipulation on the part of women, but to demonstrate that the overall course of their lives is as much a product of their own actions (albeit in the face of serious constraints) as is the course of men's lives. Following the theme of this book, I will pay particular attention to middle-aged women, but I will argue that "middle age" is not a culturally recognized category in Mayotte and has no exclusive privileges or obligations associated with it. Hence, the question becomes one of assessing the degree to which the period of later adulthood represents the "fruition" of earlier plans, decisions, and interests. My aim is to present a broad picture of women's lives in rural Mayotte--one that emphasizes continuity, as well as change, and incorporates the range of diversity in the experience of women within the society.

AGING IN MAYOTTE

Mayotte is a tropical island of some 45,000 inhabitants, located approximately halfway between the Swahili coast of East Africa and Madagascar. I worked in a pair of villages of Malagasy speakers, which were formed in the mid-19th century by a mixture of immigrants from the Sakalava states of northwest Madagascar and indentured laborers from East Africa. Two further strong influences on the communities were the indigenous stratified Muslim society and the enterprises of the French, who took control of Mayotte in 1841 and established plantations there. The plantations declined in importance around the turn of the century. Since then the economy of the villagers has been dominated by subsistence horticulture, supplemented by fishing, raising cattle and other domestic animals, and performing occasional wage labor. In the last few years the sale of cash crops by small independent producers has also been significant. It must be clear then that Mayotte is, and has been, a society in flux, and I cannot speak of a baseline of "tradition" against which to measure change. Any shifts in the positions of Mayotte women in the course of their lifetimes have doubtless come as much from changing historical circumstance as from a playing out of a traditional pattern of the life cycle. Nevertheless, I will attempt to consider the life cycle as it appeared in 1975-76.

In Mayotte there is no clearly demarcated period of "middle age." The sharpest break in a woman's life occurs with her first marriage (Lambek 1983). Thereafter, aging is a gradual process. The term *ulu be* (literally "big person") is polysemous and context dependent. At menarche it may be said that the "child" (*zaza*) is "now grown up" (*fa ulu be*). But she will still be referred to as a child until her defloration (whether properly, during the course of her first wedding, or improperly, prior to it). Defloration is a clear transformation that ends childhood. But again a woman is only a *ulu be* in reference to this event and in contrast to "children." In other contexts she will say of herself, and it will be said of her, that she is *tsendriky ulu be* ("not yet adult"). *Ulu be* also refers to both "responsible elder" (*ulu be an tanana* "village elder" and *ulu be an mraba* "family elder") and "important person" ("big man," "big woman"). These statuses only become unequivocal relatively late in life, if at all. However, the final stage of life is that of *bakoko*, which implies physical or mental infirmity. Whereas *ulu be* is a status that indicates social relevance, the *bakoko* is someone from whom the community has already begun to withdraw.

In the Mayotte scheme then, there is no clearly demarcated category corresponding to "middle age." Rather, there is gradually increasing social adulthood, constituted of a combination of age, social competence, and responsibility and followed by a decline into senescence. Menopause or cessation of fertility for other reasons (see Boddy this volume) is not a socially significant transition point.

The experience of aging and adulthood is organized largely in terms of generation, relative age, and the fellowship of age cohorts. Of these, generation is perhaps the most significant. Motherhood marks a notable achievement in a woman's life and henceforward she is addressed by a teknonym (*nindry ny fulany*, "mother of so-and-so"). A woman who does not give birth does not thereby lose in prestige (although she may be extremely disappointed) and will be given the name "aunt (or elder sibling) of so-and-so." Grandmotherhood marks another transition, but in most women this occurs during their thirties and well before they cease giving birth themselves. A grandmother is sometimes addressed as *dady* (*ny fulany*), "grandmother (of so-and-so)." When she reaches old age she is referred to either by her childhood name preceded by *dady*, thus Dady Salima, Grandmother Salima or by a nickname, e.g., Sokolon (Cyclone, noted for her volatile temper). These names are used by the entire community.

While the relationship of children to parents is marked by respect and attention that should last throughout the parents' lives, grandparents are often treated with levity by people of the grandchildren's generation (although less by those whom they have raised). Grandparents tease grandchildren when the latter are young and often have to suffer a turning of the tables when they themselves become *bakoko*, a condition for which there is not always great sympathy.

Relative age structures relationships within a single generation, so that the *zandry* ("younger sibling") should demonstrate respect for his or her *zuky* ("older sibling"), irrespective of gender. In any encounter (except where generation contradicts relative age) the younger person should initiate deferential greetings to the elder.

In community-wide ceremonial affairs, people are grouped according to age and sex. Shortly before marriage boys and girls join their respective sets of age mates, with which they will be associated until the groups disband at old age. There are approximately five or six age groups for each sex in a village (although the sets may succeed each other more rapidly in larger villages). As she or he marries for the first time, each member of a given age/sex group must sponsor a feast for the other members. In later years the groups continue to form work and commensal units on the occasion of village ceremonies and of ceremonies, such as weddings, sponsored by individuals but to which the entire community is invited and lends its assistance.[1] In general, responsibilities are divided so that elders advise, the middle-aged manage, and the young adults execute collective tasks, although there is also much overlap. For example, the age groups of older women do their share of food preparation. Respect for the wisdom and skills of the elderly is balanced by an appreciation for the energy of youth. At the same time, there is a certain tension between the old and the young, especially among the men.[2] In the arena of village politics, young adults are recognized as a significant interest group whose force must be acknowledged. The division into a number of age groups, each of which is in some competition with its immediate neighbors offsets some of the opposition between old and young.

To summarize the discussion so far, the aging process in Mayotte is gradual, emphasizing continuity rather than discontinuity. The generations succeed each other without sharp breaks, and individuals remain at the end of adulthood in much the same positions vis-à-vis significant others, parents, children, siblings, and members of the age sets, as they began. Age is essentially a matter of growth; a person gains juniors and loses seniors. The only reversal occurs in the relations between alternate generations. Grandchildren, often named for their grandparents, are viewed, in some sense, as replacing them. This offsets the authority gained with age and ensures that the greater relative influence associated with later adulthood is a matter of degree rather than kind.

WOMEN'S CAREERS

I have been speaking in the abstract, about structure rather than organization, and about men as well as women. In turning to a consideration of adult women, I will continue to emphasize continuity. I follow Myerhoff and Simic in their conceptualization of aging as a "career." They view aging as "a process by which the individual builds, or fails to build, a lasting structure of relationships, accomplishments, affect, and respect that will give meaning and validation to one's total life. . ."(1978:240). In other words, the position of women at middle age is in large part a product of their own creative endeavors (in the face of certain constraints) and of their entire lives to that point. Thus I emphasize continuity within the life cycle but point to the discontinuity among the experiences of different Mayotte women. In the remainder of the chapter, I will consider certain aspects of women's life activity, emphasizing the choices open to them as well as the constraints. In general, I am concerned with how a woman acquires and consolidates sufficient material resources, social ties, and specialized knowledge to develop by later adulthood a position of relative security and authority in domestic and public life.

Marriage

At marriage a woman leaves her parents and establishes a separate household (Lambek 1983). Henceforward, she maintains her own hearth and home until she is physically incapable of doing so. She receives a house from her parents, built by her father or brothers on land to which either her mother or father has claim and thus in the same village as at least one of them. Usually it is near her mother's house. She also receives household furnishings from her kin and a wardrobe and jewelry from her husband. No return is expected upon termination of the marriage.[3] This means that in the event of a marital breakup a woman, no matter what her age, does not return to her parents but continues her existence as a relatively autonomous householder.

A wife is responsible for most of the childcare, cooking, washing, and cleaning; a man is responsible for supplying the basic necessities which must be purchased: kerosene, salt, soap, etc. Wife and husband both engage in subsistence horticulture. In any given year they may cultivate several plots located on land to which either party has access. It will be clear for each plot whether the yield belongs to the wife, the husband, or both jointly, but in general it is the wife who controls and distributes subsistence products. By contrast, if cash crops are planted, they are usually the husband's responsibility and he is entitled to dispose of the earnings. For example, if a man marries a woman whose father has planted ylang ylang trees, he can choose to work with his father-in-law, who will then split the proceeds. The wife receives indirectly, as the result of her husband's purchases on her behalf. Nevertheless, it is she, along with her siblings, who inherits (inheritance is bilateral), and should the marriage break up, the land and the crops planted on it remain in her control. Thus she has a certain amount of leverage to ensure she receives sufficient support, and in the event of termination of the marriage can manage the ylang ylang herself if she so chooses. Her husband has the right to manage the cash income, but only so long as he fulfills his responsibilities. Likewise, in the case where a man is earning income from his own land, his wife expects adequate support; if it is not forthcoming, she may end the relationship.

Marriages in Mayotte are brittle, and a good marriage is defined as one in which the partners show mutual respect (*ishima*). This means that they should refrain from adultery and cooperate in the management of the household. A good marriage is thus one in which trust grows and in which the parties recognize that mutual respect and interest predominate. After a few years either the wife gains assurance that the husband dispenses the income fairly or the husband begins to share money management with his wife. In most cases a woman also has a minor source of income of her own, perhaps from a small cash crop or craft. Whereas a husband has the duty to draw from his income to maintain the household, a woman is under no such obligation.

Both women and men are economic actors in their own rights and both can own property, spend money on themselves, aid their kin, and contribute to various public activities. For some of the larger ceremonial exchanges entailing the provision of feasts to which all village members are invited, wife and husband may function as an economic unit, thereby fulfilling their individual ceremonial obligations by jointly producing the feast. The completion of these ceremonies is a major step in an individual's social career. A husband and wife who trust each other may engage in other joint projects, such as the construction of a new house or the purchase of land. If they do not trust each other, they will put relatively more resources into projects of their respective sibling groups.

The growth of trust also means greater mobility for the wife. In the early years her husband may be reluctant to see her travel much (although even then, she is hardly house or village bound), but older women pay frequent visits to kin and friends in other villages and travel to ceremonies and political meetings.

One career path for a woman, then, is the construction of a solidary relationship with a husband based on mutual trust and respect. The conjugal unit becomes a basis for joint social action, for building a family, social links, a material estate, and prestige. The main threat to a woman who invests in her marital relationship and looks to it for security is that the trust may break down, her husband may choose to initiate a second, polygynous union, or to abandon her entirely. In fact, although most men are tempted by polygyny, especially when they reach middle age and feel they can afford it, the chances of this sort of outcome appear to decline the longer the marriage lasts. Aside from feeling hurt, a woman will be outraged that her husband is choosing to direct his cash elsewhere, especially if he had little enough to begin with.   A woman has three choices when faced with this situation: to convince her husband to abandon his plans, to throw him out, or to put up with the situation.   Many attempts at polygyny fizzle as the husband realizes that the new marriage poses too great a threat to his own investments in the previous relationship.   Indeed, a slighted wife often successfully holds out for a large compensation before agreeing to resume the marriage as before. There is also a great deal of moral pressure among women not to accept the overtures of a man who is already married in the same village, especially if it is to a kinswoman.   Thus a polygynous man must be mobile and capable of pursuing his social and economic interests simultaneously from two locations. It is often much easier to simply stay with the first wife should she make an ultimatum.[4]

A middle-aged woman who is left without a husband may or may not be in a difficult position, depending in large part on the ties she has made or maintained beyond the conjugal relationship.   As a member of a sibling group, she has access to subsistence resources, and as an adult woman, she owns her own house and utensils.   She may have a problem with a cash and labor supply, forcing her into dependence on brothers and adult sons until she can find a new husband or lover.   On the other hand, she may have amassed sufficient skills or resources to support herself.   Some townswomen become wealthy in real estate, renting out their houses and investing in new ones (see also Ottino 1964).[5]

I said earlier that Mayotte marriages are brittle. Divorce is very easy and means simply that the parties no longer live together or support one another.   A woman has a little more difficulty asking a man to leave than a man has in leaving; nevertheless, it is always possible to force him out, if necessary by conducting an affair under his nose.   A number of marriages break up early, as a result of one or both parties growing tired of the union. Women often divorce because their husbands fail to provide adequate economic support. Most divorced women remain in close contact with their kin and continue their subsistence pursuits in the village.   However, a young divorcee is considerably more mobile than her married counterpart, and in fact there is no one with direct authority over her.   She may close up her house and disappear for lengthy visits to kin and friends in other villages or in town.   Some women engage in a series of relatively short-lived marriages, possibly as many as 20 or more in a lifetime.   They diversify rather than consolidate their relations.   Some travel off the island in the course of their marital adventures.   Although they usually continue to return home for various periods of residence and often do marry co-villagers, by middle age their position in the village is marginal unless they have children there.

Some women place (or claim to place) a high value on the diversity of their marital experiences and scorn their sisters who remain loyal to a single spouse. In middle age they are often willing parties to polygynous unions, seeing their husbands intermittently and thus retaining a good deal of autonomy.

In sum, it is difficult to compare the positions of older and younger women in the domestic economy. Wives are not objects of exchange and have the right to break free of a union, marry elsewhere, or live independently. The major constraint on all adult women is the fact that although access to subsistence resources is relatively open, men have an easier time acquiring cash. As the cash sphere becomes ever more significant, so the position of the majority of women inevitably declines. On the other hand, it must be remembered that acquiring a steady source of cash is by no means easy for village men either and is viewed by most of them as a constant source of worry. Moreover, in the recent past most of the cash was immediately transformed into goods that were either consumed on ceremonial occasions or given to women and which they accumulated (also see Ottino 1964). This too is changing with the increasing penetration of the cash economy. On the one hand, men are forced to invest in further productive resources, and on the other, they are purchasing an increasing array of consumer goods for their own use. Many households have a running argument as to who owns the shortwave transistor radio.

Finally, although women are not particularly encouraged to participate in and have far less opportunity for wage labor than men, a few of them choose to operate as part-time entrepreneurs. For example, a number of women maintain small shops in the village. The owner of the longest-running, largest, and most successful of the village shops is an energetic woman in her mid-thirties who has also begun to produce her own ylang ylang cash crop. She travels to town a good deal more frequently than most of the men in the village and pursues her interests among numerous business contacts there.

Child Rearing

Kinship in Mayotte is bilateral and children belong equally to wife and husband. Moreover, because child transfers are easily arranged, no one need remain with or without children should he or she desire otherwise. Child rearing is an activity that women can pursue throughout their lives; alternatively, they can avoid it. In the circulation of children, middle-aged women play a major role, although men, young women, and the children themselves may also have an interest in the matter.

A young mother is not usually left to care for her children alone. A woman helps her inexperienced daughter in the tasks of motherhood and occasionally removes an infant or toddler from the latter's care entirely. Or a young mother without sufficient adult assistance takes in a younger sibling, niece, or nephew to help her in child care and other domestic tasks. Women often begin to have grandchildren before they have stopped giving birth themselves; at this time their compounds may be full of children. Once weaning has begun, child care may be shared informally by a group of closely related women.

Child transfers are common, ranging from informal or impermanent arrangements such as those mentioned above to those that are less frequent and more permanent. Women can ask one another for children and the requests are often difficult to turn down, especially when they come from senior kinswomen, such as a mother or mother-in-law. Some young women find themselves constrained to give up their first few offspring to the various people who ask for them. Mothers who have a history of losing infants to disease may be said to be unable to raise children and will send out subsequent births fairly automatically. Usually this is considered to be a matter of fate rather than fault. Because stepparents are considered not to have the best interests of stepchildren at heart, the offspring of divorced or widowed parents are often taken in by a relative. In these ways infertile women or those whose children are already grown can acquire children to raise.

A few women do not wish to raise children and give them to relatives as soon as they can. An example is Fatima, a young woman living with her third husband. She has no full siblings and both her mother and her mother's mother are dead. Her two children from her first marriage are being raised, respectively, by her mother's father's sister (who also raised Fatima) and by her mother's mother's brother, who is also the child's father's father's brother. Fatima's child from her second marriage lives with his father's kin in his village. Her newborn baby will go to its father's relatives as soon as it is a few weeks old. In explanation, Fatima says she just "can't handle children." She becomes angry with them very quickly; moreover they hinder her when she wants to travel. Another woman doesn't like to raise children because she "doesn't know how to raise her voice."

Older women also make decisions about child rearing, and many of them choose to take in children. For example, when Amina died leaving a toddler and a baby no more than a few weeks old, her mother-in-law Velu immediately accepted them, bringing to seven the number of grandchildren she was then raising. Velu had left her latest husband because he refused to help support so many children; instead, she was being financially assisted by her own adult children. Amina's mother, Hamba, was married but raising no children at the time of Amina's death. However she declined to take the children on the grounds that the spirit who possessed her could not stand the smell of urine and would make her sick were she to be in close contact with infants. Other people suggested this was actually Hamba rather than her spirit speaking. Four years later Hamba took in the two children (both well past the age of toilet training) of her other daughter, who had left her husband for a man in another village.

None of these women is typical. Velu was much admired for her love and patience with children--at one point she had even raised the child of a co-wife--while Hamba was considered somewhat selfish and unsociable. Nevertheless, the point is that women are not tied to child care and middle age does not make a difference in this regard.[6]

More burdensome than child rearing is the care middle-aged women must provide for aged and ailing parents (*bakoko*). This is considered to be the responsibility of a daughter first, although a son will contribute financially and will look in on his mother frequently. The relationship between a middle-aged woman and her aged mother is full of ambivalence. People have little patience with the very old, but a daughter is supposed to respect her mother and would be ashamed to reject her and be criticized for doing so. If she has no sisters, a middle-aged daughter cannot rely on much assistance from others and may be quite tied to the household. For example, Rehema felt guilty whenever she spent several days away from home working in distant fields. Her adult daughters, who helped willingly with the care of small children, looked after Rehema's mother very grudgingly and often neglected her. Care of the elderly, then, is a constraint placed upon middle-aged women but not upon younger ones.

By contrast, far from being a constraint that keeps a woman anchored to the home, motherhood in Mayotte is an activity that provides women with an extra source of domestic labor and widens a woman's ties. One of the primary reasons for taking in children is to have a helping hand. Moreover, a mother exchanges services with close kinswomen who are also raising children. The ties established with her husband and his kin will be continued even if the couple separate. Thus people say that "a marriage with children never dies." If the mater is not the genetrix, she reinforces links with the latter and with the genitor and can expect assistance from them. Fosterage helps to cement marriage alliances and maintains links despite divorce. Women can also restructure kin ties through the establishment of "fictive" kin relationships and reinforce these links by means of child transfers. The more children she raises, the more a woman can participate in arranging marriages and subsequent child transfers. As time passes she becomes the center of an ever expanding *mraba* ("family") with ever greater links to other members of the community. By maintaining an active interest in children and grandchildren, she can in turn expect their respect and support. Thus women's manipulation of social relations can partially offset their unequal access to cash. Moreover, the greater a woman's authority within the family, the more significant her role in mediating between the family and the community, acting in support of either family interests or public morality (for example, by monitoring the propriety of proposed marital unions of junior members of the family).

Let us briefly consider two women in their fifties who may be said to have made a career of motherhood. Dady Mwana (Figure 1) is a widow who has had three husbands. She has raised a daughter by the first husband, three daughters by the second husband, two male and two female junior kin of her third husband, four grandchildren, and one son of one of her foster children. One of her daughters has only a single child and lives next door to Dady Mwana, participating in her daily activities. Dady Mwana also arranged the marriages of her third husband's kin to her own relations (Figure 2), thus consolidating her family. Dady Mwana runs a small shop and makes use of one of her foster sons to replenish the stock. As a widow, she is now the focal member of a large kin group.

Halima Kolo is the middle one of three sisters. Only the eldest of the three was fertile, but while the youngest sister, whom the villagers consider slow-witted, has never raised children, Halima has raised many (Figure 3). Halima is divorced from her third husband. She cultivates ylang ylang planted by her deceased second husband on land belonging to her sibling group, is head (*ulu be*) of her kin group (*mraba*), chief of the village women, and a renowned curer.

Public Life

Finally, we may compare the roles of older and younger women in public life. It should be clear from the preceding discussion that both women and men are viewed as

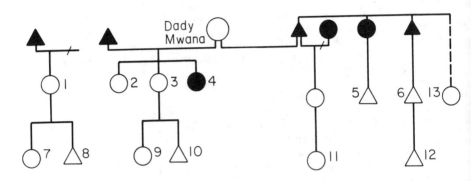

Figure 1. Children Raised by Dady Mwana

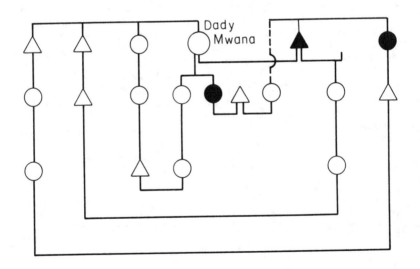

Figure 2. Marriage Links Among Dady Mwana's Kin

Key: Numbered individuals are those who were raised by Halima. Black figures indicate deceased individuals.

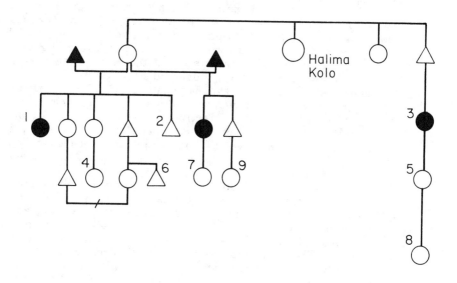

Figure 3. Children Raised by Halima Kolo

autonomous actors, as "social adults" who can engage in multiple activities beyond the domestic sphere and who can determine in large part where the boundaries of the domestic sphere are to lie. Older women (like older men) play a more important role than younger women in public life, but this seems to be a function of the value attributed to relative age rather than to conditions specific to being female.

All women belong to the village age groups mentioned at the beginning of the chapter. A woman becomes a full member of the village organization only in the third year after her wedding. When women participate in public work, their young daughters stay at home to carry out domestic chores. Each age group has a leader and the leader of the senior group is referred to as the "chief" of the women of the village. She and her assistants act as the spokespersons for the entire body of adult women and can often exert strong pressure on the men. The main function of the age groups is the regulation and implementation of ceremonial activity, and the chief of women negotiates with the men concerning decisions of scheduling and the like. The women determine and collect each household's contribution to an affair and redistribute the raw materials so that they may be processed by each age group working as a unit. Women are considered far better at extracting household contributions than are men. The names of each age group assert the women's views of themselves. The "Lightning" are so called because they work quickly. Other names include "Airplanes" and "Chatterboxes."

In general, the women's groups maintain a tighter control over their members than do the men's groups. This was particularly evident in the organization of the two political parties found in Mayotte in the 1970's, especially the Soldat, which advocated modernization through closer ties with France and separation from the other Comoro Islands. In the decade before Comoran independence, Soldat women led a vigorous campaign. On one memorable occasion women from throughout Mayotte gathered to surround road-building machinery and prevented its removal to one of the other islands. They spent several days and nights there and sent messengers asking their menfolk for more provisions. Men agree that women provided the force behind the movement and that men only began to take an active role when victory appeared imminent. During 1975-76 I attended several large political congresses at which the number of women present appeared roughly to equal the number of men. The middle-aged female party leaders of each village played key roles in maintaining support for the cause and in building the inter-village party organization. During the referendum, they sat next to the ballot boxes in each village and woe betide anyone, male or female, observed by them to vote for the opposing party. The women utilized the inter-village ceremonial system to ensure broad participation. Women's political meetings were held in conjunction with performances of the *Maulida Shengy*, a lengthy religious text sung by women in honor of the Prophet. Each village had to send a specific number of performers; absent villages were threatened with having to host the next *Maulida* themselves, a considerable expense. In this way too, the skills of leadership were tied to traditional religious knowledge, a domain in which the middle-aged were likely to be preeminent.

Middle-aged women were also much more active than men and younger women in celebrating political victory. They rented all the bush taxis on the island one day and drove around singing, clapping and ululating. In many villages the adult women planted a French flag and performed victory dances. However, with the achievement of their first aims, separation from the remaining Comoro Islands and a reassertion of the French presence in Mayotte, the women took second place to men in the party and in the government. In 1980, after the reorganization of the village administrative system, two out of the seven councillors who represented the villages in which I worked were women. One of the women was the successful shopkeeper mentioned earlier, the other an ambitious woman who operated entirely through the manipulation of kinship ties and through her position in the age group system. There is also inequality in that the two women represent "women" whereas the men represent the entire community. Most of the representatives, male and female, were not much older than 40, reflecting the division of political roles between elders as advisers and younger adults as executors. Village authority is vested ultimately in the *ulu be*, the "elders." These include senior women as well as senior men, but the public role of the former is slight.

The key female leader remains the head of the women's age group organization. She is in later middle age. Women identify with her and respect her. Occasionally they labor collectively in her fields on their own initiative, not out of any obligation, they say, but to repay her for all her efforts in managing village ceremonial affairs.

Middle-aged women also predominate over younger women as curers, midwives, and so on, although women can begin to learn these skills at virtually any age. Women's role in spirit possession (Lambek 1980, 1981) is particularly significant here. Possession by a spirit, especially a male one, gives a woman a new basis for communicating with her husband and other males. Some women are possessed by spirits who act with a great deal of authority and direction in the affairs of the family (*mraba*) or as diviners and curers with reputations that stretch beyond the confines of the village. Such authority is built up gradually and only flourishes when a woman reaches middle age.

Finally, we may speak of women's participation in Islam. This is one area in which their status is explicitly subordinate to men, in terms of both ideology (which the women by and large do not accept) and practice. For example, in the commonly performed rituals such as the *shidjabo*, a kind of blessing, women cannot take an active role in uttering the prayers but must sit with their children as objects of the prayers. Women frequent the mosque much less than men, but many mosques do have separate women's sections. Older women go to the mosque more often than younger ones, although interest also varies by family. Women with small children say it is too much effort to keep the clothes clean enough for the mosque, but the real reason is probably that they receive no encouragement to attend. Women do play an active role in certain aspects of Islam, such as primary education, maintaining the fast, and performing liturgical music.

CONCLUSION

In Mayotte there is no clear distinction between the positions of older and younger women in the domestic sphere, except to the degree that a senior woman can count on the support of her juniors. Her authority over other women is not automatic since every adult woman maintains her own household and thus a strong basis for autonomy. A woman's authority must be built up through the creation of moral obligation. A woman may attempt to build a marriage that grants her certain rights and security. The ties a woman builds with her husband(s), with her children, her foster children and their parents, her affines, and her children's affines mutually reinforce each other, granting her greater authority in a more tightly bounded cluster of kin. But a woman may also be successful if she lacks either a good marriage or children. In the public sphere the superior position of middle-aged women over younger women is more clear-cut, although only certain women can emerge as leaders in any age group.

The relationships between women of various ages are characterized by mutual support. It is my impression that younger women avoid appearing to put themselves ahead of their elders. Thus they hold back from an active participation in the mosque, in curing, or in politics, citing embarrassment and saying they are too young. This is less true of men, who are more openly in competition with one another (and who also restrict the degree of women's participation in prestigious activities). Women may adhere to a hierarchy based on age more closely than do men, but it is one that is tinged by the solidarity of the relationship between mothers and daughters.

Brown (1982) argues against the idea of a decline in women's status at middle age. The Mayotte data support this. However, they show no sudden changes but rather a pattern of continuity, growth, and florescence. Changes appear to be due more to the Mayotte conceptualization of age than of gender, but they are also grounded in the cumulative endeavors of women constructing their individual careers.

NOTES

The research on which this chapter is based has been supported by the Canada Council (now Social Sciences and Humanities Research Council), the National Science Foundation (Grant #GS-42337X, Conrad Kottak and Henry Wright, principal investigators), and the University of Toronto. I would like to thank Judith Brown and Jacqueline Solway for their encouragement.

[1] This is an oversimplification of the exchange system. In general, public work is distinguished according to gender. One man participated in both men's and women's age sets. His wife belonged to the age set of another village and since he wanted to sponsor a ceremony in his own village that would require women's work, he felt he had to contribute "women's labor" on other occasions. He worked and ate with both women and men on ceremonial occasions, thereby acquiring double portions of meat. People considered his behavior in this one regard rather eccentric (though by no means shameful), but it represents a logical playing out of the rules regarding labor in the production of ceremonies.

[2] A comparison of male and female intergenerational competition and hostility could profit from cross-cultural study. As far as I know, most of the work on this subject concerns only males.

[3] The expenses of the groom are not bridewealth but function rather in the prestige system.

⁴ For an example of a successful strategy on the part of a wife faced with polygyny, see Lambek (1980).

⁵ One extremely successful divorced middle-aged townswoman who saw no reason to remarry was dubbed the "financial wizard of Mamutzu [the town]" by a disgruntled anthropologist tenant.

⁶ On the other hand, menopause is often welcomed by fertile women for bringing relief from the frequent burden of pregnancy.

REFERENCES

Brown, Judith K.
   1982   Cross-cultural Perspectives on Middle-aged Women. Current Anthropology 23(2):143-156.
Lambek, Michael
   1980   Spirits and Spouses: Possession as a System of Communication among the Malagasy Speakers of Mayotte. American Ethnologist 7(2):318-331.
   1981   Human Spirits: A Cultural Account of Trance In Mayotte. New York: Cambridge University Press.
   1983   Virgin Marriage and the Autonomy of Women in Mayotte. Signs 9(2):264-281.
Myerhoff, Barbara G., and Andrei Simič, eds.
   1978   Life's Career--Aging: Cultural Variations on Growing Old. Beverly Hills: Sage.
Ottino, Paul
   1964   La Crise du Système Familial et Matrimonial des Sakalava de Nosy Be. Civilisation Malgache I:225-248.

6 Sexuality and Social Control among the Garífuna (Belize)

Virginia Kerns

For Garífuna (Black Carib) women in Belize, middle age marks the end of childbearing. By their early forties, women have borne their last child; most of them also have a grown child, or several.[1] Their major duty as mothers, in middle age as in youth, is to care for their children and protect them from harm. Middle-aged women offer protection by representing their grown sons and daughters in ancestral ritual. Young women fulfill this duty by observing a number of restrictive "rules," as they call them, which middle-aged women largely enforce. Because so many of the rules pertain to childbearing, older women are exempt from most of them. The perceived reason for many of the rules is that they protect children. An unperceived effect is to limit social contact between men and young women who are potential (but illicit) sexual partners.

The social control of female sexuality is primarily a concern of middle-aged women, the mothers of grown children. In their view a young woman who is sexually unfaithful is an irresponsible mother. If she conceives, either with her spouse or her lover, the child will suffer physical harm, they say. (Her action is also thought to be socially harmful in a number of ways discussed below.) Older women do not speak of infidelity as a violation of male proprietary rights in

87

women, nor do they show much concern about suspected
infidelity by any woman past the age of childbearing.

The next section of this chapter contains a summary of
some major aspects of mating, reproduction, and kinship.
The subsequent one outlines cultural beliefs about female
sexuality and reproductive capacity, and perceived changes
in these at middle age.   The final section deals with the
apparently disparate cultural "rules" that apply largely to
young women.   The manifest purpose and meaning of these
customary beliefs and practices varies, but together they
have the effect of limiting the daily association of young
women with men and promoting female fidelity and paternal
certainty.

At middle age and after, when they no longer bear
children, women cease to follow many of these rules themselves and begin to enforce them instead.   As women grow
older and their reproductive powers decline, their personal
liberty and social powers increase.

ETHNOGRAPHIC BACKGROUND

Culturally and biologically, the Garífuna are of mixed,
Afro-Indian origins.   The British deported them from their
homeland, the West Indian island of St. Vincent, at the end
of the 18th century.   Today some 80,000 people live in the
50-odd settlements scattered along the Caribbean coast of
Central America, from Belize (formerly British Honduras) to
Nicaragua.

Several facts of social life pertain directly to perceived
biological facts of life (outlined in the next section).   The
first of these is that maternal and paternal relatives, traced
through one's biological mother and father, comprise a full
set of kin.   In this bilateral system, people routinely distinguish between maternal kin (*tiduhenu nuguchun*, mother's
relatives) and paternal kin (*liduhenu nuguchin*, father's
relatives).   The specific terms of reference and address,
however, are the same for both sides.

Most women and men reproduce, and virtually all say
they want children.   People speak of children in terms of
their emotional, social, and material value.   Children love
and are loved in return.   They signify one's social identity
as an adult.   When grown, they are supposed to "help" their
parents, especially their mothers, with money and food.
These women, in return, provide food and shelter for their
grown children when needed, and many help by fostering
grandchildren as well.   For most, but especially for the
women without a supporting spouse, these exchanges represent their daily work and daily bread.

While some adults never have children, virtually all women and men are socially eligible to reproduce, and marriage and co-residence are not prerequisites of sexual relations and childbearing. The decision to initiate sexual relations is a personal one, made without need for the consent of kin, legal ceremony, shared living quarters, and very often without open acknowledgement of the relationship. A common but by no means fixed sequence of events is this: a man and woman, finding each other attractive, have sexual relations; later, the woman becomes pregnant (if she is of child-bearing age and fertile); either before or after she gives birth, the couple begin to live together; after some time they may decide to marry. This pattern is subject to great variation however, depending on such factors as the couple's age, compatibility, financial means, and fidelity to each other. One or the other may decide at any point to end the relationship on grounds of incompatibility, nonsupport, neglect, or infidelity. Such separations are more common among young men and women than among older couples.

While the sequence of events and duration of the relationship vary, sexual relations are said always to precede marriage or (extralegal) co-residence, and initially, the lovers usually meet secretly. Eventually, often quickly, others suspect them of doing so; and sooner or later both the man and woman--or just the man--openly acknowledge the relationship. While most adults admit to having had more than one sexual partner, men often claim to have had both simultaneous and sequential relationships. Women admit to sequential relations only. Nearly everyone criticizes any woman suspected of infidelity, but opinion is divided about a man who "plays" with a second woman. Other men usually admire him. Most women shake their heads and predict trouble between the two rivals.

Finally, female fidelity and paternal acknowledgement assure a child a full set of kin and an unambiguous social identity. The concept of legitimacy is an alien one. It is quite common and acceptable for an unmarried woman to bear a child and for a woman to bear children by more than one man.[2] Although rumors of infidelity are rife, actual cases of paternal uncertainty are extremely rare.[3]

FEMALE SEXUALITY AND FERTILITY

At the time of my fieldwork in Belize, I was in my mid-twenties and childless. Many women asked pointed questions about my health and suggested local remedies---various medicinal plants--that might "cure" my presumed infertility. (It did not occur to them that any woman might choose to delay childbearing until her late twenties or thirties or to remain childless.)   In the course of answering their questions and countering with my own, I found that all the women I knew shared a set of beliefs about the basic "facts of life."   Certain women, however, "knew a lot" more. Knowledge tended to be related to age.   Young women sought guidance from their mothers and other middle-aged or old women; and in many cases it was offered even if they did not seek it.   Older women took this as their "duty."

Most women spoke quite openly about sexuality and reproduction, which they regard as "natural" and "good." None of them ever avoided or hesitated to answer questions I asked.   (I did detect wonder at my apparent naiveté in raising some of these questions.)   Older women made the following observations about female sexuality and fertility, often with supporting evidence drawn from their own experience or that of female kin and acquaintances.   I have summarized below these shared beliefs, supporting evidence, and, where possible, corroborative data from medical sources.   Many of these beliefs are in general accord with findings of Western medical research.   (The indigenous and Western medical explanations of these facts do not necessarily correspond.)

1.   Menarche generally occurs between the ages of 12 and 15 and signals that a girl is or will soon be fecund; several years usually elapse between menarche and initial pregnancy.

Women's evidence: They cited their own experience and that of kinswomen and acquaintances.   Some attributed the delay between menarche and first pregnancy to the fact that a young girl's body is "not ready to make the baby," even if she is sexually active.   Others explained that mothers supervise their adolescent daughters rather closely in order to prevent a premature pregnancy.

Medical evidence: The age at menarche varies within and between human populatons but is very rarely under 10 or over 18 years.   "The first several menstrual cycles are usually irregular and anovulatory.   Regular ovulatory cycles are usually established within two years after menarche, and full fertility is attained a few years after the first menstruation. . .   The period of adolescent infertility enables the girl to attain greater maturity before reproduction" (Hafez 1978:72,78).

2.   Pregnancy may occur as early as the age of 14, but this is uncommon and also undesirable because it puts the mother's health at risk.

Women's evidence: They cited one case of a young girl who had recently given birth at the age of 15; she was 14 when she conceived the child.   This was the only such case known to have occurred in the recent past.   A number of women shook their heads with disapproval when they talked about it. Most expressed surprise that both the pregnancy and delivery were normal.

Medical evidence: "Adolescent pregnancies are associated with increased incidence of toxemia, uterine inertia, contracted pelvis, prolonged labor, prenatal mortality, fetal anomalies or premature labor" (Hafez 1978:77).

3. Sexual relations are both enjoyable and necessary to good health. Prolonged abstinence (for more than a few months) can cause headaches and low backaches, as well as weight loss.

Women's evidence: Women who abstain from sexual relations for a prolonged period of time (either because they have no sexual partner or are being faithful to migrant spouses) commonly suffer these symptoms.

Medical evidence: Headaches, backaches, and changes in appetite are among the symptoms of premenstrual syndrome, which is generally assumed to be a biologically based disorder (Abplanalp 1983:109,113). One well-known theory is that premenstrual syndrome is due to a deficiency of progesterone during the premenstrual phase (Dalton 1964). Treatment studies do not offer conclusive support of this theory (Abplanalp 1983:115). The suggestion has been made that some symptoms of premenstrual syndrome are related to unrelieved sexual tension (Masters and Johnson 1966:119-20). Apparently this has not been a subject of empirical study.

4. Women engage in sexual relations because they "naturally" possess a sexual drive but they also "naturally" have the strength to control this drive and confine themselves to one sexual partner.

Women's evidence: They have "felt for (wanted) sex" quite often, and virtually all of the women they know have engaged in sexual relations and regard intercourse as pleasurable. Many consider men to be "naturally" promiscuous ("like dogs," as some put it), but they say that women have the strength to be faithful to one sexual partner for an extended period of time. No woman admitted to me that she had ever been unfaithful, yet many confided that they suspected other women of infidelity. When I asked why those women had been unfaithful (given alleged powers of self-restraint), I was told that the self-control of some women wavers sometimes and that of most men most of the time.

5. The sexual drive does not diminish greatly as fertility declines, and it persists after menopause.

Women's evidence: They named older women who had ceased to bear children but who (by self-report) remained sexually active. (As one postmenopausal woman put it succinctly and directly, "I'm still hot!")

Medical evidence: According to Masters and Johnson (1966:246), "there is no reason why the milestone of the menopause should be expected to blunt the human female's sexual capacity, performance, or drive."   They find no physiological basis for any decline in the frequency of sexual activity at menopause or after.[4]

6.   All young women are "naturally" fecund.   Infertility and other reproductive problems (miscarriage, stillbirth) are due ultimately to "unnatural" (that is, supernatural) causes.

Women's evidence: They pointed out that most women reproduce.   They   named   several   childless   women   and explained that they were the victims of sorcery or malicious spirits; or they had caused their own reproductive problems by (allegedly) once aborting themselves or by ignoring various supernatural taboos.

7.   If a woman spends an extended period of time alone with a man (other than a close relative) it can be assumed that he made sexual advances, which she accepted; if she meets him secretly at night, she obviously intends to have sexual relations with him.   (To be "alone" with him means to be out of public view, especially in a place where others are unlikely to find them; an "extended period of time" means more than a few minutes.   Only close relatives are prohibited as sexual partners.   They include all lineals, and also classificatory lineals: first cousins and lineals' siblings.)

Women's evidence: Such a man and woman, they say, have no other reason to spend time alone together.

8.   If a woman has multiple sexual partners, and if pregnancy results, determining paternity--and hence, the paternal relatives of the child--is problematic; no method of determination is absolutely conclusive.

Women's evidence: They cited the few cases of "washpan babies," a term they use when referring to children who are the suspected issue of extramarital relationships.   (Some also applied the term to babies born to single mothers whom they suspected of having had two sexual partners at the time of conception.)   When paternal identity is in doubt, older women informally examine the child.   Most of them are thought to be able to identify newborn infants as "for" their sons or not.   (This is a skill that men and young women claim not to have.)   The infant's facial features are said to provide the most important evidence, but other physical features also provide clues.

Older women implied that only female fidelity absolutely insures paternal certainty.   Infidelity, they said, puts a child's paternity in doubt, and there is no means of entirely dispelling it.   Years later "people will still have a lot to say" about the circumstances of conception and birth.

Medical evidence: Blood tests can demonstrate that a particular man is not the father of a particular child--but they cannot prove that he is.

9.   The age at menopause varies from the mid-thirties to the mid-fifties, but 50 is about average.

Women's evidence: They cited the case of one woman who had stopped menstruating in her early thirties. (I questioned the woman, who was then in her late thirties, and she confirmed this.)   Hers was the earliest age they knew of.   Women generally mentioned "about 50" as the age at menopause, when menstruation was highly irregular or ceased altogether.

Medical evidence: "The average age of onset of menopause is 50 years (range: 37 to 56 years). . . Menopause is completed after one year of amenorrhea, normally by 55 years of age" (Hafez 1978:215).

10.   Fertility declines before menopause.   Women may reproduce in their early forties, but not after the age of 45.

Women's evidence: They named a number of women who had borne their last children in their early forties, but they knew of no case in which the mother gave birth at the age of 45 or after.

Figures that I collected in one community support this claim.   Every woman between the ages of 45 and 60 who had reproduced had borne her last surviving child by the age of 44.   Most of them (about two-thirds) did so by the age of 38. [5]

Medical evidence: "Declining fertility in aged women is partly due to less frequent ovulation.   In women aged 40 to 45 years, 70% of menstrual cycles are ovulatory and the percentage drops to 60% after 45 years of age. . . It is estimated that 1 out of 20,000 to 60,000 births occurs past the age of 50" (Hafez 1978:223). [6]

FOLLOWING THE RULES

Initially, Garífuna women of all ages struck me as remarkably independent in mind and manner.   I was to find that they are not bound by certain restrictive customs that so obviously limit the personal liberty of women in many cultures.   (For example, they need not be married to engage in sexual relations and to bear children.   They do not require the consent of kin to marry, earn money, travel, and so on.)   Over time, however, I did learn of various restrictive "rules," as they are called, that apply to women.   Most of these are situational, and thus temporary, rather than absolute and enduring restrictions.   They pertain to various phases of the female reproductive cycle (menstruation, pregnancy, and the postpartum period), hence to women of childbearing age. Middle-aged and old women, who have ceased bearing children and are approaching or have passed menopause, are exempt from most of these. They are also avid exponents and enforcers of such "rules."

Nearly all of the rules are perceived as protective devices. A woman who follows them protects herself or her children or other people from physical harm, which takes various forms: sickness, loss of specific physical powers and senses, or even death. In some instances a malevolent spirit is the agent of harm, but the woman's failure to follow the rule is the root cause. Such a woman brings physical suffering upon herself, her child, or other people, and her name suffers as well. She also has to contend with reproach and repeated warnings from her mother and other middle-aged and old women. Some young women scoff openly at a number of these rules, dismissing them as "superstition." Yet most do as they are told, if only to keep the peace.

As examples, here are several of the rules that apply to women during menstruation, pregnancy, and after childbirth. A menstruating woman should stay close to home and avoid social gatherings. The scent of menstrual blood is said to attract malevolent spirits, who then attack someone near the menstruating woman (but not her directly). A pregnant woman is also advised by older women to stay at home in order to avoid seeing strange sights that may "mark" her unborn child. She should also avoid conflict, they say, since her anger can "spoil" the fetus in some way. After giving birth, the woman customarily stays inside the house or near home for nine days. This is said to protect her own health.

Such rules are situational, temporary, and pertain to women of childbearing age. One rule that might be considered absolute, however, is that of sexual fidelity. But the most dire consequences of female infidelity are said to occur at conception, during pregnancy, or soon after giving birth. Older women say that a pregnant woman who is unfaithful risks becoming infertile, and can also cause congenital defects in the child she bears. (The father's semen, in contrast, is said to "nourish" the fetus.) If the woman is unfaithful later, before the child is weaned, she will suffer a wasting illness, and her child may sicken as well. Aside from causing such physical harm, a woman's infidelity is viewed as socially damaging to her children, and in a lasting way. Specifically, a woman who conceives a child while she is suspected of "playing" with a second man creates uncertainty about which man is the child's father. She thereby denies the child a full set of kin and future certainty about who is permitted or prohibited as a sexual partner.[7] Since a man may justifiably leave an unfaithful woman, the children she has already borne will suffer the loss of his financial support. Older women speak of infidelity as dereliction of maternal duty. They cite the variety of suffering that it may cause children (and sometimes the unfaithful woman). Infidelity does not cause serious harm (defined as sickness, other physical affliction, or death) to men or to women past the age of childbearing.

A subtle and complex system of incentives and constraints, largely directed toward young women and enforced by older women, limits illicit sexual relations that may result in children of uncertain paternity. The major incentive is the approval of other women, the wish to avoid their criticism and to keep one's name out of the "news" (the community rumor mill). The last seems nearly impossible in villages. Virtually every woman has fallen under suspicion at some point in her life, and some quite a few times.

Various sorts of constraints also exist. (These include the aforementioned beliefs about the suffering caused by female infidelity.) Certain social devices serve to limit the opportunities for illicit relations by regulating the nature and frequency of contact between men and young women. Segregation and surveillance are the most important of these. The customary division of labor by gender has the effect of physically separating women and men for most of the day. Men work at a distance from home (fishing or doing wage labor), while most household tasks are allocated to women. Moreover, a young woman is supposed to work in the vicinity of her house and to leave her yard only with a specific destination in mind. Stopping to engage in "idle talk" (say, a lengthy tête-à-tête, even in public view) with an unrelated man raises suspicions that she is arranging a tryst with him. Most women claim not to "drift about" in the community; in fact, however, middle-aged women visit quite freely, and old women do so without the least fear of critical comment.

Generally speaking, the younger the woman, the more others take note of where she goes and with whom. When young women leave their houses at night (to attend a ritual or social event, for example, or to buy something at a shop) they routinely take children or female companions with them. If they leave the village during the day to work at their "farms" (swidden plots) or to collect firewood or coconuts, they also go in company. The stated reason for taking companions to the bush is that a lone person is more likely to be "bothered" (harmed) by malevolent spirits who live there. Some of these spirits also frequent the community at night, hence the need for companions after dark. By going about in company, young women protect themselves from gossip and criticism, as well as from bad spirits.

Middle-aged and old women are noticeably less concerned about surrounding themselves with companions, although they clearly value companionship. (Nearly everyone does. Solitude is not valued or sought by most people.) If expedience demands, an older woman will leave a ritual event (at night) by herself, or go off alone to collect firewood, and without expression of fear. Immunity from supernatural harm is said to increase with age.

In short, a variety of customary beliefs and practices restrict the personal liberty of young women, but not middle-aged and old women. They promote female fidelity and paternal certainty, in part by limiting the nature and frequency of contact between men and young women. If a woman of childbearing age commits an act of infidelity, she may inflict harm on the child she conceives, those she has already borne, herself, and even her mother. (In the event that the young woman's spouse leaves her, she and the children lose his support. Her mother will be obliged to "help" them with food and shelter.) An act of infidelity by a middle-aged woman does not have such serious social consequences, nor is it said to cause physical suffering. She will not conceive a child, and some or all of her children are grown (and probably contributing to her support). While "people always have a lot to say" about any young woman whom they suspect of being unfaithful, they show noticeably less concern about a middle-aged woman whose eye wanders. The female sexual drive is not thought to diminish sharply at middle age, but women's childbearing capacity is known to have ended by their mid-forties.

The personal liberty of women increases at middle age, and the emphasis of female power shifts from negative to positive. All women, whatever their age, have a perceived power to create or sustain the lives of others (by fulfilling culturally defined obligations) or to harm or destroy others (by neglecting these duties). Young women are thought more able and likely to cause serious, lasting harm by neglecting or willfully breaking restrictive rules that apply to them. Older women act together to enforce these rules and others that support moral and social order. Theirs is a perceived power to protect and preserve and so to serve the common good.

NOTES

I am grateful to the Wenner-Gren Foundation for Anthropological Research and to the Fulbright-Hays Commission for supporting my fieldwork in Belize during 1974-75 and 1976.

[1] Elsewhere I have used the term "older women" to refer to those past the age of childbearing (over 44) but not yet elderly (under 70). Such women fit Brown's (1982) definition of middle age; they are mothers of grown children. Young adults usually refer to their mothers and other women of this age as "old" (*waia*) and to elderly women as "old old" (Kerns 1983:94ff.).

[2] In two communities, slightly over half of the women of postreproductive age (60 women, 45 years and older) who had borne two or more children had done so by two (45 percent) or more (7 percent) men.

[3] In two communities, there were 71 women of postreproductive age who had borne children. Three of these women were each suspected of having produced a child by an extramarital liaison (a so-called "washpan baby"). These children comprised less than 1 percent of all children borne by the postreproductive women.

[4] Kinsey and his colleagues also found little evidence that the physical processes of aging cause a woman's sexual capacity to decline "until late in her life," by which they seem to mean the sixties or after (see Kinsey et al. 1953:353,715).

[5] There were 27 women in this age category who had given birth to one (7 percent) or more (93 percent) children.

[6] Demographers use various age intervals to define the childbearing period: 15 to 49, 15 to 44, 20 to 44. In general, however, "so little childbearing takes place after age 44, even in high fertility populations, that almost no distortion results from attributing all such births to the age group 40-44 years of age" (Bogue 1971:5-6).

[7] As an example, many people cited the case of a young man who for a time unwittingly courted his half sister. He carried the surname of his mother's husband, but relatives of the husband doubted that the young man was kin. His mother was said to have conceived him by a man other than the one she lived with at the time and later married.

REFERENCES

Abplanalp, Judith M.
  1983   Premenstrual Syndrome: A Selective Review.   *In*
  Lifting the Curse of Menstruation: A Feminist Appraisal
  of the Influence of Menstruation on Women's Lives.
  Sharon Golub, ed. pp. 107-123.   New York: The
  Haworth Press.
Bogue, Donald
  1971   Demographic Techniques of Fertility Analysis.   Chi-
  cago: Community and Family Study Center.
Brown, Judith K.
  1982   Cross-cultural Perspectives on Middle-aged Women.
  Current Anthropology 23:143-156.
Dalton, Katharina
  1964   The   Premenstrual   Syndrome.   Springfield,   Ill.:
  Charles C. Thomas.
Hafez, E. S. E.
  1978   Human Reproductive Physiology.   Ann Arbor, Mich.:
  Ann Arbor Science Publishers.
Kerns, Virginia
  1983   Women and the Ancestors: Black Carib Kinship and
  Ritual.   Urbana: University of Illinois Press.
Kinsey, Alfred C., et al
  1953   Sexual Behavior in the Human Female.   Philadelphia:
  W. B. Saunders.
Masters, William, and Virginia Johnson
  1966   Human Sexual Response.   Boston: Little, Brown.

7 Bucking the Agnatic System:

Status and Strategies
In Rural Northern Sudan

Janice Boddy

The reaches of the Upper Nile north of Khartoum, Sudan, are bounded by a chain of settlements, mud-brick hamlets strung end to end, interspersed with larger villages at railway depots and now and then an administrative town. These settlements cling tenaciously to the river, forming a barrier between fertile, cultivable Nile silts and desert sand. Their inhabitants are Arabic-speaking Muslims whose traditional occupation, farming, has been eclipsed for some decades by labor emigration owing both to a shortage of arable land[1] and to the perennial urban promise of comfort, adventure, and better wages.

Hofriyat (a fictitious name) is one such village whose population is depleted of men between the ages of 15 and 50 for much of the year. Roughly half of its 89 households are comprised of adult women and young children supported by remittances from husbands and male kin, whose presence is felt only during vacations, religious holidays, funerals, and weddings. Some men move away permanently, find wives in distant locales, and neglect their kinship responsibilities in Hofriyat; but these are few. Despite the lures of the city, the majority remain firmly attached to the village area where they were born and feel keenly the obligation to select a wife from within its confines. Marriage among Hofriyati ideally takes place between close kin, between a man and a woman whose families are previously bound by a thick net of moral obligation. Should a man wed a nonrelative from outside the village area, he is scorned by his neighbors as one whose wife is a ewe or she-goat from the market, so uncertain is her pedigree, so greatly has he relied on the word of unrelated individuals to vouch for her character. Just as the market ewe might seem to be a good deal at the time of its purchase only to prove otherwise once its owner gets it home, so the wife formerly unknown to villagers might appear sweet, honest and hard working at the time of her wedding, but prove difficult, demanding, and worst of all, untrustworthy shortly thereafter. Similarly, a village woman who marries a nonrelative or outsider takes a greater chance than does one who marries close. Harmony and cooperation in social relations are highly valued qualities and most threatened by marriages between villagers and nonkin.[2]

But a hidden dimension in all of this is the issue of fertility. In Hofriyat human fertility is appropriately exercised only between close kin, for morality inheres in kinship, and social life, consisting as it does of patterned, controlled behavior, depends upon the bearing and nurturance of offspring by people who are obligated to each other both naturally and contractually. Socialization, in a sense, begins in the womb and is bound to be successful only if the womb has been impregnated by a morally appropriate and legally designated sire.

The fertility of Hofriyati women is at once their most valuable and, as we shall see, their most elusive asset. Since reproductively active women are effectively barred from occupations outside the home and are, with the remainder of Hofriyati, party to the cultural conviction that the role of a woman is to produce descendants for her husband, fertility is the salient feature by which feminine self-image is defined. The following pages are devoted to exploring the implications of this state of affairs for women of middle age. I suggest, as do other authors in this volume, that a woman's entry into middle age is determined by the state of her fertility: it is the post-reproductive phase of life. Yet in Hofriyat there is a subtle difference, for here the state of a woman's fertility is judged not only in terms of her biological capacity to reproduce but also by her legal status. Furthermore, a legally post-reproductive woman in Hofriyat may share with her chronologically senior counterpart a certain freedom from constraints and also opportunities for acquiring power and social recognition that middle-aged women in non-Western settings seem typically to enjoy. Not surprisingly, in the case at hand such opportunities have much to do with fertility: middle-aged women may attain the power to manipulate the fertility potential of others either by arranging their first marriages or by becoming the focal points for future marital alignments. Since descent among Northern Sudanese Arabs is agnatic and marriages ideally are contracted between people who are related through males, some consideration of where women figure in this scheme is necessary if we are to understand the type of power available to them and the strategies they might use to achieve it.

WOMEN IN THE SOCIAL STRUCTURE

The residents of Hofriyat are organized into several related patrilineages, few of which presently exhibit corporate characteristics. Ideally these lineages are endogamous; preferred marriages are those between patrilateral parallel cousins or *awlad 'amm*. In practice, however, lineages are endogamous only to the extent they are corporate.[3] First marriages usually involve close cognatic kin irrespective of descent affiliation, the salient criterion of marriageability being the demonstration of some prior relationship, whether patrilateral, matrilateral, bilateral or purely affinal. Most first marriages, those held to be morally appropriate because they unite "close" kin, are based on a cross or a parallel sibling link in the second or third ascending generations. Significantly, Hofriyati make no real distinction between agnatic and uterine links when determining the relative closeness of kin.

Yet a distinction is made when it comes to future genealogical reckoning. Because of a secondary system of kin classification, which assigns cousins of the same generation the status of siblings, marriages that ultimately are based on relationships traced through women may be brought forward in time, thereby in most cases erasing all traces of uterine kinship. For example, a prospective couple whose fathers are the sons of female matrilateral parallel cousins are spoken of as *awlad 'amm* because their fathers are classed as brothers (Figure 1). In future generations these may be considered real brothers, the original classificatory designation, as preserved in the marriage, providing grounds for bringing village genealogy into line with present realities.

Moreover, though kinship is traced bilaterally through the living, in ascending generations the doctrine of patrilineality takes precedence, encouraging a progressive suppression of close uterine relationships in favor of more remote agnatic links (Boddy 1982a; cf. Kronenberg and Kronenberg 1965). Here again marriages that originally were contracted between cognates will appear to their descendants as marriages of *awlad 'amm*.

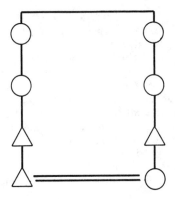

Figure 1. A marriage between classificatory <u>awlad 'amm</u> based on a kinship link traced ultimately through women, in the future to be considered a marriage of the children of brothers.

In thus rewriting the past, Hofriyati both generate future marriages and reinforce the ideological fiction that lineages are endogamous and unambiguously agnatic. Though links traced through women are indispensable to contemporary social arrangements, rarely are they remembered as such when traced beyond the grandparental generation. Further, women's names usually disappear from genealogical memory within a generation or two of their deaths. To be incorporated into genealogies on a more permanent basis is to be immortalized--a coveted status and the province of reproductively successful men. The social recognition permitted to women is both elusive and temporally limited.

These features of Hofriyati social organization bear relevance for the ways by which a middle-aged woman might work to attain or to surpass her allotted potential following divorce or the death of her husband. The dissolution of her first marriage usually jeopardizes a woman's quest for elevated social status relative to her peers (Boddy 1981). Yet some women are able to profit by it, to seize the chance for a second beginning which, if tempered by equal amounts of skill and luck, might enable them to achieve positions of influence later on. But, before I go on to discuss the problems and strategies of women in middle age some background is needed about Hofriyati women in general and their concept of the ideal life career.

WOMEN AND THE LIFE CYCLE

The sexes in Hofriyat are segregated; women are pharaonially circumcised[4] and relatively secluded. They inherit both as wives and as daughters and may pass on property to their husbands and children. A woman's property, both movable and immovable, whether inherited, received as a gift from her husband, or occasionally, earned, is hers alone. In her lifetime it may be disposed of as she desires, however constrained she might feel to conform to the wishes of male kin.

She has no rights over the allocation of her fertility, however, at least in her younger years. A woman's first marriage is arranged by her parents and elder brothers with an eye to the possibilities for marital arrangements in future generations, especially should significant amounts of heritable property be at stake (cf. Peters 1978). Bridewealth (*mahr*, sometimes translated as "dowry") is nominal, and is said to be held in trust by the woman's father for her use or upkeep in the event of divorce. Importantly, a woman remains an active member of her natal family after marriage.

Her close male agnates retain life-long moral and economic responsibility for her, which is shared in part by her adult sons should she be widowed or divorced. She is expected to return to her parents' home at the dissolution of her marriage. Moreover, though virilocal residence is said to be the rule, a woman often lives in her natal household most of her married life. She is home for extended periods of time surrounding each pregnancy and, should her husband work outside the village, may remain there indefinitely. In sum, while rights to use a woman's fertility are conferred upon her husband at marriage, jural rights and obligations are not similarly transferred and remain with her own minimal descent group.

It is necessary to stress that marriage in Hofriyat is best viewed not as an end in itself but as a means for both parties to attain elevated social status through reproductive success. In marriage a man acquires access to his wife's fertility, and she acquires legitimate means to activate it. Reproduction for village women takes place solely in the context of a marriage. Alternatives not only are unthinkable, but a grave affront to family honor, punishable by death at the hands of her agnates.[5]

When a woman marries for the first time, usually between the ages of 14 and 18, her symbolic status is high. As a virgin bride, she is the idealization of femininity and the embodiment of key cultural values (Boddy 1981). Enclosed by pharaonic circumcision, her womb is the locus of morally appropriate, socialized fertility that has been rendered potent through marriage (Boddy 1982b).

However, the corresponding social status of a bride is low: she is a married woman, yet childless. She can expect a gradual improvement of her position relative to affines and peers as she produces children for her husband in the course of a stable and preferably monogamous marriage, especially if most of her offspring are sons. Her ultimate goal is to become, with her husband, the co-founder of a lineage section. Her claim to prestige rests with her demonstrated fertility and subsequently with the prominent role she plays in arranging her children's marriages. When they themselves reproduce, she is assured of becoming a respected *haboba*, literally, "darling," the grandmother of a patriline and a woman who might speak her mind in public, who is listened to, who is reputed to be skilled at social maneuverings.

The respect that she commands at this point is often well deserved, for to become a powerful *haboba* is no small feat. It requires diligence and a long and fruitful marriage, the likes of which are difficult to secure in Hofriyat. Women alone bear responsibility for the reproductive problems that so frequently plague a marriage. If she suffers stillbirth, miscarriage, the death of an unweaned infant, or the birth of a daughter as her first child, a woman's procreative ability may be called into question and her marriage terminated. If she is young, she may quickly remarry at the insistence of male kin, provided a suitable spouse can be found and she can be pressured to comply. For importantly, the dissolution of her first marriage guarantees a woman an increased measure of personal autonomy at the same time as it brings about a diminution of her status. She now has the ostensible right to choose among her suitors or to remain unwed.

Presuming a woman passes the crucial test of demonstrating her fertility, the next hurdle in her marriage is likely to come at any time between her late twenties and her forties when menopause signals the end of her reproductive career. It is then that a Hofriyati woman might well find the marriage she has worked so hard to establish threatened by divorce or co-wifery. Perceived fertility dysfunction is not the only provocation for such action on the part of village men. For it is a mark of a man's prosperity to have a wife unencumbered by childcare concerns, who has time to spend ministering to her husband's personal wants. Thus he may take a second, younger wife as much to enhance his prestige as to increase his descendants.

But since few men have sufficient means adequately to support two households,[6] such gambits regularly fail and divorce of the first wife often results. Should she remain unrepudiated, the first wife will nonetheless see her quest for *haboba* status menaced by the diversion of her husband's procreative attentions and the impending division of his estate among a greater number of heirs. Co-wifery that results in permanent separation and withdrawal of financial support is perhaps the most devastating blow to a woman's aspirations, for without divorce she is precluded from resuming her reproductive career through remarriage. Finding herself in this predicament, a woman might seek the intervention of her brothers in order to secure her liberty.

Divorce, separation, and co-wifery do not exhaust the range of career crises a woman might experience. She might, of course, be widowed. Should her husband die while their children are still young, a leviratic marriage is usually arranged. However, depending on the circumstances, she may refuse her husband's kinsman, preferring the relative autonomy that postmarital status brings.

MIDDLE AGE OR POSTREPRODUCTIVE STATUS

What seems to emerge from the foregoing discussion is that the crisis that Hofriyati women are apt to face prior to menopause is the official or legal cessation of their reproductive careers. The status of a divorcée or a widow precipitates--whether for good or for ill--many of the changes that a woman who remains stably married throughout her reproductive years experiences when she is no longer able to reproduce. Should a divorcée or a widow remarry (as is likely to happen when she is young and no serious fertility disorders have been discerned), her newfound mobility and autonomy will be curtailed to some extent. Yet the choice of husband is largely her own. She now has the freedom to allocate her fertility where she will (though her male kin ought to be consulted) or indeed, to withhold it. Both options have important implications for a woman's long-range goals, a point to which I will return.

What I wish to emphasize here is that if we adopt the view that middle age for women universally refers to the time of life surrounding menopause, we succumb, in essence, to a Western biological model according to which physical changes provide absolute reference points in the course of a woman's life. For us the onset of menses, loss of virginity, pregnancy, and the cessation of menses have traditionally signaled momentous alterations of social context, a re-situation of relationships and of feminine self-image. In Hofriyat, to focus on menopause as the crucial criterion of middle age is to miss the point. Much as virginity in Northern Sudan may be socially defined as potential but unactivated fertility (Boddy 1982b) and is a status that can to a certain extent be renewed through reinfibulation[7]--as Hayes (1975:622) suggests--so too might middle age be defined in social terms as the deactivation of procreative ability, as a status that can, under certain conditions, be partially reversed. In Hofriyat a woman's "social age" is linked inextricably to the state of her fertility. Menopause is but one event among several that might usher her into midlife, a status variously intermediate between bridehood and senescence, heralded either by legal or by physical cessation of reproduction and bringing with it increased personal autonomy and enhanced opportunity to manipulate the social environment for her own ends. However, if midlife is not coincidental with menopause, the status might also bring a loss of prestige.

POLITICAL STRATEGIES AND OPPORTUNITIES FOR ADVANCEMENT

Whatever the individual circumstances, the termination or suspension of a woman's reproductive career frequently jeopardizes her aspirations to become a powerful and respected *haboba* later on. Middle age in Hofriyat is marked, in part, by a narrowing of former career possibilities and available strategies. It may sometimes affect women in dramatically negative ways, particularly if male kin are absent or deceased. One woman of my acquaintance who has twice been married and twice divorced, whose only child is a daughter herself divorced and childless, and whose close male kin are no longer living must rely on the charity of her neighbors in order to survive. For this she suffers the chides and barbs of her juniors and the pitying looks of her contemporaries.

Yet most Hofriyati women in the postmarital midlife status are better advantaged, having male kin who are committed to their financial support. Indeed, some welcome the status in spite of its ominous implications, seeing in their comparative autonomy fresh possibilities for social advancement. For such a woman might, in a sense, circumvent the agnatic system earlier described and both achieve a position of respect and, like the conventional *habobat* (plural), assure herself a passing place in village genealogies.

Previously I discussed some peculiarities of kinship calculation in Hofriyat, noting that despite the undeniable significance of uterine relationships in determining marriageability and inheritance, the doctrine of patrilineality, plus a system of generational classification, operates to suppress the memory of such links in ascending generations. Thus, even if she is co-founder of a lineage section, a woman's name and achievements are seldom remembered for more than a few generations, unlike those of her male counterparts. Moreover, should she have experienced a prevenient end to her reproductive career, it is doubtful that a woman's memory will survive a generation after her death. In her later years she can expect to exert little influence over the disposition of the fertility of others. She is unlikely to become a key figure in the negotiations of future marriages whether during her lifetime or thereafter.

However, should she be in a position to remarry, she might alter her prospects significantly. Hofriyati entering their second marriages are far less constrained to marry close kin than they are in their first. This, coupled with the fact that a previously married woman is quite free to choose among her suitors, means that she might opt for a lineage-exogamous union. Her choice, if astute, might counterbalance any drawbacks (e.g., co-wifery) in the conjugal arrangement, for she might now become the point of articulation between two and in some cases three patrilines that do not acknowledge close relationship due to a lack of known intermarriages in previous generations. Her second marriage might thus provide the link necessary for future marital considerations among unrelated descent groups. For if a woman provides just one child for each of the lineages into which she was wed, then all children of her consecutive husbands are considered siblings, hence unmarriageable. But a marriage prohibition between individuals in one generation ensures preferred marriageability among their offspring in the next. Thus might a woman who is precluded from becoming the *haboba* of a patriline come to exert influence over the marriages of her husband's descendants by his other wives for generations to come. In a sense, then, her central position allows her to usurp prerogatives of the legitimate *habobat*.[8] Even should her second marriage prove infertile, it nonetheless creates possibilities for intermarriages between her husband's and her own natal groups, for marriages occasionally are contracted on the strength of demonstrated prior affinity between lineages.

Furthermore, a woman who becomes a pivotal figure in village genealogies also becomes a reference point for the potential alienation of heritable property, a notable consideration when her siblings and her husband's siblings negotiate marriages for their respective offspring. A woman who comes to occupy a node in the descent structure of Hofriyat might also gain influence as a result. In posthumous recognition of the continuing significance of her position, her name is not soon suppressed in the constructions of village genealogists. Indeed, in contrast to the vertically organized and segmented patrigenealogies commonly recounted, there exists a second type of genealogy in Hofriyat, constructed horizontally and known as a *nisba awlad khalat*, a genealogy of matrilateral parallel cousins. This form is wholly devoted to tracing, for a single generation, the intricate web of kinship that obtains between lineages due to the first and subsequent marriages of related women.

However, many premenopausal women who are propelled into the status of "middle age" do not remarry. For some, especially those with several children, this is a matter of preference: one widowed woman told me she had provoked the dissolution of her leviratic marriage because she resented its constraints; she viewed it as incompatible with her vocation in the *zar* spirit possession cult.

On the other hand, women who are deemed infertile are likely to remain unwed whatever their desires. Yet the relative jural minority of these women and their expanded mobility and autonomy in certain domains have permitted a few of them to pursue other interests advantageously. Two of these are worthy of note. One woman, a childless divorcée, undertook government sponsored training in midwifery and is presently the only licensed practitioner in the district. She derives a substantial income from her salary and from gifts from those she assists. Since her job takes her into nomad camps in the desert and into neighboring villages where she has no kin, she would be hard pressed to function in this capacity were she married and secluded. It is only because her reproductive career is now officially behind her that she has the autonomy she requires.

The second instance concerns an older woman who was divorced when fairly young after producing a daughter as her first child. This woman returned with her child to live in her parents' home after her husband left the village; upon her parents' deaths, she was allowed by her siblings to retain possession of that house and at the time of my field-work was considered its sole owner. She and her daughter were supported by her brothers from their father's small farm and she worked to supplement her income by selling cooked food to villagers. Then, with the proceeds of her business, she began to purchase and distribute raw materials for the cottage crafts that occupy women in their spare moments, dealing with itinerant traders or placing orders through male kin. Next, she made use of her relative freedom from seclusion to sell finished basketry in the local market. Over the years she has otherwise diversified her trade. Through her entrepreneurial activities, she has amassed considerable wealth; twice now she has taken herself on the pilgrimage to Mecca.

Though she is not the *haboba* of her husband's descendants, this woman is widely respected, for she is on her way to becoming the actual, if not formally accredited, founder of a lineage section. She was instrumental in arranging the marriage of her daughter to her brother's son, a landless but industrious sharecropper, then gave the couple money with which to buy a plot that someone no longer living in the village wished to sell. With her help, this family has continued to acquire land little by little, both through mortgage and through outright purchase. Marriages recently arranged between her daughter's daughters and her brothers' descendants point to the gradual crystallization of a corporate descent group. What is significant here is that an endogamous patrilineage is emerging that is focused on the financial success of a woman, based upon the future inheritance of her daughter, and is directly attributable to the premature curtailment of her reproductive career (Figure 2).

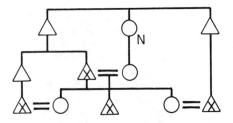

(x : cooperate in farming)

Future rewrite:

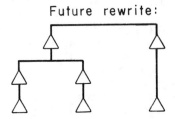

Figure 2. A Corporate descent group crystallizing around the entrepreneurial success of a woman, N, and the eventual disappearance of her position from future genealogies.

CONCLUSION

In Hofriyat marriage inaugurates a woman's reproductive career: divorce, widowhood, or menopause may bring it to a permanent or temporary close. Middle age for Hofriyati women is neither identified with a specific chronological age nor absolutely associated with a particular physical manifestation. Instead, it is the social status accorded a woman whose fertility is no longer active, whether jurally or biologically. Much as Brown (1982) has described, the status of "middle age" is characterized for a woman by enhanced personal autonomy, that is, the capacity to make certain decisions for herself and a relaxation of some of the constraints by which she was bound in her childbearing years. It is also associated with her expanded maneuverability in the social arena, frequently leading to the furtherance of uterine kinship ties in future marital arrangements, however fleeting their recognition in village genealogies.

Postmarital middle age status coupled with ongoing jural minority in certain respects means that village women with close male kin are assured of economic support while being freer to explore a limited range of career alternatives. These in turn may enable them to approximate the position of *haboba* in other than usual ways. This is the positive side of things. Middle age can, however, bode disaster for a woman cast adrift who has no male kin. These circumstances, plus the fact that middle age generally implies the narrowing of former possibilities even as it implies the broadening of others, suggest that this period of a woman's life is approached with ambivalence, if not with trepidation.

NOTES

[1] The reasons for the perceived scarcity of land for cultivation are numerous: periodic changes in the course of the Nile through its floodplain may either cause good silts to be lost to inundation or remove the source of water for flood-bank irrigation. Added to this are the problems of land fractionation due to formalized land registration and adherence to Islamic inheritance rules, desertification and the stated decline in productivity of *wadi* (stream bed) plantations, increasing population pressure in certain areas, and the expense and uncertain availability of fuel for diesel irrigation pumps.

[2] Co-villagers are considered to be kin of some sort by definition, however tenuous their genealogical links in recent generations.

[3] Lineages in Hofriyat appear to go through cycles of consolidation and dissolution. Families often "incorporate" when their members acquire land or some other lucrative resource (e.g., a diesel pump), but since all heritable property is individually owned and strictly divided among heirs, they tend to dissolve when their membership proliferates and ownership becomes fractionated.

[4]   Pharaonic circumcision as practiced in Sudan involves surgical removal of the clitoris, labia minora and all or part of the labia majora. This is followed by infibulation, whereby skin from either side of the wound is pulled together and held in place by thorns or by suture. A small opening often no broader than the circumference of a matchstick is left for the elimination of urine and menstrual blood; once healed the genital area is covered by a layer of thick, resistant scar tissue. For further consideration of this operation, its implications, functions, and significances, see Boddy (1982b), Dareer (1982), Gruenbaum (1982), and Hayes (1975).

[5] Since sexual segregation is the norm in Hofriyat and tensions between spouses frequently run high over the issue of honor, companionship in a marriage is both rare and unexpected. It may develop with age, however, should the union prove stable.

[6] According to the tenets of Islam, a polygynous man must treat his wives equally. In Hofriyat this is taken to mean that each must have her own house.

[7] When a woman gives birth, the opening left in the scar tissue of her circumcision wound (see n.4) must be surgically enlarged to release the child. Once delivered, her wound is immediately closed up again (reinfibulated), she is given gifts of jewelry similar to those she received at her wedding, and she is re-presented to her husband as a "bride."

[8] Thus, the power available to older women in Hofriyat is a kind of "limited good": the acquisition of power for oneself entails the loss of power for others, a system which tends to pit women against each other competitively.

REFERENCES

Boddy, Janice
  1981 Clever Virgins Make Good Grandmothers. Paper
  presented to the Canadian Ethnological Society, Ottawa.
  1982a Parallel Worlds: Humans, Spirits, and *Zar* Possession in Rural Northern Sudan. Unpublished Ph.D. dis-
  sertation, The University of British Columbia, Vancou-
  ver, B. C.
  1982b Womb as Oasis: The Symbolic Context of Pharaonic
  Circumcision in Rural Northern Sudan. American Ethnologist 9(4):682-698.
Brown, Judith K.
  1982 Cross-cultural Perspectives on Middle-aged Women.
  Current Anthropology 23(2):143-156.
Dareer, Asma El-
  1982 Woman, Why Do You Weep? Circumcision and Its
  Consequences. London: Zed Press.
Gruenbaum, Ellen
  1982 The Movement Against Clitoridectomy and Infibulation
  in Sudan: Public Health Policy and the Women's Movement. Medical Anthropology Newsletter 13(2):4-12.
Hayes, Rose Oldfield
  1975 Female Genital Mutilation, Fertility Control, Women's
  Roles, and the Patrilineage in Modern Sudan: A Func-
  tional Analysis. American Ethnologist 2:617-633.
Kronenberg, A., and W. Kronenberg
  1965 Parallel Cousin Marriage in Mediaeval and Modern
  Nubia, Part 1. Kush 13:241-260.
Peters, Emrys L.
  1978 The Status of Women in Four Middle Eastern Commu-
  nities. *In* Women in the Muslim World. Lois Beck and
  Nikki Keddie, eds., pp. 311-350. London: Cambridge
  University Press.

8   A Study in Pride and Prejudice:

Maori Women at Midlife

Karen P. Sinclair

Maori women approach middle age with far more responsibilities than at any other point in the life cycle. But they now possess commensurately more power and authority with which to execute them. No longer completely constrained by pollution beliefs or burdened by the demands of young children, they are free to assume a more prominent, public position (Flint 1975; Kerns 1980). Ceremonial and ritual roles, hitherto limited to men, are now, to some extent, available to women. But it would be a mistake to characterize this point in the life cycle as discontinuous with women's previous experiences. Clearly, the diminishing of gender distinctions reported so extensively elsewhere (Brown 1982a, 1982b; Griffen 1982) contributes to the authority of Maori women. But women who now find themselves operating in these heady new dimensions have in fact been preparing for the prestige and independence that will characterize their later years. Continuity and consistency mark women's lives. In a colonial situation, such as exists in contemporary New Zealand, the importance of coherence in female experience cannot be minimized.

Although there are exceptions, women's lives seem to improve dramatically at middle age. As Brown points out, "Overwhelmingly the cross-cultural evidence indicates positive changes. Middle age brings fewer restrictions, the right to exert authority over kinsmen, and the opportunity for achievement and recognition beyond the household" (1982b:143). In a similar vein, both Griffen (1982) and Kehoe (1973) have commented on the restrictions inherent in maternity; child-care not only limits social opportunities, but women of childbearing age are often imputed attributes deemed contrary to the exercise of supernatural power. In middle age these constraints are relaxed. In short, women become more effective social actors, capable both of managing resources and manipulating their ideological and social worlds to lend meaning to their performance (Dominy 1983:2).

By virtue of their position as an indigenous minority, Maori women are called upon to operate in two contexts: one defined by Maori rules and traditions, the other by the conventions that govern the European social system. Gender and social identities are therefore enacted in different arenas.

As Maori men and women age, they participate more fully in ritual and ceremonial affairs. At this time of life, social, ritual, and political responsibilities supplant earlier concerns with domesticity and wage labor. Maori elders are expected to preside over crucial aspects of Maori social life; their responsibilities and obligations make them focal points at feasts, funerals, and on all occasions that distinguish the contemporary Maori situation. For it is at these times that Maoris may celebrate, mourn their dead, and demonstrate their commitment to their place as Maoris in New Zealand society. To participate merely by attendance requires very little; to take an active role requires years of training, expertise, and dedication.

Middle age finds the Maori male at the apex of his social power. If he has learned and practiced his task well, he is a skilled speaker, capable of persuasive public oratory and decisive behind-the-scenes manipulation. In addition, he has the advantage of an ideology that unequivocally asserts the superiority of men. Few women would question the formal structure that stresses the ascendancy and public dominion of men. At the same time they clearly recognize their own contribution to the informal, not always acknowledged, aspect of ceremonial and ritual life. Indeed, the organizational and ritual importance of middle-aged and elderly women is a critical counterpoint to an ideology of masculine preeminence. As women age, they depend increasingly on other women to buttress their public position. Thus the cooperation and assistance that women grant one another throughout the life cycle provide a necessary impetus to wider female participation. Women have forged close, intimate bonds, not only by working with and alongside one another--for men do this as well--but by making the subtleties of social relations their province. Thus as they reach middle age, they have more than allies and support; they have become the arbiters of community standards.

Without the security and pride of high status so often associated with men, women have been more prepared to deal with Europeans. Whatever humiliations were attendant upon such transactions, women now have an understanding of the larger culture that men lack. Furthermore, because they have maintained closer ties with their own children, they can use their knowledge of the Pakeha (the New Zealand term for individuals of European descent) to guide the younger generation through the difficulties of culture change. It is these skills that have made women, rather than men, mediators in the intricate social fabric that confronts the contemporary Maori.

The women who are the subjects[1] of this chapter are members of a religious movement, *Maramatanga*. Involvement in the movement accelerates and reinforces their growing importance and influence; for to participate in a movement like this is to participate actively in the definition and formation of Maori identity. Middle-aged women use their spiritual expertise to embark on new careers (as healers for example), to travel abroad as members of church groups, or simply to consolidate and justify their increasing prestige and influence. Religious activity does not change but rather reinforces the authority that maturity grants to women.

This chapter then is an investigation of why women's status increases at middle age. That it does in the Maori case is at first glance somewhat surprising. For colonialism often diminishes the stature of women (Boserup 1970; Bell 1981) and Maoris already have in place an ideology that affirms female inferiority. But the confluence of tradition and innovation has worked in this instance to enhance the position of women. The fusion of traditional rules, which accorded women greater authority as they aged, with the ambiguities of colonialism, which permit them greater scope to exercise this influence, has allowed women to fashion a significant social contribution.

MAORIS IN CONTEMPORARY NEW ZEALAND

In slightly over two centuries, New Zealand has been transformed from the stratified Polynesian chieftainship of the aboriginal Maoris into a complex Western democracy. This process has placed the burden of accommodation on the Maoris, who have had to respond to social and political forces that laid siege to their former way of life. The adjustment has been neither uniform nor painless; calls to battle and religious innovation have taken their place next to judicial land reform, passive conversion to Christianity, and more recently, organized political protest. Two hundred years after the arrival of Captain Cook, Maoris acknowledge only reluctantly European hegemony over their ancestral lands.

Their discomfort is not without justification.[2] On most measures that indicate standard of living or quality of life, Maoris emerge considerably below Europeans. Moreover, the situation tends to be self-perpetuating, as Forster and Ramsay point out:

> Entering the labor market with few skills and less than the Pakeha standard of education, they must take those jobs which pay least; their standard of living restricts the potential opportunities and encouragement that can be given to their children. Without supported opportunities or unusual circumstances, the children are likely to find themselves in a position not unlike that of their parents. Thus the situation can all too easily become self-perpetuating (1971:202).

Today only 10 percent of the New Zealand population identifies itself as Maori. But this represents a larger proportion since the last census, and growth appears to have come from an increase in the number of children born. Thus the Maori population is much more youthful than the Pakeha populace and is growing at a much more rapid rate. These demographic changes will inevitably affect relations within Maori society and between Maoris and Europeans.

Another significant change in Maori life is the increase in urbanization. Continuing a movement away from rural areas that began shortly after World War II, young Maoris have looked to the cities for employment and stimulation that is absent in rural areas. Too often, however, they are ill equipped to make the necessary adjustments, and urban life frequently fails to meet their expectations. Rather, a host of social problems emerges. According to Walsh,

> Over two thirds of the Maori urban population is under the age of 25. Between 1961-66 three-quarters of the Maori youth aged 16-19 years went to live in urban areas. In 1967 over half the Maori children born were born in urban areas. This poses serious questions of adjustments to city living additional to those expected for any migration to a strange environment. First generation migrants all over the world tend initially, to live in the decaying central core of the city and overcrowded conditions and high crime rates are not unusual (1973:12).

Under these circumstances, many relationships have to be redefined. The links between town and country Maoris must be reassessed. The traditional leadership of rural elders seldom reaches effectively into the urban milieu.[3] Yet the connections between youth in the cities and their families in rural areas are far from tenuous. Moreover, these ties are made and reinforced by women, who have demonstrated their ability to adapt and make themselves significant in the contemporary Maori world. Indeed the Maori family continues to be important. The resilience of this particular pattern has been discussed by Ritchie:

> After suffering almost every major impact that culture change can bring we still find that the Maori family preserves its own model and that Maori individuals seek to recreate the kind of community that family model best fits. Currently, neither education, entrapment in the affluent society, discrimination, nor inducement has been potent enough to destroy Maori patterns....For such times ahead as we need to consider, it is likely that the satisfactions of Maori family and community life will make these alternatives attractive and habitual for a very large number of those who call themselves Maoris (1972:75).

Relationships between Maoris and Europeans have, apparently, become more problematic. It is difficult to know whether the problem has actually intensified or if it is only now that difficulties in this area are being acknowledged. Anti-Maori prejudice can no longer be denied. St. George affirms its existence: "Prejudice in New Zealand there is, and the studies show that Pakeha New Zealanders do direct prejudice against Maori New Zealanders, and that they also hold prejudicial attitudes towards various other national groups that are distinctly negative where color of skin is concerned" (1972:15). Widespread stereotypes further distort ethnic relations (Metge 1976; Arbuckle 1976). Pakehas view Maoris as musical, happy-go-lucky children while they are perceived by Maoris as selfish and individualistic, without the commitment to kin and community that makes Maori life valuable. Perhaps the most poignant aspect is to be found in the fact that Maoris have come to accept these negative stereotypes of themselves, frequently maintaining that they are unattractive failures (Archer and Archer 1970).

New Zealand society, then, confronts the Maoris with many uncomfortable situations. Unwilling and unable to emulate Europeans, they have discovered that their own culture is not valued by the larger society. They have learned that pride in Maoriness must come from within their own group; only through concerted efforts will traditions be sustained. Underemployed in rural areas, with little expertise in understanding the perplexities of urban life, Maoris face serious problems of adjustment. Indeed the strains evidence themselves in many ways. There has been an increase in domestic violence, crime, and admission to mental hospitals. Walsh attributes the rise in diagnosed schizophrenia to "difficulties in maintaining dual cultural identity or in choosing between different sets of cultural values" (1973:30). Solutions have tended not to be enduring; each generation has had to come to terms anew with the difficulties of being Maori in contemporary New Zealand.

GENDER IDEOLOGY

Gender ideology traditionally affirmed the superiority and preeminence of Maori men. While some aspects of gender asymmetry have been muted over time, the priority of men remains axiomatic. Thus women, who in their own right command considerable respect, will automatically defer to men. The source of men's position in general derives neither from their accomplishments nor from their abilities, but from a cultural ideology that views men as ritually undefiled and women as dangerously polluting. While these beliefs have many consequences, one is the greater freedom accorded men and the commensurately stronger restrictions placed on women.

Female sexuality and reproduction traditionally carried implications of chaos and destruction. In Maori mythology, women were presented as ambiguous creatures, embodying notions of life and death, fertility and sexuality. As befitting such anomalous beings, women were circumscribed by rules that limited and restricted their social participation. Pollution beliefs kept women in their place and narrowed their spheres of social action. On one level, notions of female pollution erected boundaries between male and female domains: women were prohibited from all building sites and excluded from all major ritual activities. Heuer maintains that "the presence of women, or more precisely of the female organs, was deemed destructive to sacredness, as was the presence of cooked food. For this reason, there were no female priests; women were, however, not infrequently seers or mediums for lesser gods" (1969:477-478).

The reproductive capacity of women was subject to great cultural elaboration. Women could purify sacred areas by walking over them or restore a warrior's lost courage in the same manner. Thus female genitals, if defiling, were also clearly powerful. Their ambiguous life-giving powers were handled with suitable gravity. Menstruating or pregnant women were denied access to entire areas of the social and physical landscape. Were they to violate these rules, the results threatened to be immediate and spectacular: crops would fail, animals would flee, warriors would fall in battle (Best 1905:215; Heuer 1969:466-467).

While such beliefs and proscriptions clearly make use of Maori conventions regarding life and death and blood and fertility, there is also a message with a clear sociological dimension. Women are disruptive to the harmony and order of social life (Douglas 1978:61). They must be controlled and contained. Moreover, the checks and limitations placed upon the activities of women make a clear public statement expressing female inferiority. Pollution beliefs not only attest to the difference between men and women but express as well the cultural conviction that legitimacy is a male preserve. To require a menstruating woman to keep away from male activities can make this point quite effectively. "To blame her carelessness in this repect for his failure in fishing or hunting or farming is a way of using the cosmos to constrain other people" (Douglas 1978:62).

Many of these prohibitions are no longer relevant or effective in the contemporary context. However, notions of female contamination continue. Young girls are taught never to bare their genitals nor to step over a male. Sitting on a table, while indelicate behavior in a man, is a deliberate defilement when done by a woman. If hot water is in short supply and baths are to be shared, it goes without saying that men, who come in with dirt from the fields, have the first bath. Women must take the second bath, for grime and grease are not as dirty or as polluting as whatever women will leave behind in the water.

Officially, gender ideology stresses complementarity. There is no presumption of equality. While there is a strong emphasis on interdependence, the public and symbolic quality so often associated with the role of men suggests a dimension that is lacking in female experience. Thus Salmond writes:

> Women do have a role to play in the ceremonial area. They call, wail and chant ancient songs. But theirs is largely a supporting role and in most areas they are excluded from the central activity of speechmaking (1975:43).[4]

Women, however, derive some benefit from this separation: it affords them opportunities to establish ties with other women and to create a network of alliances that will serve them well in their later years. These networks are formed early and become stronger over the life cycle. To a large degree they are a response to the enduring boundaries between men and women.

GENDER ROLES AND FEMALE NETWORKS

From a child's earliest years, there is a separation of male and female domains. Peer groups, becoming important first in childhood, continue to be significant throughout the life cycle. Even before adolescence, boys and girls begin to exist in separate but proximate social worlds; young girls are more constrained by domestic responsibilities while young boys are freer to range further afield. More significantly, however, young girls are far more attuned to one another's feelings and develop more intense emotional attachments than do boys of the same age (Ritchie 1972; Earle 1958).[5]

Married by their late teens, most women spend the next two decades involved with a growing number of young children. Despite the availability of birth control, women who are now middle-aged refrained from family planning. Consequently, they have frequently produced anywhere from 6 to 13 children. Although Maori family patterns preclude the isolation of young mothers so typical in other Western societies, most women described this point in their lives in distinctly negative terms. They expressed feelings of loneliness and desolation that were mitigated only by their closeness to and dependence upon other women. In rural areas such women depended far more on one another than on their spouses. Indeed, in addition to assistance with cooking and child care, women often provide one another a refuge from the afflictions of marriage: neglect, unrealistic demands, and verbal and physical abuse. Women feed, dress, and care for one another's children, thereby lessening the tyranny of domestic preoccupations. Clothing and food are rapidly redistributed, allowing scarce resources the widest application. Thus mothers aid daughters, aunts support nieces, cousins and sisters attend one another. Contemporary Maori households, then, are managed by a cooperative network of women who prepare and distribute food, shop, and tend to the needs of children.[6]

These networks are not confined to mundane events. At feasts and ceremonials, they are activated to accomplish the many details involved in the extension of Maori hospitality. When young, girls perform menial tasks; as middle-aged women they initiate and control the ritual occasions so crucial to modern Maori sensibility.

The participation of young women in ceremonial occasions is confined to the tasks of dishwashing, table setting, waitressing, shopping, and food preparation. While the work often borders on drudgery, young women nevertheless witness the effectiveness of female management and the importance of women's contribution. In the face of their own experience, they are not daunted by a formal ideology that only recognizes male accomplishment. At this time they are also being prepared for the more active ritual role that they will be expected to assume as they mature.

In ceremonial affairs women have a supportive, auxiliary role, at least while they are premenopausal. Men continue to dominate public ritual events by their expertise in oratory and genealogy. By singing and chanting, women give group confirmation to individual male performances. It is significant that women always appear publicly in a group while men, in general, engage in individual productions. Women bestow group sanctions, or in rare cases, signal group approbation.

The ritual and formal status of men and women changes as they progress through the life cycle. In old age, they are *kaumatuas*, elders. Men are referred to as *koro*, women as *kuia*. Both terms denote grandparenthood, as well as respected elder. Most middle-aged individuals will accept *Koro* or *Kuia* as a term of address from grandchildren but eschew the general label. They do not want to be seen as fitting too snugly into the elder category. For Maoris, middle age connotes a period of vigor and visibility that may be contrasted to the ceremonial, but relatively inactive, importance of elders.

As women reach middle age, the focus of their activity broadens: they now participate more publicly and effectively than do younger women.[7] By raising the call to the dead and welcoming new arrivals onto the *marae* (the ceremonial courtyard), older women mark the commencement of ritual events. But the competence of middle-aged women is best seen in the manipulations that go on in preparation for a major ceremony. Here years of mutual cooperation have achieved a finely honed machinery that goes smoothly into action, almost without thought, when the occasion warrants. Women depend on their peers and on their daughters and nieces for performances that will ensure the essential order of Maori ritual. Stores are brought in, cakes and breads are baked, meals are prepared, tables are set, dishes are washed, beds are prepared, meeting houses arranged, and children cared for. In addition women also "make flax mats, embroider pillow cases, purchase mattresses, order linen, crockery, and cooking utensils" (Salmond 1975:170). By sounding out the early cry for the dead, by weeping with those closest to the deceased, women engineer many of the details that demand attention at times of community crisis. The prominence of middle-aged women in *marae* ritual as well as their back-stage domination of the details that facilitate such events, translate into effective control over both domains. Without them visitors would be neither welcomed nor fed and much of the distinctiveness of Maori ceremonial would be lost.

Moreover, middle-aged and elderly women serve as *pani*, the formal mourners who, for the intervening days between death and burial are removed from ordinary social life with its mundane concerns and remain with the deceased. The traditional structure asserts itself here, since women are involved with the details of death. But only those who are past childbearing age carry this burden. Significantly, the mourning ritual (*tangi*) is a major marker of Maori ethnicity; the domination of women at this time bestows on them a critical role in passing down tradition. The colonial situation has transformed a necessary, if inevitable encounter with the defilement of death into a socially sanctioned positive assertion of ethnic identity. Its main practitioners, believed in the past to be already contaminated, have emerged as significant social actors.

In addition, many middle-aged women are involved in the political lives of their communities. By serving on the numerous tribal committees that direct the various currents of social life, women make a direct contribution to decisions regarding the structure of Maori affairs. Fundraising, the organization of major cultural events, and the maintenance of the *marae* are often accomplished under the competent gaze of older women. Their political influence is buttressed by the kind of support they derive from their network. Women will often reach a decision among themselves. There are few areas in Maori life where consensus on the part of older women can afford to be ignored. Furthermore, organizations such as the Maori Women's Welfare League provide women a path to local and even national recognition.

In church affairs, women, and not men, serve on district and parish committees. Maintaining ties with the church reflects more than the domestication of religion, for in such tribunals, which are often overwhelmingly European, the tricky area of interethnic relations is an explicit item for discussion. The church has also come to depend on women to do most of its community public relations work.

At middle age, a woman's nurturant role is far from over. The relative poverty of most Maoris makes the autonomous, self-supporting nuclear family an elusive ideal. Grandmothers baby-sit or take over the long-term care of their grandchildren, and for most, domestic life is incomplete without at least one young child at home. Women also persist in mediating and adjudicating the difficulties of culture change faced by their adult children. Their continued closeness to their offspring and their awareness of the difficulties they face have provided middle-aged women both with allies and with a precise knowledge of the contemporary social situation. By contrast, few men concern themselves with the problems of drug possession, urban gangs, or domestic disputes that routinely confront their children.

In groups or individually, these women also instruct the community in traditional arts and crafts. They teach weaving and basketry, mat making and flax dying, Maori songs and language to schoolchildren, church groups, their own youth, and curious Europeans. For Pakehas, they often provide examples of a noble heritage distilled for contemporary New Zealand consumption. But for Maoris, these women represent a capacity to use traditions to define, but not to limit, a behavioral and symbolic repertoire that is exclusively Maori. Their continued intimacy with their grown children and their awareness of the complexities of the contemporary situation draw the younger generation to them.

Traditional gender ideology, therefore, no longer constrains middle-aged women, but it frames the nature of their experience. Women who are today middle-aged have learned to operate in an essentially female universe and have grown adept at executing the responsibilities defined as suitable for such individuals. As women age, the restrictions of gender diminish. Female solidarity, the result of a lifetime of sexual segregation, has been transformed into control over younger women and into political influence within the community.

The contingencies of the colonial situation have enhanced the authority and influence that Maori women were traditionally permitted to claim. Institutions outside the community--e.g., the church and the schools--generally gain access to Maoris through women. By their continued involvement in these institutions and by their enduring commitment to their children and grandchildren, women have come to understand a social world dominated by Europeans. They are not always pleased by what they see, but they are prepared to adapt to it, for flexibility has been necessary throughout their lives. They are therefore willing both to uphold tradition and to ease its passing. Thus the colonial situation, which has so often diminished the stature of Maori men, has enhanced the prestige of Maori women.

MARAMATANGA

Becoming a cultural minority in the land of their ancestors has been a difficult adjustment for Maoris. In the past 200 years, many prophets have come forward. Some have offered deliverance from the tyranny of the Pakeha, others have presented their followers with the means to accomodate the intruding presence. All have attempted to create a

meaningful social order, one in which to be a Maori is to be
a valued social participant. The middle-aged women discussed in this chapter belong to one such movement.
Through the ideology of the movement and by adherence to
its ritual, these women are more prepared than most to
assume an active voice in the determination of Maori affairs.

The movement is nominally Catholic. But its ideology
depends on traditional religion and on the Maori prophetic
heritage as much as it relies on the dogma of the orthodox
Catholic Church. The members of *Maramatanga* (the name
suggests knowledge and enlightenment) see themselves as the
logical culmination of the Maori prophetic tradition. They
refer to themselves as the *kaimahi* (the workers), the *hun-
garuarua* (the chosen few), and to their beliefs as the
tikanga (the correct way). The 300 people who constitute
the movement, although geographically dispersed, are all
related to one another and are all descendants of the original
prophet. While he was an individual clearly endowed with
spiritual gifts, it is his legacy that sets his followers apart.
For he is seen as the "last of the prophets." In subsequent
years no leader has been necessary, for members hold that
they now all have access to the spiritual world. Deceased
friends and relatives (known as *wairua*, the spirits of the
dead) commune with their descendants, warning of coming
adversity, counseling in times of trouble and supplying the
living with a continuous source of songs, which win them
acclaim in major cultural competitions.

The history of the movement, going back 50 years, is
dominated by women. Although men participate, it is women
who today tend to receive messages, who return as *wairua*,
and who maintain a close monitoring of human/spiritual relations. This is not surprising, for women's participation in
Maramatanga gives them a voice equal to that of men. Women
can and do engage in public speechmaking and have moved
into many domains previously reserved only for men. Middle-aged and elderly women, who are free from domestic
pressures, participate more vigorously than any other segment of *Maramatanga's* membership.

The rituals of the movement depend largely on a knowledge and understanding of traditional art forms; oratory,
singing, and chanting must be performed with skill and
facility. The extent to which women participate competently
indicates their capacity to master and to retain traditional
cultural forms. Such activities clearly preserve the past,
but far more importantly, they sustain the value of the present. By defining the work of the ancestors as worthwhile,
as worthy of preservation, they have legitimated their position as Maoris in contemporary New Zealand. Moreover, the
triumphs that accompany participation (the successful pilgri-

mages, the admired songs, the victories in cultural competitions) all enhance women's status and prestige in the eyes of the membership.

On several occasions throughout the year, kinship ties and individual commitments are activated in a series of cele-brations, known as *ras*, which commemorate important events in the spiritual history of the movement. At such times, the members who are able, gather to discuss spiritual matters and to avail themselves of Maori hospitality. Commensality and solidarity are often explicit themes; traditional inequali-ties based on rank, genealogy, and gender are deemed insignificant.

At the *ras*, the participation of middle-aged women is especially marked. As the most mobile group, their atten-dance is far more regular. More significantly, their organi-zational skills facilitate the feeding and housing of several hundred people over several days. Middle-aged women, therefore, sustain and are sustained by their participation in *Maramatanga*.

Many women attribute the ease with which they are able to assume their increased ritual obligations to spiritual assistance. But the *wairua* have done more than assist them in the execution of their anticipated duties. Under their auspices, several women have become healers. Others have less spectacular gifts. Nevertheless, it is assumed that each has something to contribute and should therefore be accorded the respect due to an important, productive member of the community.

To a much greater degree than men, women use what they have learned from *Maramatanga* to take an active role in the affairs of the wider society. Several women participate at all levels of church organization. Far from being alien-ated from Catholicism, members have assumed an elite role in the administration of the Maori Mission. Such positions have led them to take trips abroad (to Samoa, to the Philippines) and to travel extensively in New Zealand. The assurance that they can depend on the guidance and counsel of their *wairua* helpers, grants many the confidence to journey freely. Men, who are usually employed and therefore unable to leave their jobs, are not as likely to participate as fully or to derive the benefits that full participation conveys.

Membership in *Maramatanga* allows women to confront and overcome their marginality. As Maoris and as women, they are at a serious social disadvantage. However, these liabilities become somewhat less significant in the face of women's demonstrated spiritual ascendancy. Religious activ-ity thus encourages women to redefine their roles; they have ceased to be passive complements of men. Both because of the easing of restrictions as they age and through the avenues opened to them by *Maramatanga,* women at middle age can embark on a new social identity.

CONCLUSION

The confluence of social change and aging has frequently proved devastating for women. But Maori women living in rural areas have found that the individual life process and the larger social process have together increased their prestige.

In both its traditional and contemporary forms, Maori society has used age and gender as principles of social differentiation. For women, the liabilities inherent in one are overcome by the other as they approach middle age. At this point in their lives, they are free in a number of ways and from a number of constraints; pollution rules, child care, and male monopolies no longer inhibit them. However, their independence is relative. Women are still perceived as defiled and defiling, grandmothers continue to oversee the young, and certain areas remain proscribed regardless of a woman's age. Nevertheless, when compared to the confined and circumscribed lives of younger women, their gains are considerable.

The women discussed in this chapter have the additional advantage of religious experiences that reinforce their authority and provide channels for their accomplishments. The equality accorded to them as members of the movement, along with the preparation they receive in ceremonial forms, facilitates their assumption of a more active role in the wider community. In this manner, women have assisted the process of accommodation between two different cultural traditions.

Despite the dramatic social change that these women have witnessed, there has been considerable continuity in their lives. Women rather than men have been prepared to assume an expanded social role. This is in keeping with the fact that these women have spent an entire lifetime in accomodation and cooperation. Early in the life cycle, women learned to depend on one another and to exercise cooperative control over their domain. In middle age these youthful allegiances are transformed into political alliances, while the informal influence of earlier years becomes recognized formal authority.

Certainly women seldom command the respect that is given to men as a matter of course. Their virtues pale in the face of more manifest masculine accomplishment. Yet as they age, women gain status and influence in the Maori community for precisely the same reasons that they gain respect and attention from Europeans. Their authority in one sphere informs their performance in the other. Within these complex contexts, middle-aged women are important social actors. For men the reverse is true. High prestige in the Maori community does not assure their appreciation by Europeans. On the contrary, the colonial situation would seem to make failure inevitable for Maori men since succeeding in one sphere preordains failing in the other. Thus the effect of colonialism in New Zealand has been the reverse of what we have come to expect. The importance of Maori men is no longer assured, whereas the contribution of Maori women appears to be guaranteed.

NOTES

[1] The research presented in this chapter was gathered over a two-year period, 1971-73, and during the summer of 1982.

[2] In a preliminary report of the 1981 census, 10 percent of Pakeha men were classed as professional/administrative while a bit over 2 percent of Maori males fell into that category. Similarly, less than a third of European males were laborers while almost half of the Maori men were so labeled.

In 1969 (the 1981 statistics are not available at this time) Maori infant mortality was 29.8/1000 compared to 18/1000 for Pakehas. Similarly, while a European man can expect to live 69.2 years, the life expectancy for Maori males is 59. In education, 47.3 percent of the Europeans had a school certificate or more while only 13.1 percent of the Maoris had reached this level of educational attainment (cited by Walsh 1973).

[3] In the rural area in which I have worked, there is more continuity and stability. Women are therefore able to take their place in the community with greater confidence. Since middle age represents the culmination of many themes initiated earlier in the life cycle, the relative stability of the rural setting assures their position.

It is important to point out that while middle-aged rural women do make a comparatively successful adjustment, Maori women are clearly subject to great stress. Their death rate from lung cancer is the highest in the world, while hypertension is a very common affliction (Blank 1980).

[4] Older women comment freely on the content and imagery employed by speakers. Salmond writes:

> It is notable that whenever a man oversteps the bounds of *marae* protocol, it is nearly always the women who carry out corrective action...if a speaker becomes insulting or cuts across major rules of *maraes* procedure, the older women apply the ultimate sanction of the *whakapohane*. They stand, turn their backs on him, then bend over and raise their skirts in pointed derisory comment (1975:127).

[5] Evidence for a more widespread occurrence of this phenomenon may be found in Whiting and Edwards (1973).

[6] A similar point is made by Stack (1974) for black women in the United States.

[7] It is commonly reported that the status of women is likely to improve when there are important roles available (Bart 1969; Griffen 1977; Datan, Antonovsky, and Maoz 1981).

REFERENCES

Arbuckle, Gerald
　　1976   The Church in a Multi-Cultural Society.   Greenmeadows Seminary, Hastings, New Zealand.   Unpublished manuscript.
Archer, D., and M. Archer
　　1970   Race, Identity and the Maori People.   Journal of the Polynesian Society 79:201-218.
Bart, Pauline
　　1969   Why Women's Status Changes in Middle Age.   Sociological Symposium 3:1-18.
Bell, Diane
　　1981   Women's Business Is Hard Work: Central Australian Aboriginal Women's Love Rituals.   Signs 7:314-337.
Best, Elsdon
　　1905   The Lore of the Whare Kohanga.   Journal of the Polynesian Society 14:205-215.
Blank, Arapera
　　1980   The Role and Status of Maori Women.   *In* Women in New Zealand Society.   P. Bunkle and B. Hughes, eds. pp. 34-51. Sydney: George Allen and Unwin.

Boserup, Ester
   1970   Woman's Role in Economic Development.   New York:
   St. Martin's Press.
Brown, Judith
   1982a   A Cross-cultural Exploration of the End of the
   Childbearing Years.   *In* Changing Perspectives on Menopause.   A. Voda, M. Dinnerstein, and S. O'Donnell, eds.
   pp. 51-59.   Austin: University of Texas Press.
   1982b   Cross-cultural Perspectives on Middle-aged Women.
   Current Anthropology 23:143-156.
Datan, N., A. Antonovsky, and B. Maoz
   1981   A Time to Reap.   Baltimore: Johns Hopkins Univer-
   sity Press.
Dominy, Michele
   1983   Gender Conceptions and Political Strategies in New
   Zealand Women's Networks.   Unpublished Ph.D. disserta-
   tion, Cornell University, Ithaca, N.Y.
Dougherty, Molly
   1978   An Anthropological Perspective on Aging and Women
   in the Middle Years.   *In* The Anthropology of Health.
   Eleanor E. Bauwens, ed., pp. 167-176.   St. Louis: C.
   V. Mosby.
Douglas, Mary
   1978   Implicit Meanings.   London: Routledge and Kegan
   Paul.
Earle, Margaret
   1958   Rakau Children from Six to Thirteen Years.   Wellington: Victoria University of Wellington Publications in
   Psychology, no. 11.
Flint, Marcha
   1975   The Menopause: Reward or Punishment?   Psychoso-
   matics 16:161-163.
Forster, J., and P. Ramsay
   1971   Migration, Education and Occupation.   *In* Social Process in New Zealand.   J. Forster, ed., pp.   198-232.
   Auckland: Longman Paul.
Griffen, Joyce
   1977   A Cross-Cultural Investigation of Behavioral Changes
   at Menopause.   Social Science Journal 14:49-55.
   1982   Cultural Models for Coping with Menopause.   *In*
   Changing Perspectives on Menopause.   A. Voda, M.
   Dinnerstein, and S. O'Donnell, eds. pp. 248-262.   Austin: University of Texas Press.
Heuer, Berys
   1969   Maori Women in Traditional Family and Tribal Life.
   Journal of the Polynesian Society 78:448-494.

Kehoe, Alice
  1973   The Metonymic Pole and Social Roles.   Journal of
  Anthropological Research 27:266-274.
Keith Jennie
  1980   The Best Is Yet to Be: Toward an Anthropology of
  Age.   In Annual Review of Anthropology, 9.   Bernard J.
  Siegel, Alan R. Beals, and Stephen Tyler, eds. pp.
  339-364.   Palo Alto, Calif.:   Annual Review Press.
Kerns, Virginia
  1980   Menopause and the Post-Reproductive Years.
  National Women's Anthropology Newsletter 4(2):15-16.
Metge, A. Joan
  1976   The Maoris of New Zealand.   London: Routledge and
  Kegan Paul.
Ritchie, James
  1972   New Families, New Communities.   In Racial Issues in
  New Zealand.   G. Vaughan, ed., pp. 89-96.   Auckland:
  Akarana Press.
Ritchie, Jane
  1957   Childhood in Rakau.   Wellington: Victoria University
  of Wellington Publications in Psychology, no. 10.
Salmond, Anne
  1975   Hui: A Study of Maori Ceremonial Gatherings.
  Wellington: A. H. & A. W. Reed.
St. George, Ross
  1972   Racial Intolerance in New Zealand: Problems and
  Insights.   In Racial Issues in New Zealand.   G. Vau-
  ghan, ed. pp. 9-18.   Auckland: Akarana Press.
Stack, Carol
  1974   All Our Kin: Strategies for Survival in a Black
  Community.   New York: Harper and Row.
Walsh, A. C.
  1973   More and More Maoris.   Christchurch: Whitcombe
  and Tombs.
Whiting, Beatrice, and Carolyn Edwards
  1973   A Cross-Cultural Analysis of Sex Differences in the
  Behavior of Children Aged Three Through 11.   Journal
  of Social Psychology 91:171-188.

III   COMPLEX SOCIETIES

In many complex societies, such as India and traditional China, the new bride has an unenviable position at marriage, when she takes up residence within the household of her husband's kin. Only after the birth of sons and with their increasing maturity does a woman's status gradually improve. The data Raybeck provides for Kelantan Malaysian women differ from this pattern and present a more egalitarian instance, traceable to the economic role of these women, according to Raybeck.

Yet the major themes of this book persist. Older Chinese women can accede to certain special statuses. Middle-aged women of Kelantan have considerable geographic mobility and observe fewer restrictions than younger women. And Vatuk notes that the groom's mother exercises a certain amount of control over the sex life of the young married couple.

Although both authors remark on the enhanced position of middle-aged women in the societies they describe, both also point out that middle age brings certain liabilities. Vatuk reports that once an Indian woman becomes a mother-in-law, she is expected to renounce her sexual attractiveness and even her sex life. And Raybeck suggests that greater opportunity for achievement also creates the possibility of failure. Thus both authors view middle age as conferring both advantages and disadvantages.

9 South Asian Cultural Conceptions of Sexuality

Sylvia Vatuk

In a recent article, Judith Brown observes that in many non-western societies women's lives "appear to improve with the onset of middle age," rather than becoming less satisfying, as is commonly the case in our own society (1982:143). One reason for this, she suggests, is that restrictions on a woman's physical mobility and on her freedom to interact socially with others that may be imposed in earlier periods of her life are often relaxed in middle age. A key factor in the increased freedom and independence enjoyed by the older woman is her inability any longer to conceive and bear offspring. In cultures that regard the processes and substances exuded in menstruation and childbirth ritually contaminating to males, it is easy to see that the attainment of menopause might entail social advantages.

Furthermore, in cultures characterized by what Mediterraneanists have called an "honor and shame" complex (see, for example, Peristiany 1965; Schneider 1971), the perceived need to control women's sexuality by imposing limitations upon their freedom of movement should lose much of its urgency when they become infertile. As Brown explains, "once their sexuality can have no consequences, women are often regarded as asexual. Beyond childbearing, a woman can no longer bring dishonor upon her family by sexual adventuring" (1982:144). While Brown's statement to the

137

effect that a postmenopausal woman cannot shame her family with an illegitimate pregnancy needs no further elaboration, the same is not true of the notion that the loss of reproductive functions means the end of a woman's sexuality in the broader sense. This cultural assumption is worth exploring in greater depth.

Many ethnographers, from research in various parts of the world, have reported such conceptions: the postmenopausal woman is considered "asexual," treated "like a man," thought to be sexually unattractive to men and/or lacking in the desire or ability to be sexually active. However, I have not been able to discover in the literature any attempts to examine or analyze the content or the internal cultural logic of such conceptions. Most ethnographers, indeed, seem to take for granted, as obvious and self-evident, the idea that female sexuality ceases at menopause. This may be, at least in part, because the ethnographers are themselves members of cultures in which the asexuality of the postmenopausal woman is also popularly and widely assumed; therefore they may regard the issue as unproblematical--a cultural restatement of a biological given. Yet we know from recent studies of the physiology of female sexuality that although aging brings about distinct changes in the mechanism of sexual responsiveness and functioning, under favorable personal and cultural conditions women can and in fact do remain sexually active for many years after the climacterium (see Masters and Johnson 1966). Such scientific findings from disciplines other than our own prompt a closer look at the assumptions underlying the notion that women cease to be sexual persons when they lose the ability to bear children.

For this purpose I propose to look at cultural constructions of female sexuality in South Asia, where, as in the societies Brown refers to in her article, there is a prominent concern for the sexual modesty of women, and a concomitant plethora of social institutions designed to restrict young women to the "private," domestic arena, limit their physical mobility, social contacts, and activities, and make them generally dependent on and subordinate to the authority of the male members of their families. In South Asia, too, as many observers have noted, female seclusion and veiling, demands for deferential behavior toward males, and limitations on women's freedom are gradually relaxed as old age approaches (see, for example, Mandelbaum 1970:88-90; Jacobson 1977:105-107; Vatuk 1975:155-158, 1981:22-30). These changes are associated with increasing ability to exercise power and influence over others and carry out decision making within the family and kindred, particularly after a woman's sons mature and marry and their wives take over the more burdensome and confining household chores.

Some scholars of South Asian societies have made the specific association suggested by Brown between the older woman's improved social status and her physiological status as one whose childbearing capacity has ended. David, for example, speaking of the loosening of restrictions on the behavior of older women among Tamil-speaking Sri Lankans, suggests that this is related to the fact that the postmenopausal woman is "incapable of affecting family honor by improper behavior with males" that might lead to a pregnancy (1980:99). Hershman makes a similar point about the position of the Punjabi woman after menopause: "With the shedding of her shameful sexuality a woman becomes more like a man and she has the ability to exercise power according to the strength of her own personal character" (1977:275). In order to put these statements into their broader context, let us examine in greater detail South Asian cultural conceptions about the nature of men and women as sexual persons and about the effects of the aging process, and menopause in particular, upon female sexuality in its various manifestations. In order to do this, it will be necessary to draw very widely on a variety of ethnographic, literary, mythological, and psychoanalytic sources, in addition to my own field research, which has not focused directly on this issue. Unavoidably, the ensuing discussion will contain sweeping generalizations and display a seemingly careless disregard of regional and subcultural variation within South Asia as a whole. However, some insights should emerge that can provide an impetus for more solidly grounded empirical investigations by others.

ATTITUDES TOWARD SEXUALITY

With respect to South Asian attitudes toward sexuality in general, most scholars who have concerned themselves with the matter seem to agree that sexual desire is accepted rather matter-of-factly as an impulse whose satisfaction provides an incomparable source of pleasure for women and men alike. There is no sense that sexuality is bad, dirty, or sinful in itself. It is regarded as a positive force, not only for the transitory delight it affords, but more importantly, for its unique ability to bind together man and wife for the foundation of the family unit and the procreation of offspring. However, it is recognized that because of the very compelling strength of physical desire, those under its sway may be impelled to behave in ways that have potentially destructive consequences--for the individual, for the social groups to which he or she belongs, and/or for society at large. Thus, when directed at socially inappropriate objects, incestuous, adulterous, or intercaste matings may result; when desire for the love object leads to an exclusive preoccupation, other socially significant relationships or obligations may be neglected. Furthermore, sexual feelings may distract an individual from the pursuit of other important worldly or spiritual goals. And while beneficial and even necessary in moderation, sexual activity when indulged in to excess, can even be physically harmful and debilitating, especially for the male. It is hardly surprising, therefore, that there should be considerable cultural emphasis in South Asia upon the proper and careful regulation and control of sexual impulses--not only for women, but for men as well.

On the one hand, the control of sexuality is achieved through a variety of social practices, including varying degrees of seclusion and veiling of women and the enforcement of strict standards of modesty and decorum in mixed-sex gatherings. A major purpose of these is to ensure that sexual expression is confined, as far as possible, to the marital relationship, between partners selected by their parents from within the appropriate social units, and according to customary rules concerning prohibited degrees of kinship. Even within marriage the frequency and timing of opportunities for sexual relations are considered a legitimate area for social control, especially in the early years of marriage, when most couples live within an extended family setting. Thus a newlywed pair's access to privacy is limited by elders--an extended working day is imposed upon the young bride, open display of interest or affection in the presence of other people is proscribed, and space within the house is rarely allocated to the couple for their exclusive use on a long-term basis. While it is recognized that sexual concerns are paramount for a recently married couple, and properly so, it is felt to be important for the integrity of the larger family group that such preoccupations not interfere with the even routine of household affairs or the solidarity of previously established relationships among its members. The fact that in the long run the latter is almost inevitable perhaps gives even greater force for this imperative in the early stages of married life.

THE STAGES OF LIFE

Not only in social institutions, but also in cultural conceptions about the ideal life course of the person, the theme of control of sexuality is prominent, at least in the Hindu traditions of the region. The most familiar textual formulation of this, from the Manusmrti, outlines four stages of life for a man and, after his marriage, for his wife as well (see Bühler 1886). While such a schema is not, of course, rigidly adhered to in practice as a detailed guide for action, it nevertheless provides a conceptual framework for appropriate role performance at each major stage of the family developmental cycle, which has considerable immediacy for men and women at all social levels, even for those not directly familiar with the textual materials from firsthand reading.

The textual description of each of the stages of life--the four *asramas*--includes specification of the appropriate attitudes and activities for that period. These specifications pertain to various facets of life--work, food, abode, etc. But at each stage central attention is paid to appropriate sexual behavior. An active sexual life, in this schema, is appropriate only to one life stage, that of married adulthood, the years of rearing offspring. In the first stage of life, up to the time of marriage, a man's primary duties are to learn and to serve his religious preceptor faithfully; he must strictly abstain from sexual activity of any kind. During the second stage of life, on the contrary, a man and his wife are positively enjoined to engage in sexual relations and to procreate, while concerning themselves with the associated matters of supporting and managing a household and becoming involved in wider social and community affairs. The third stage begins when a couple's sons marry and begin to have children in their turn. Now a man ought to begin turning over the management of the household to the younger generation and devote most of his attention and time to the spiritual quest. This is a transitional stage: a man should gradually begin to loosen the bonds of affection and reciprocity that tie him to others by physically leaving his home and by subjecting himself to an increasingly ascetic regimen. While a man may take his wife with him upon his departure from home, he should not permit her presence to distract him from his spiritual aims--they may live together, but should not engage in sexual activity. In the fourth and final stage of life, a man should cut all ties with family and society, including his wife, and spend his remaining days roaming homeless in the world, renouncing all pleasures and attending single-mindedly to the goal of salvation. It is significant, insofar as this life-cycle model sheds any light upon conceptions of *female* sexuality in South Asian Hinduism, that the period of a woman's active sexual life is delimited by the requirements and timing of her husband's worldly and spiritual needs, rather than by any physiological changes in her body or any secular or religious aspirations of her own.

As this model of the ideal life cycle illustrates, the expression of sexuality in South Asian cultures is subject not only to social, or external control, imposed upon the individual by others, but there is also a very strong emphasis on self-control in the sexual realm. In general, as I shall show, these cultures tend to place more emphasis on the former mechanism in the case of women, while stressing the latter more heavily as a means of regulating males' sexual conduct. The reasons for this difference in emphasis are related to differences in male and female sexual natures, as culturally conceived. These in turn are comprehensible within the context of broader ethnomedical theories about the makeup of the human body and its various processes, of which I have room here to give only the sketchiest account.

TRADITIONAL MEDICAL VIEW

According to traditional Hindu medical texts (see Filliozat 1964), which outline a humoral theory of bodily constituents and functioning, the ultimate source of bodily strength and vitality, as well as of the sexual fluids themselves, is contained in the blood, which is in turn equated with somatic "heat." Semen is regarded as a kind of distilled "essence" of blood--its loss, like the loss of blood in its ordinary form, involves the inevitable draining away of a man's strength. While it is not desirable or practical for most men to avoid losing any semen at all in sexual intercourse, this theory clearly suggests that a man can retain a high level of vitality to the extent that he is able to control the expression of sexual impulses. In fact, a major and recurrent theme in Hindu mythology centers on the potentialities of the use of ritual heat, generated by sexual abstinence, by gods and ascetic holy men for powerfully creative or destructive purposes (see for example, O'Flaherty 1973; Danielou 1964; Cantlie 1977.) Such notions are not restricted to the ancient classical texts--similar ideas are present in the various local folk medical theories reported by ethnographers who have worked in different regions of India and Sri Lanka. The following quotation from McGilvray, summarizing the words of some of his Tamil-speaking Hindu informants on the east coast of Sri Lanka, is typical of these explanations of the relationship between sexuality and health reported from all over the subcontinent:

> The loss of semen through sex, masturbation, or nocturnal emission drains the body of valuable blood, while the retention of semen, particularly during adolescence and young manhood, promotes a man's physical, and ultimately his spiritual development. The body of an ascetic young bachelor should glow with good health (1982:33).

While males, according to this theory, must take special care to preserve their supply of strength-giving blood, postpubertal women are thought to have an overabundance of blood. As McGilvray's informants put it, "the monthly flow,...is a safeguard...insuring that a woman's natural surplus of blood (and hence physical strength and vitality, including sexual desire) is regularly drained away" (1982:31). This conception of the relationship between menstruation and level of sexual desire is obviously pertinent to the issue of the image of the postmenopausal woman as one who is no longer sexual. It is also relevant to the widely reported view that women are "naturally" more passionate, and thus sexually demanding, than men. This notion is found not only in the explicit statements of informants (as cited, for example, by such scholars as Hershman 1977; Carstairs 1967; Harper 1969), but also in the indirect evidence provided through analyses of ritual symbolism (see Beck 1969; David 1980; and Babb 1970).

Because of woman's lustful nature, she presents a dual threat: to the honor of the men of her family and to the well-being of potential sexual partners. On the most superficial level, the latter threat arises out of the notion that the act of sexual intercourse inevitably drains a man's vitality.

A lustful woman, particularly a woman who is not one's legitimate sexual partner in marriage, can thus be envisioned, in the extreme case, as a threat to a man's very existence (see Vatuk and Vatuk 1975). Some psychoanalytically oriented discussions of conceptions of female sexuality in South Asia have suggested furthermore, that underlying a widespread fear of the consequences of female sexuality among Indian and other South Asian men is the possibility that one may prove unable to fulfill adequately a woman's sexual demands. Both Kakar (1978:95) and Carstairs (1967:167), for example, have associated this fear with what they regard as an unusually severe and prevalent concern with impotence, particularly among young males (see also Obeyesekere 1976:213-215; Lannoy 1971: 114-118).

While woman as sexual partner is thus conceptualized as passionate and therefore untrustworthy and threatening to men, a counterpoised image of woman as mother and sister sees her as pure, self-sacrificing, selfless, and ever-faithful. Kakar, describing what he regards as a severe ambivalence in this South Asian male attitude toward women, says that "underlying the conscious ideal of womanly purity, innocence, and fidelity, and interwoven with the unconscious belief in a safeguarding maternal beneficence, is a secret conviction...that the feminine principle is really the opposite: treacherous, lustful and rampant with an insatiable, contaminating sexuality" (1978:93). Harper notes a similar ambivalence in attitudes toward women in rural Karnataka, south India (1969:81-86), as does Hershman with reference to Punjab (1977) and Hart for traditional Tamilnad (1973).   In the work of these writers, the major focus is on the implications of such ambivalence for male psychological development and sexual functioning.   Roy is almost alone in considering in depth the impact of this divided conception of femininity for female psychosexual processes over the life cycle. Among the conclusions to be drawn from her extended discussion of personality development and social adaptation among urban, elite, upper-middle-class Bengali women is that, particularly as middle age approaches, this culture provides substantial rewards to a woman who denies the sexual side of her being and accepts an essentially asexual, motherlike identity, even vis-á-vis her own husband (1975:117-121).   Jacobson's (1978) interesting analysis of life history data from an elderly central Indian woman, though providing a somewhat different perspective, nevertheless also supports such an interpretation.

THE AGING WOMAN

When one turns to the question of how, in South Asian cultures, the aging process is thought to affect the nature of female sexuality, the evidence is not entirely clear.   On the one hand, according to indigenous medical theory, the aging process is thought to involve an overall "cooling" of the body.   This gradual dissipation of somatic heat in later life is linked to a supposed decline, for both sexes, in the supply of blood that represents the source of youthful strength and vitality, as well as sexual desire.   In the case of women, this process is made evident by the ending of the menstrual flow.   Thus, for a female there is a clear ethnomedical rationale for equating the infertility of the postmenopausal period with asexuality in the broader sense.

However, somewhat inconsistent with the notion that women become gradually less sexual as they age, until menopause causes their sexual desire to dissipate altogether, is the widely reported belief in South Asia that sexual intercourse with an older woman is far more dangerous for a man than is intercourse with an adolescent or young adult woman. McGilvray, for example, notes that according to his informants intercourse with an older woman can kill a man (1982:65-66).   (Presumably this is the case if indulged in on a regular basis.) Kakar maintains, based on experience in his psychoanalytic practice, as well as on folklore and myth, that there is among Indian men a widespread "fear of mature female sexuality.   The fantasy world of Hindu men is replete with the figures of older women whose appetites debilitate a man's sexuality" (1978:91). He connects this dread with feelings of ambivalence toward the mother, aroused in the context of early socialization. Although there is no suggestion in the literature that these images of the sexually aggressive *older* woman refer to the *postmenopausal* woman, their prominence in this culture is nevertheless of relevance to the broader issue of what happens to female sexuality with age (see below).

One might expect that, since in the South Asian view the onset of menopause brings about a fundamental alteration in woman's nature, involving as it does the loss of the two key aspects of her gender identity, this physiological transition might be ritually or symbolically marked in some way. Such is not the case with menopause, and in this respect South Asia is not an exception.

Might menopause serve as an essential criterion of eligibility for significant ritual or social roles? In fact, it seems quite clear that the social status transitions that accompany middle age--the acquisition of increased power, authority, and autonomy referred to above--are tied in with family developmental processes rather than with chronological age, reproductive capacity, or sexuality. The obvious distinctions made by Hindus and Buddhists for ritual purposes are among the virgin (*kanya*), the married woman whose husband is living (*suhāgin*), and the widow. The last is typically excluded from ritual participation, while the former two play distinct and often central roles in a wide variety of ceremonial contexts. The classification of women for ritual purposes is thus based in South Asia upon marital status--a "sociological" characteristic--and in part also upon physiology, insofar as the *kanya* is understood to be a pre-pubescent girl and the *suhāgin* a physically mature and sexually active woman.

Physiological status is not relevant, however, in the definition of the widow, and her ritual exclusion is not, explicitly at least, associated with the matter of sexuality or its absence. As for the postmenopausal but still married woman, I have found in the literature reference to only one minor ritual in which she is specified as the appropriate *central* character. This is a Sinhalese domestic ritual in which seven "grandmothers" are the recipients of sweets-- their consumption of these offerings is supposed to assure family prosperity (Gombrich 1971). Even in this rite the qualifications for eligibility do not involve specific reference to physiological status, although Kemper (1980:750-751) is perhaps justified in suggesting that the quality of beneficence attributed to the grandmothers in this ritual derives from the fact that they are no longer menstruating.

Furthermore, the loss of the ability to conceive and bear children--and the accompanying bodily changes--do not appear to be culturally construed as problematical or traumatic for South Asian women. By contrast we may note that in the Western societies in which this matter has been investigated, the menopausal transition period is generally felt, by men and women alike, to be fraught with physical and psychological stresses of various kinds (see, for example, Davis 1982; Skultans 1970; Bart 1969; but also Neugarten, et al 1963). While evidence on this point from South Asia is scanty, the available literature confirms my own observations that older women in this society do not explicitly associate any physical or psychosocial difficulties with the physiological processes of menopause. This does not mean that late middle age is regarded as a necessarily healthful or problem-free time of life, but rather that any difficulties that a woman experiences during this period are not consciously perceived as being a consequence of the climacterium per se (Vatuk 1975:161-163; Flint 1975).

The end of childbearing and of the menstrual cycle is generally welcomed--despite the fact that it is childbearing that gives a woman in this culture her major source of positive gender identity. Perhaps, however, this should not be too surprising: aside from the strictly practical considerations involved, it is clear from the preceding discussion that it is the social status of motherhood, rather than biological fertility itself (with its vaguely threatening and ritually contaminating sexual associations) that is culturally valued and socially rewarded. A middle-aged woman who has successfully achieved this status by bearing one or more still-living children need not regret reaching the point when she can bear no more--particularly when by doing so she is able to overcome the disadvantage that her active sexuality presented during her years as a young mother. Only after menopause, in the context of these South Asian cultural conceptions of female sexuality, would a woman be able to attain the ideal and idealized image of a pure (because sexless), wholly beneficent, and trusted mother figure.

RESTRICTIONS AND CONSTRAINTS

Up to this point the picture I have painted is internally consistent--the postmenopausal woman as clearly asexual, freed from the social constraints made necessary by her lustful sexuality in earlier years. However, there are other elements in the picture that do not fit so well. It has frequently been noted that the widow in this part of the world is subjected to a variety of sumptuary restrictions and ritual disabilities--the former, at least, seem explicitly designed to neutralize her sexuality, as part of a process of enforced renunciation. These restrictions are imposed regardless of the age or physiological state of the woman involved: as David puts it, the symbolism of widowhood ignores menopause as a biological event (1980:98). It has rarely been noted in the literature, however, that women in late middle age--regardless of whether their husbands are living--are also subjected to restrictions on dress and physical adornment and upon sexual activity itself that have much in common with those imposed upon women who have lost a mate. Thus even though at one level the woman at this stage of life is said to be asexual, the most prominent constraints on a woman's behavior continue to center on the issue of sexuality.

First, the middle-aged woman, particularly one whose son has married, is subject to negative social sanctions if she dresses in such a way as to heighten her physical attractiveness. While she is expected to dress cleanly and to keep her hair bound and oiled, she should not attempt to adorn her person in any way. In the part of India in which I have done research--Western Uttar Pradesh and the Delhi area--this means wearing only white or light-colored clothing (no deep or bright colors) of inexpensive cotton fabric. Preferably, she should wear hand-me-downs from a daughter-in-law, and her clothing should be worn until it has totally outlived its ability to cover the body. New clothes, even if of the required color and fabric, are only considered suitable for a woman of this age on special ceremonial or holiday occasions. For these she should still avoid silk or synthetic fabrics and should not wear jewelry (except that considered normal, everyday wear) or use makeup. If she wears a sari (rather than the traditional shirt and full skirt formerly worn in this region) her blouse should not be of the tight, stomach-revealing cut preferred by younger women but long and loose, the sleeves wrist-length. To dress otherwise in middle age is to risk ridicule and the suspicion that one is attempting to attract male sexual attentions.

This kind of dress code appears at first glance contradictory in terms of the often reported observation that postmenopausal women are permitted a casualness of dress and a degree of license in behavior that is proscribed for the young and sexually active. It is not considered immodest if a woman of this age reveals her breasts, even in front of males, and she may be seen with her skirt or sari hiked up to her knees when working--something that a younger woman would carefully avoid. Modesty of dress is not an issue at this age--in a sense, perhaps, because the outward signs of modesty also represent signs of the existence of sexuality. For an older woman to be excessively modest could thus legitimately be interpreted as a kind of sexual gesture or even an invitation. To put this another way, a woman is encouraged to abandon modesty standards in order to make her reinforce the cultural definition of herself as a nonsexual person, regardless of how she may personally feel. The same applies to the lewd and bawdy talk and gestures that are such a source of amusement to others when they come from an older woman. Especially significant is the fact that they are prescribed in certain ritual and ceremonial contexts--as when the women of the bride's family greet the male wedding party of the groom before the marriage ceremony. On an informal level, this kind of talk may also be heard from middle-aged and older women and is tolerated and even encouraged in a way that it would not be were the speaker still in her reproductive years. It seems to me that to allow a woman to behave in a way that is the very antithesis of the way that genuinely sexual women would behave, and even to reward such behavior by appreciative laughter and attention, is a way of encouraging her to deny the very thought that she might still be a woman in the sexual sense. From such a perspective this license is at least a double-edged sword.

A second kind of constraint that is imposed on both men and women at this time of life takes the form of strong social pressure to cease having sexual relations, even within marriage. The decision to stop being sexually active when a son marries and brings his bride into the household is consistent with the scriptural prescriptions for an ideal life plan. It is typically presented, by men particularly, in terms of spiritual considerations. My female informants usually explained this later-life celibacy as motivated by "shame" (*sharam*): it is embarrassing and even "wrong" for two couples, related as parent and child, to be simultaneously sexually active in the same household. However, those who provided details about the timing and other circumstances of their own decision to refrain from further sexual activity, uniformly reported that the husband had taken the initiative--the implication usually was that they had had little choice in the matter.

It is significant that the issue of whether to continue sexual relations after the marriage of a son is not one that is necessarily considered a very private, personal one. There is a strong social expectation that sex should end at this time, regardless of the personal preferences of the pair. Physical arrangements within the home are not conducive to an older couple's continuing to sleep together. They do not normally share a private bedroom, and as soon as grandchildren cease to nurse they begin to sleep with a grandparent as their own parents seek sexual privacy at night. Any attempt on the part of the older couple to have sex would be difficult to arrange without other members of the family becoming aware of it and without it becoming more general public knowledge and a source of disapprobation. Occasionally, of course, a couple fails to conform to this norm, and even more rarely, a woman with grandchildren becomes pregnant herself in middle age. Such an event causes great embarrassment, especially for the woman--the man may still be the object of some admiration for his continuing virility but the woman is only considered "shameless."

It should be pointed out that the control of a young couple's opportunities for being together privately and engaging in sexual relations and other forms of intimacy, which I referred to earlier, is exercised primarily by the groom's mother. The fact that at this time the mother has herself been forced to renounce her active sexual life, by reason of her son's marriage, sheds a new light on this phenomenon and on the family dynamics at this period.

If, as the logic of South Asian ethnomedical theories suggests, the woman after menopause is no longer a sexual person, why should her sexuality continue to be the focus of social and symbolic controls, even while the earlier forms of control over her sexuality have been relaxed? The answer to this question may be sought in further exploration of cultural images of women and their powers, as found in ritual symbolism and myth, as well as in beliefs pertaining to the supernatural. There seems to be a clear and consistent tendency in South Asia to fear the power of women who are not under external control. Babb (1970) has pointed this out in his discussion of the qualities imputed to unmarried, as opposed to married (male-controlled) deities. Harper makes a similar point in connection with beliefs in ghosts and witches, who are typically female, often widowed and old. He reasons that fears of women are projected into the images of these supernatural beings; in turn, he explains the fear itself as arising out of the knowledge that women in ordinary life are kept in a weak and dependent position. And one of the unconscious reasons for so keeping them is the fear that they are in fact powerful beings (1969). This analysis can perhaps help us to understand the persistence of sexually focused restrictions on the middle-aged woman. It does not seem unreasonable to hypothesize that as a woman in later life finds herself working free of male authority, for a variety of reasons related to the dynamics of the family cycle, and as she becomes increasingly powerful and independent, this process should be perceived as unleashing potentially threatening forces and should call up attempts at control. Since the destructive powers of women are so inextricably associated with their sexuality in South Asian cultural conceptions, it is then perhaps not entirely surprising that these new controls should continue to center on sexual issues even though the logic of cultural theories about female sexuality requires that the restrictions placed on the woman when she was younger now be abandoned.

REFERENCES

Babb, L. A.
  1970   Marriage and Malevolence: The Uses of Sexual Opposition in a Hindu Pantheon.   Ethnology 9:137-148.
Bart, Pauline
  1969   Why Women's Status Changes in Middle Age: The Turns of the Social Ferris Wheel.   Sociological Symposium 3:1-18.
Beck, B. E. F.
  1969   Colour and Heat in South Indian Ritual.   Man 4:553-572.
Brown, Judith K.
  1982   Cross-cultural Perspectives on Middle-aged Women. Current Anthropology 23:143-148.
Buhler, J. B., transl.
  1886   The Laws of Manu. Oxford: Clarendon Press.
Cantlie, A.
  1977   Aspects of Hindu Asceticism.   In Symbols and Sentiments.   I. Lewis, ed. pp. 247-267.   London: Academic Press.
Carstairs, G. Morris
  1967   The Twice-Born.   Bloomington: Indiana University Press.
Danielou, A.
  1964   Hindu Polytheism.   London: Routledge and Kegan Paul.
David, K.
  1980   Hidden   Powers: Cultural   and   Socio-Economic Accounts of Jaffna Women.   In The Powers of Tamil Women.   Foreign and Comparative Studies/South Asian Series, No. 6.   S. S. Wadley, ed. pp. 93-136.   Syracuse, N.Y.:   Maxwell School of Citizenship and Public Affairs, Syracuse University.
Davis, D. L.
  1982   Women's Status and Experience of the Menopause in a Newfoundland Fishing Village.   Maturitas 4:207-216.

Filliozat, J.
1964   The Classical Doctrine of Indian Medicine.   Delhi: Munshi Manoharlal.
Flint, Marcha
1975   The Menopause: Reward or Punishment?   Psychosomatics 16:161-163.
Gombrich, Richard
1971   Food for Seven Grandmothers: Stages in the Universalization of a Sinhalese Ritual.   Man 6:5-17.
Harper, E. B.
1969   Fear and the Status of Women.   Southwestern Journal of Anthropology 25:81-95.
Hart, G. L., III
1973   Women and the Sacred in Ancient Tamilnad.   Journal of Asian Studies 32:233-250.
Hershman, P.
1977   Virgin and Mother.   *In* Symbols and Sentiments.   I. Lewis, ed.   pp. 261-291.   London: Academic Press.
Jacobson, Doranne
1977   The Women of North and Central India: Goddesses and Wives.   *In* Women in India: Two Perspectives.   D. Jacobson and S. S. Wadley, eds.   pp. 17-111.   Columbia, Mo.:   South Asia Books.
1978   The Chaste Wife: Cultural Norm and Individual Experience.   *In* American Studies in the Anthropology of India.   S. Vatuk, ed.   pp. 95-138.   New Delhi: Manohar.
Kakar, S.
1978   The Inner World.   Delhi: Oxford University Press.
Kemper, Steven
1980   Time, Person, and Gender in Sinhalese Astrology.   American Ethnologist 7:744-758.
Lannoy, R.
1971 The Speaking Tree. London:Oxford University Press.
Mandelbaum, David
1970   Society in India.   Berkeley: University of California Press.
Masters, William H., and Virginia Johnson
1966   Human Sexual Response.   Boston: Little, Brown.
McGilvray, D. B.
1982   Sexual Power and Fertility in Sri Lanka: Batticaloa Tamils and Moors.   *In* Ethnography of Fertility and Birth.   C. P. MacCormack, ed.   pp. 25-73.   London: Academic Press.
Neugarten, Bernice et al.
1963   Women's Attitudes towards the Menopause.   Vita Humana 6: 140-151.

Obeyesekere, Gananath
    1976   The Impact of Āyurvedic Ideas on the Culture and
    the Individual in Sri Lanka.   *In* Asian Medical Systems:
    A Comparative Study.   C. Leslie, ed. pp. 201-226.
    Berkeley: University of California Press.
O'Flaherty, W. D.
    1973   Asceticism and Eroticism in the Mythology of Śiva.
    London: Oxford University Press.
Peristiany, J.G., ed.
    1965   Honour and Shame: The Values of Mediterranean
    Society.   Chicago: University of Chicago Press.
Roy, Manisha
    1975   Bengali Women.   Chicago: University of Chicago
    Press.
Schneider, Jane
    1971   Of Vigilance and Virgins: Honor, Shame, and
    Access to Resources in Mediterranean Societies.   Ethnol-
    ogy 10:1-24.
Skultans, Vieda
    1970   The Symbolic Significance of Menstruation and the
    Menopause.   Man 5:639-651.
Vatuk, Sylvia
    1975   The Aging Woman in India: Self-Perceptions and
    Changing Roles.   *In* Women in Contemporary India.   A.
    deSouza, ed. pp. 142-163.   New Delhi: Manohar.
    1981   Authority, Power, and Autonomy in the Life Cycle of
    the North Indian Woman.   Paper presented to the Annual
    Meetings of the Association for Asian Studies, Toronto.
Vatuk, V., and Sylvia Vatuk
    1975   The Lustful Stepmother in the Folklore of Northwest-
    ern India.   Journal of South Asian Literature 11:19-43.

10 A Diminished Dichotomy:

Kelantan Malay and Traditional Chinese Perspectives

Douglas Raybeck

There is a marked disparity between the status of Malay women in West Malaysia and the status of women in traditional Chinese society. A number of anthropologists describe the situation of women in Malay society as one of relative equality (Raybeck 1981; Strange 1981; Winzeler 1974), where women can control important economic resources, participate in important domestic decisions, and influence public political behavior. In contrast, authorities describe the status of women in traditional Chinese society as one of severe inequality, where women "were considered to be minors throughout their lives, subject first of all to the men of the family into which they were born, then on marriage to the men of their husband's family, and finally on widowhood to their sons" (Baker 1979: 21-22; cf. also M. Wolf 1972, 1974; Lang 1946; Yang 1945). In Kelantan, Malaysia, it is recognized that a woman is in several respects the social equal of a man and fully capable of conducting her own affairs, while in traditional China, Confucius asserted that "women indeed are human beings, but they are of a lower state than men and can never attain to full equality with them" (Burton 1911:18-19). Thus, Confucius also stated, it was " a law of nature that woman should be kept under the control of man and not allowed a will of her own"

(Burton 1911:29). I believe I can shortly demonstrate that the dichotomy between the status of women in traditional China and among Kelantan Malays diminishes considerably as women enter middle age, and I wish to examine the causes for this diminished dichotomy.

Brown argues that across cultures women entering middle age generally encounter positive changes in their circumstances. These changes often include fewer restrictions on behavior, greater authority over kin, and better opportunities for achievement and recognition (Brown 1982:143-145). She cites a number of alterations in the circumstances of middle-aged women that help to account for these improvements. These changes include the end of fertility, continued personality development, a lessening of narrowly defined feminine parenting behavior, and a woman's increasingly influential relationship with her adult children (Brown 1982:146-148). I will refer to these factors in this chapter and will attempt to evaluate their utility for explaining the positions of middle-aged women in Kelantan Malay society and in traditional China. By middle age, I refer to the period that generally begins near the onset of menopause in the mid-to-late thirties and gradually ends with the decline of physical vigor around the mid-to-late fifties. Throughout this effort, it will be useful to distinguish between the jural status of women and their usual social situations, for the accepted social circumstances of women do not wholly reflect cultural ideals (cf. Baker 1979; Raybeck 1981).

The following description of Malay women refers principally to the state of Kelantan where I conducted 18 months of fieldwork. Kelantan is similar to another east coast state, Trengganu, studied by Strange (1981), who has provided a useful description of the position of Malay women, which I will employ to complement some of my own observations.

While Kelantan differs considerably from the more developed states of the peninsula, where wage labor and increased urbanization have altered many of the circumstances described below, there remain some rural west coast villages, such as Jendram Hilir, described by Wilson (1967), which can provide still more supplementary material on the position of Malay women.

The description of traditional Chinese society refers to circumstances obtaining before 1911; however, considerable ethnographic information is drawn from recent studies conducted in Taiwan. There is ample precedence for viewing elements of Taiwanese society, particularly those concerned with family structure, as very similar to such elements in traditional China (Cohen 1976; Freedman 1979; M. Wolf 1972, 1974). Further, a concern with the situation of women in traditional Chinese society has considerable relevance for their current position in the People's Republic. There are

clear indications that older customs still influence the position of Chinese women and hinder their full participation in
the communist state (Baker 1979:200ff; Parish 1975:615; Parish and Whyte 1978: 215).

KELANTAN MALAY WOMEN

The state of Kelantan on the east coast of the Malay
Peninsula is noted as a stronghold of traditional Malay customs and cultural practices that are disappearing from the
more developed states on the peninsula.   Ethnic Malays
constitute approximately 92 percent of the state's population,
and the great majority of them reside in rural nucleated villages, where they practice wet rice agriculture.   Their social
structure is bilateral and results in the formation of relatively stable kindreds, which provide important material and
emotional support for members.   Most social life occurs within
the confines of the rural village and is strongly influenced
by cultural values that emphasize the importance of individual dignity and interpersonal harmony (Raybeck 1975).
Virtually all Malays are Sufi Moslems and view themselves as
sincere participants in the religious system.
The general position of women in Kelantan society is
defined by a combination of traditional custom (*adat*) and the
rules of Islam.   Elsewhere (Raybeck 1981), I have described
the manner in which Kelantanese villagers resolve conflicts
between these two codes.   Briefly, the indigenous perspective on women and their rights is one of rough equality with
men.   A woman is entitled to full economic participation,
equal inheritance rights and participation in major domestic
decisions, as well as an active and influential social life.   In
contrast, the laws of Islam require a wife's deference to her
husband, limit her rights in such important social matters as
divorce, and entitle her to an inheritance half the size of
her brothers'.   Nonetheless, the social circumstances of
women remain close to the indigenous perspective, for the
Kelantanese have adopted behavioral strategies that largely
uphold the letter of Islamic law while maintaining traditional
village social organization and the important role of women in
that organization (Raybeck 1981:15-17).
The status of young Kelantanese men is somewhat
superior to that of young women.   However, women's status
increases more dramatically with age than does men's and
reaches its zenith in middle age, when it achieves rough
equality with that of men.   Thus, it is instructive to examine
the positions of women at various stages in their life cycle.
The Kelantanese highly value children and refer to
them as "the gift of God" (*hadiah Tuhan*).   Families are

equally pleased by the birth of a girl or boy, and parents sometimes express a preference that the firstborn be a girl, who can be of greater assistance in the household and who, when older, may be of greater assistance than a male in the parents' old age (Djamour 1959; Firth 1966). Young boys and girls are initially treated in a similar fashion, but by the age of six or so, girls start to assume domestic duties and are encouraged to remain close to home while boys of this age have no responsibilities and are somewhat freer in their movements.

As girls approach puberty, their freedom of movement is further restricted, and the importance of their chastity and of modest behavior is impressed upon them. During this period, they are taught that they should exhibit deference to males, including their future husbands, yet they often observe that the behavior of their mothers does not conform to this admonition. A girl's first marriage is usually arranged by her parents, but she may often influence the choice of her spouse, and she is almost always able to veto the match if she disapproves. She may disapprove if she dislikes the proposed groom or because of the proposed postmarital residence. While marriage residence is technically ambilocal, women prefer to be close to their natal family, and most couples establish residence near the bride's parents (Raybeck 1975; Strange 1981:127).

A young bride will generally receive from her parents her brideprice (*mas Kahwin*) and often an additional sum, which she will bring to her marriage along with whatever property she may have inherited. Throughout her marriage she retains her right to the property she brought with her, and should she become divorced, she is entitled to her original property and half of everything she and her husband acquired during the marriage. A young wife still has some constraints on her freedom of movement, but she usually takes an early lead in managing the family finances and in selling goods at the local market (Firth 1966; Strange 1981). Thus, while a young wife is ideally expected to be obedient to her husband and to defer to him, her active economic role encourages both her independence and assertiveness in domestic decisions. As Strange has noted, "Both women and men talk about a wife's obedience more than they expect or practice it in the family milieu" (1981:135). As a wife grows older, her participation in village affairs increases and the restrictions on her movements and activities continue to decrease.

As a married woman approaches middle age, she usually becomes a more active participant than her husband in several aspects of village life, particularly in the sphere of economics (Firth 1966; Raybeck 1975; Strange 1981; Wilson

1967). It is she who manages the household finances and monitors the family budget. She also works in the rice fields at times of planting and harvesting, and she may maintain her own garden, in which she often raises cash crops for sale in the village market. She may also sell handicrafts that she and her husband have made, as well as other items such as snacks, shellfish, etc. Such economic activity on the part of women is not confined to Kelantan: rather it is common throughout Southeast Asia (Boserup 1970; Strange 1981; Winzeler 1974). However, in Kelantan women dominate the marketing and tend to control the distribution of many forms of produce (Firth 1966:116; Strange 1981:198).

A woman's economic activities require her frequent participation in the village market, where she encounters other women sellers, who provide her with information on such socially relevant matters as prices, local politics, the availability of marriageable girls and boys, etc. A woman's access to such extradomestic information provides her with a lever with which she can widen her social participation. A wife is often more aware of the intricacies of village affairs than is her husband, and she takes an active role in major domestic decisions involving such concerns as the marriage of children, the purchase of land, and even political matters (Raybeck 1981:16; also cf. Firth 1966:26ff.; Wilson 1967:105). Further, a wife may rely on members of her kindred for emotional support and for assistance in caring for her children.

A middle-aged woman is not expected to be as modest as a younger woman and is free to travel beyond the village for economic and other purposes. Social visits to relatives in other states may last for several weeks while travel for business purposes seldom takes more than a day. Many Kelantanese women engage in trading operations that require travel throughout the state, and often across the neighboring border with Thailand. Middle-aged women are also among the most active small-scale smugglers engaged in moving long-grained rice from Thailand to Kelantan (Raybeck, in press). Such women are also free to pursue other business concerns from which a younger woman would be barred. The most popular coffee shop (*kedai kopi*) in the village was owned and run by a middle-aged woman, although Islamic-influenced village morality holds that it is generally improper for women to frequent coffee shops.

Both older and younger wives may sometimes gain greater freedom through divorce. Divorce is extremely common in Kelantan, and while the rules of Islam make it difficult for a woman to obtain a divorce, there are social mechanisms a wife can employ that will force her husband to

divorce her (Raybeck 1981:16-17).   A divorced woman is free
of both parental restrictions and those of her former husband.   A divorcée may arrange her own remarriage, and she
often establishes a specific contract, which assures her of
rights she would not enjoy in a standard marriage.
Although divorce often frees a woman to take a more active
role in village life, younger women usually soon remarry as
the status *divorcée* also carries an undesirable connotation of
sexual license and impropriety.   Older women, however, may
choose to remain single, especially if they have property,
kindred support, and adult offspring (cf. Strange
1981:232-33).   Firth has noted that the single status of older
women "illustrates their assertion of their own independence,
rather than the casting of them off by the rest of the community" (1966:11).

Despite the highly visible participation of middle-aged
women in economic activities, their roles in the religious and
political spheres are more circumscribed.   Women can arrange
for Islamic feasts and other religious events, but they may
not publicly participate in them.   Similarly, at the village
level it is not considered appropriate for a woman to hold
office or to be publicly active in politics.   However, many
middle-aged women display an interest in public politics and
a pronounced ability to affect such politics (Raybeck
1981:16).

A Kelantanese woman experiences a gradual increase in
status and in social participation from the time of her initial
marriage through middle age.   There does not appear to be a
marked discontinuity between youth and middle age.   Indeed,
as Strange has noted, there is "no view of 'middle-age' as a
discrete segment of the life cycle" (1981:76).   The relatively
high status accorded Kelantanese women in general and middle-aged women in particular seems best explained by their
active economic role in village society (Firth 1966:32ff.;
Strange 1981:198-99).   However, it also seems likely that as
a woman assumes greater economic responsibilities and experiences the demands of attendant increasing participation in
domestic decision making and village social life, the female
personality would become stronger and more assertive, as
Brown suggests (1982:147).   Certainly, the most assertive
women I encountered in Kelantan were middle-aged or older
and differed markedly from younger women in this respect.
As women age, there also appears to be a lessening of narrowly defined feminine parenting behavior, as Brown notes
Gutmann would predict (1982:147-48).

Although the circumstances accounting for the relatively high status of middle-aged women in Kelantan support
much of Brown's model, their status does not seem to be
particularly dependent on the relationship they have with

their adult children.   Since the mother-offspring bond is an important element in Brown's argument, I will discuss it further in the conclusion of this paper.

TRADITIONAL CHINESE WOMEN

Traditional Chinese society was consistently patricentric.   Descent was patrilineal, residence patrilocal, and authority patriarchal.   Although China had a complex literate society for thousands of years, most Chinese were illiterate peasants residing in rural villages and engaged in the raising of wheat in the north and wet rice in the south.   Their patrilineal rule of descent formed corporate lineages that often owned land and were among the most influential elements in Chinese social life.   While the Chinese could and did participate in a variety of religious traditions, ranging from animism and Taoism to Buddhism, the dominant values of traditional China focused on the family and wider lineage. These values were clearly reflected in Confucianism, which exalted the importance of the family and described appropriate behaviors for each family member.   The belief in and practice of ancestor worship continually emphasized both the importance of maintaining a family line and the importance of males for this purpose.

The general position of women in traditional Chinese society, as defined by kinship rules, Confucian ideology, and the legal code, was quite low (Baker 1979; Freedman 1979:245; Lang 1946; Levy 1963: 149ff.; M. Wolf 1974; Yang 1945).   A woman was jurally a minor throughout her life, and although she had a right to her dowry, she had no inheritance rights to land (Freedman 1979:258; van der Sprenkel 1977:17), nor did she have much opportunity to participate in economics (Boserup 1970:89; Lang 1946).   She was expected to defer to her husband in all domestic matters, and she was not expected to play any active role in the social life of the village or of the wider society.   However, Arthur Wolf (1975) and other authorities (Freedman 1979; M.Wolf 1972) have argued that the circumstances of women in China were quite varied, and Margery Wolf (1972) has noted that women's situations changed markedly as they passed through various stages of their life cycle.   Thus, as for Kelantanese women, it is appropriate to examine the manner in which the circumstances of traditional Chinese women change as they age.

Unlike the Kelantanese, traditional Chinese express a strong preference for male children.   Males are necessary to perpetuate the family line, to provide for the parents' old age, to worship their spirits after death, and to carry on the economic fortunes of the family. Females, in contrast, are seen as mouths to be fed that will contribute little to the future of the family and will leave it upon marriage. Both male and female children are usually loved and treated tenderly (Levy 1963:68; Lang 1946:238), but a family lacking boys or with too many children may actively resent the birth of a girl and give her a derogatory name as a sign of their displeasure (Yang 1945:125). Not surprisingly, boys were generally better nourished and better cared for than girls. Indeed, Ho finds evidence for extensive female infanticide in traditional China among both poor and wealthy families (Ho 1959:58ff.). Among poor families concerned with subsistence, a newborn girl might be drowned, sold to another family, or when older, sold into prostitution (Levy 1963:69). Wealthy families appear to have practiced female infanticide to avoid the expense of future dowries (Ho 1959:60).

During childhood, young girls are often disciplined with greater severity and frequency than are their brothers (Levy 1963:71; M. Wolf 1972:53-79). They are expected to assume domestic responsibilities by the age of five or six and soon learn to defer to all males of the family, even younger ones (cf. M. Wolf 1972:66). As a young girl approaches puberty, she is kept under constant observation and her freedom of movement is severely restricted. Her marriage is arranged by her parents, who usually attempt to further their interests by making a connection with a desirable family. Unlike her Kelantanese counterpart, the young Chinese woman does not have the option of vetoing the proposed marriage.

As a young bride enters her husband's family, her status in Chinese society is at its nadir: "her marriage cut her off economically and as a legal person from her own family and transferred the rights in and over her to the family receiving her" (Freedman 1979:245). Not only was a young bride required to defer to her husband and his father, but she was also under the constant supervision of her mother-in-law, who often treated her with great harshness. During the first year of marriage a bride's position was very insecure. She could be divorced for barrenness, neglect of her parents-in-law, or simply garrulousness (Baker 1979:45). At the same time, she had no right to initiate divorce, and if she abandoned her husband or repudiated him, she could be legally put to death (Baker 1979:46; van der Sprenkel 1977:144).

The major means by which a young bride may improve her circumstances is to bear a son. Her mother-in-law will be less inclined to beat her severely since the welfare of the child is tied to his mother's health. The production of a male heir also assures the continuity of the husband's family and may gradually provide the wife with some leverage in domestic matters. Frequently, her increasing influence exacerbates family tensions, for she will be more interested in the welfare of her husband and children than she will be in concerns of the wider family (Freedman 1979:246; M.Wolf 1972). The resulting friction is widely viewed as one of the principal causes of family fissioning, an event that the senior generation will attempt to postpone as long as possible.

A wife can gradually improve her situation largely by playing upon the affection of the children, particularly her sons. Margery Wolf, in a sensitive and insightful book, has described the manner in which mothers manipulate the emotions of their children so that the father is often seen as a rather remote and sometimes punitive authority figure while she is perceived as the confidante and protector (1972:158-170). During this period, as their children are maturing, many women are able to expand their influence on their husband and his family, even though the jural status of wives remains low (Baker 1979:47; Cohen 1976: 91-92; Parish and Whyte 1978; M. Wolf 1972).

As wives enter their thirties, several elements contribute to an improvement in their circumstances in addition to their influence on their children. They begin to receive some status from the ideal kinship rules, which define the hierarchy of family relationships through generation, age, and sex, in that order (Baker 1979:16). This advantage could be somewhat muted since the strong emphasis on male superiority sometimes allows sex to override the significance of age, but the principle of generation is never challenged (Baker 1979:16-17). Although Chinese wives do not take a significant part in economic activities as Kelantanese women do, they increasingly assume responsibility for household management, particularly when their mothers-in-law become infirm or if the wife's nuclear family establishes a separate residence (Cohen 1976:60-61, 91-92). Also, while the male head of the family is supposed to be in charge of ancestor worship, the daily domestic ancestor worship is usually managed by a woman, who may manipulate the family's perception of ancestral behavior for her own ends (Freedman 1979: 283,308).

When a middle-aged woman in traditional China becomes a mother-in-law, her status undergoes a marked improvement. She not only continues to influence the behavior and attitudes of her sons but also controls her daughters-in-law. Further, her influence over her sons becomes more important as they take on more responsibility for the economic and social welfare of the family. As the family head grows older, he continues to receive respect from his sons, but his authority tends to wane as theirs waxes (Baker 1979:38).

Margery Wolf has noted that "although young women may have little or no influence over their husbands..., older women who have raised their sons properly retain considerable influence over their sons' actions, even in activities exclusive to men. Further, older women who have displayed years of good judgment are regularly consulted by their husbands about major as well as minor economic and social projects" (1972:40). Indeed, as a mother and father age, it is not uncommon for the woman to become the de facto head of the household (Baker 1979:47; Freedman 1966:66-67; Parish and Whyte 1978; M. Wolf 1974: 159; Yang 1945:56-57).

A middle-aged woman is capable of playing an active and important role in the social life of traditional China even though her jural status has not appreciably improved. In addition to the greater amount of participation they have in domestic decision making, older women increase the amount of time they spend in extradomestic activities (M. Wolf 1972:38). They may serve as go-betweens, arranging local marriages, and they often become more involved in local religious activities (M. Wolf 1972:224-225). There are even reports that women have exerted significant influence on lineage affairs (Yang 1945:188) and on the social life of their village. Margery Wolf makes it clear that middle-aged women may influence others through their sons and through their own force of character. Assertive middle-aged women can develop a reputation for being quite outspoken and can "terrorize the men of their households and their neighbors with their fierce tongues and indomitable wills" (1974:157). The concern about such sharp-tongued women was sufficiently common that a book of precepts for local administrators included the admonition not to summon women to court without good reason. This precept was sustained partly by the desire to protect the good name of refined women and partly so that "women who might otherwise become fierce and violent are kept within the bounds of decency and prevented from becoming troublesome, and showing fits of temper" (van der Sprenkel 1977:146).

The authority of a middle-aged woman tended to reach its zenith with the death of her husband. Although widows were supposed to defer to their adult sons, such women often acted as the household heads, expecting and receiving the obedience of their offspring (Freedman 1966:66-67, 1979:259; M. Wolf 1972). Many women found themselves widowed in early middle age, often because their husbands were considerably older or because men were exposed to more hazards than were women. Significantly, many widows in Taiwan were reluctant to remarry since this would have meant giving up their children and their claim to a share in their deceased husband's estate (M. Wolf 1972). Instead, they could enjoy greater independence and social leverage by remaining single and having virtually unchallenged influence over their children. Arthur Wolf found that during a 50-year period in a Taiwanese community the great majority of widows over 30 did not remarry despite opportunities created by a shortage of women (1975:107-108).

Although a woman in traditional China experienced a gradual increase in status and in social participation following the birth of her first son and continuing through middle age, her experiences of the role of mother-in-law, and later widow, usually marked significant and relatively abrupt improvement in her social position. The circumstances accounting for her improved status conform closely to Brown's model, for a woman's social success depends heavily on her ability to influence her adult children, particularly her sons. Further, as Brown would anticipate, a middle-aged woman who has successfully dealt with the structural and interpersonal problems presented by traditional Chinese society may often develop a stronger and more resourceful personality. Margery Wolf has noted that "the contrast between the terrified young bride and the loud, confident, and often lewd old woman who has outlived her mother-in-law and her husband reflects the tests met and passed by not strictly following the rules and by making purposeful use of those who must" (1972:41). As in the Kelantanese situation, there also appears to be a lessening of narrowly defined feminine parenting behavior, as Brown and Gutmann would expect.

A DIMINISHED DICHOTOMY

If we compare the social positions of women in Kelantan and in traditional Chinese society, significant differences are manifest right from birth. While the Kelantanese are equally pleased by the birth of a child of either sex and accord them equal treatment, the Chinese express a strong preference for male children, and they raise boys with greater care than girls. The difference in the positions of women in Kelantan and women in traditional China is most apparent in early marriage. A young Kelantanese wife begins her marriage with a good social position based on a variety of rights to economic participation and on the support of her family and kindred, while a young bride in China was both jurally and situationally helpless. Traditionally, she seldom controlled significant resources and was under the complete domination of her husband and his family. As I have indicated above, this dichotomy diminishes as women enter middle age in both societies, owing mainly to a dramatic improvement in the status of middle-aged women in traditional China. However, different factors seem to account best for the improved situations of women in Kelantan and in China, and this calls for another look at Brown's arguments.

Brown suggests that, compared to a younger female, a middle-aged woman encounters fewer restrictions and more opportunities for social influence because of the end of fertility, personality changes, a lessening of the demand for stereotyped female parenting behavior, and particularly, her relationship to her adult children. These reasons fit the Chinese situation very nicely, and the single most significant factor in the improvement of a middle-aged woman's status is clearly her ability to influence her adult sons (Baker 1979; M. Wolf 1972, 1974). Elements of Brown's model are also relevant to the improved circumstances of middle-aged women in Kelantan, but here the factor that best accounts for their better status is the women's increased economic participation (Firth 1966; Raybeck 1981; Strange 1981).

It is apparent that middle-aged women may encounter the improved circumstances suggested by Brown for different reasons. Yet these differing specific reasons do not lessen the utility of Brown's model since she acknowledges that the combinations of factors affecting middle-aged women may differ across societies. Furthermore, although the primary reasons for the improved status of middle-aged women in Kelantan and in China differ, they also display an important underlying similarity. Friedl (1975), Sacks (1974), and Sanday (1974) have each argued that women's status in general is heavily dependent on their abilities to control valued resources, particularly in the public sphere. It seems likely that in societies such as traditional China, where women are barred from public economic pursuits and where adult children constitute a particularly valuable resource for the family and wider kinship group, a mother's ability to control her adult children may contribute substantially to her status. Conversely, in societies like Kelantan, where women can control more classically economic resources, the significance attributed to the mother-adult child tie may well be less. In such a society, a woman can act directly to promote her own interests rather than be constrained to operate indirectly through her children.

Although most of this chapter has dealt with the advantages that can accrue to women in middle age, I wish to end on a cautionary note. If middle age tends to lessen the restrictions on women and to provide them with greater opportunities for achievement and recognition, it can also have less pleasant consequences. Middle age can also provide women with a capacity to threaten the ideal system and with the possibility of encountering a greater degree of failure.

Across cultures a middle-aged woman's threats to the ideal cultural system can result in accusations of witchcraft, the evil eye, etc. Ahern notes that the Chinese conceptual system holds women to be ritually unclean and dangerously powerful. A middle-aged woman was seen as losing her reproductive power to do great good while retaining her power to threaten male ideals through pollution (1975) because of her enduring association with birth and with other marginal and transitional phenomena. Even among Malays, where women's status is comparatively high, a post-menopausal woman may be referred to as "useless" (Strange 1981:76).

Middle-aged women who experience difficulty in realiz-ing the satisfaction and achievements that are possible for them may become quite despondent. In Kelantan, middle-aged women who were widowed, lacking in financial security and separated from their children frequently fell ill with a psychosomatic complaint that required the performance of an indigenous curing ceremony (Raybeck 1974:240). In China a middle-aged woman's difficulties could have more serious consequences. Margery Wolf notes that in China women's suicide rate equals that of men (1975) and that women's sui-cide tends to occur at two crisis periods: first, when a woman is newly married and helpless; and second, in middle age when the appearance of a new bride provides a challenge for the son's affection and makes it more difficult to control him (1972:163).

Apparently the price of greater opportunities for achievement and recognition is corresponding opportunities for failure and derision.

REFERENCES

Ahern, Emily
  1975 The Power and Pollution of Chinese Women. *In* Women in Chinese Society. M. Wolf and R. Witke, eds. pp. 193-214. Stanford, Calif.: Stanford University Press.
Baker, Hugh D. R.
  1979 Chinese Family and Kinship. New York: Columbia University Press.
Boserup, Ester
  1970 Woman's Role in Economic Development. London: Allen and Unwin.

Brown, Judith K.
1982   Cross-cultural Perspectives on Middle-aged Women. Current Anthropology 23:143-156.
Burton, Margaret E.
1911   The Education of Women in China. New York: Revell.
Cohen, Myron L.
1976   House United, House Divided: The Chinese Family in Taiwan. New York: Columbia University Press.
Djamour, Judith
1959   Malay Kinship and Marriage in Singapore. New York: Humanities Press.
Firth, Rosemary
1966   Housekeeping among Malay Peasants.   2nd ed.   New York: Humanities Press.
Freedman, Maurice
1966   Chinese Lineage and Society: Fukien and Kwantung. New York: Humanities Press.
1979   The Study of Chinese Society.   Stanford, Calif.: Stanford University Press.
Friedl, Ernestine
1975   Women and Men: An Anthropologist's View.   New York: Holt, Rinehart and Winston.
Ho Ping-ti
1959   Studies on the Population of China, 1368-1953.   Cambridge, Mass.:   Harvard University Press.
Lang, Olga
1946   Chinese Family and Society.   New Haven, Conn.: Yale University Press.
Levy, Marion J., Jr.
1963   The Family Revolution in Modern China.   New York: Octagon Books.
Parish, William L.
1975   Socialism and the Chinese Peasant Family.   Journal of Asian Studies 34:613-630.
Parish, William, and Martin King Whyte
1978   Village and Family in Contemporary China.   Chicago: University of Chicago Press.
Pruitt, Ida
1945   A Daughter of Han.   Stanford, Calif.:   Stanford University Press.
Raybeck, Douglas
1974   Social Stress and Social Structure in Kelantan Village Life.   *In* Kelantan: Religion, Politics and Society in a Malay State.   W. Roff, ed., pp. 225-242.   Kuala Lumpur: Oxford University Press.

1975   The Semantic Differential and Kelantanese Malay
Values: A Methodological Innovation in the Study of
Social and Cultural Values.   Unpublished Ph.D. disserta-
tion, Cornell University, Ithaca, N.Y.
1981   The Ideal and the Real: The Status of Women in
Kelantan Malay Society.   Women and Politics 1:7-21.
In Press   The Elastic Rule: Deviance and Conformity in
Kelantan Village Life.   *In* Cultural Identity in Modern
Malaysia.   Sharon Carstens, ed. Athens: Ohio Univer-
sity Press.
Sacks, Karen
1974   Engels Revisited: Women, the Organization of Production, and Private Property.   *In* Woman, Culture and
Society.   M. Z. Rosaldo and L. Lamphere, eds. pp.
207-222.   Stanford, Calif.:   Stanford University Press.
Sanday, Peggy
1974   Female Status in the Public Domain.   *In* Woman, Culture and Society.   M. Z. Rosaldo and L. Lamphere, eds.
pp. 189-206.   Stanford, Calif.:   Stanford University
Press.
Strange, Heather
1981   Rural Malay Women in Tradition and Transition.   New
York: Praeger.
van der Sprenkel, S.
1977   Legal Institutions in Manchu China.   New York:
Humanities Press.
Wilson, Peter J.
1967   A Malay Village and Malaysia.   New Haven, Conn.:
HRAF Press.
Winzeler, Robert
1974   Sex Role Equality, Wet Rice Cultivation, and the
State in Southeast Asia.   American Anthropologist
76:563-567.
Wolf, Arthur
1975   The Women of Hai-shan: A Demographic Portrait.
In Women in Chinese Society.   Margery Wolf and Roxane
Witke, eds. pp. 89-110.   Stanford, Calif.:   Stanford
University Press.
Wolf, Margery
1972   Women and the Family in Rural Taiwan.   Stanford,
Calif.: Stanford University Press.
1974   Chinese Women: Old Skills in a New Context.   *In*
Woman, Culture and Society.   M. Z. Rosaldo and L. Lam-
phere, eds. pp. 157-172.   Stanford, Calif.:   Stanford
University Press.
1975   Women and Suicide in China.   *In* Women in Chinese
Society.   Margery Wolf and Roxane Witke, eds. pp.
111-141.   Stanford, Calif.:   Stanford University Press.

Yang, Martin C.
  1945   A Chinese Village. New York: Columbia University
    Press.

IV   INDUSTRIAL SOCIETIES

A variety of options are reported for middle-aged women in industrialized societies. According to Datan, Antonovsky and Maoz, in Israel these options vary with ethnic identity and with degree of modernity. Kaufert takes into account regional differences, variations in family structure, levels of education and employment status in her study of Canadian matrons. In industrial societies there are specialists, such as medical experts and anthropologists, whose views of middle-aged women influence those of the society at large. Kaufert reviews these models and compares them to data from Manitoba, and questions the prevalence of the "empty nest" (also see the earlier chapter by Counts). Both Canadian women and Israeli women welcome the end of fertility. Datan et al. attribute this attitude to developmental factors, the subject of Gutmann's concluding chapter of this book.

In industrial societies, the meaning of middle age for women is not merely a matter of overall cultural traditions, rules and values. The meaning is likely to vary among subcultures; to be given definition by "experts"; and to be shaped by the personal concerns and circumstances of the individual woman.

11 Tradition, Modernity and Transitions in Five Israeli Subcultures

Nancy Datan
Aaron Antonovsky
Benjamin Maoz

This study of middle-aged women in five Israeli sub-cultures reflects the expectation that culture may shape the response to biological change. The study began in Kiryat Shmona, where Benjamin Maoz, on his psychiatric residency, observed that hospitalization for involutional psychosis was seen only among European women and not among women from Near Eastern cultures. Maoz, together with Aaron Antonovsky, a medical sociologist, found in the national health statistics that the observation in Kiryat Shmona was true for the entire Israeli population: that is, that hospitalization for involutional psychosis, while rare, occurred almost exclusively among European women.

Three hypotheses were proposed to explain this observation:

1. Differences in cultural patterns create varying degrees of stress in middle age, and this stress is greatest for the modern, youth-oriented European culture and manifest not only in the extreme response seen in involutional depression, but observable also as nonpathological stress among normal women.

2. Stress may be more or less equal across cultures but manifest as psychiatric complaints among European women and expressed as somatic complaints among Near Eastern women, since there are cultural differences in the permissible forms of expressed stress.

173

3. Stress may be more or less equal across cultures, but the diagnosis of involutional psychosis is only made among the European women, due to some combination of the doctor's readiness to observe psychiatric symptoms and the woman's ability to communicate psychic distress.

Antonovsky and Maoz proposed a broad-scale study to explore the consequences of cultural differences for stress in middle age. Their view was that greater stress could be anticipated among European women, who had planned and restricted childbearing. They could therefore be said to have "denied" their femininity and to view menopause as the loss of a potentiality that had not found sufficient fulfillment. Traditional women, on the other hand, could expect to enjoy raised status as they took on a matriarchal role. Support for this view was found in the psychiatric literature.

Nancy Datan brought to the study a perspective from developmental psychology that led to a contradictory view: the European women, who had coped actively throughout their lives, would find menopause and middle age a time of new freedom, while traditional women from Near Eastern cultures, whose only role had been that of childbearer and mother, would find the loss of fertility both salient and stressful. Support for this view was found in the developmental literature.

THE STUDY: PURPOSE AND METHODS

The study was designed to address two major issues: 1.) what is the relationship between the degree of traditionalism or modernity in a culture and the level of psychological well-being in women during changes of middle age, and 2.) what is the relationship between the degree of modernity (and the woman's fertility history) and the perception of the loss of fertility. These questions emerge from a comparison of the woman's life cycle in traditional and modern cultures. In traditional cultures, early marriage (at or shortly after menarche) and frequent childbearing throughout the years of fertility are the norms. In modern cultures the converse is seen: marriage--a mark of social maturity--occurs several years after biological maturity, and childbearing is limited to a few children, typically born fairly soon after marriage. It may be said, then, that the family life cycle in traditional cultures corresponds fairly closely to the biological life cycle of the woman; with increased modernity, there is increased independence of the family life cycle and the biological life cycle. The purpose of this chapter is to inquire whether the relative strength of the relationship between the biological life cycle and the family cycle in traditional and modern subcultures is expressed in women's responses to menopause.

The study was carried out in four phases. The first phase was a pilot study during which semi-structured psychiatric interviews were conducted by Maoz with 55 women of European and Near Eastern Jewish origin, and women of Israeli Muslim Arab origin. On the basis of findings from the pilot study, a closed interview schedule was constructed for the second phase of the study, a broad-scale survey among 1,148 women from five Israeli subcultures ranging along a continuum from modernity: immigrant Jews from Central Europe, Turkey, Persia, and North Africa; and Israeli-born Muslim Arabs. The survey questionnaire dealt with aspects of middle age, including demographic information, psychosexual history, attitudes toward climacterium, menopausal symptomatology, social roles and role satisfaction, and self-reported psychological well-being.

An overview of selected social characteristics of the five ethnic groups (see Table 1) reveals a consistent pattern of differences, from the most traditional group, the Arab women, through the North Africans, Persians, and Turks, to the most modern group, the Central European women. This pattern supports our general notion that the life cycle of the traditional woman more closely approximates the biological life cycle, while the life cycle of the modern woman is relatively more independent of the biological life cycle. Traditional women marry sooner, bear more children, and continue bearing children far longer than do modern women. In addition, traditional women are likely to be religiously orthodox--and both Jewish and Moslem traditions have elaborate taboo systems related to menstruation, pregnancy, and childbirth. Finally, traditional women tend to be illiterate, while literacy is universal among the Central Europeans. In short, it is probably reasonable to say that with successively greater degrees of modernity, the life cycle becomes progressively more independent of biological changes. This general tendency, in turn, leads us to anticipate culturally determined differences in psychological well-being and the response to the loss of fertility.

All women from the second phase of the study were invited to participate in the third phase, a medical examination; of the 1,148 women who agreed to take part in the survey, 697 consented to the medical examination. There was somewhat more readiness to cooperate in the medical examination among women in the more traditional groups, but this difference was not statistically significant. The medical examination included a pregnancy history, a general physical examination, the woman's self-reported assessment of her physical health, and the physician's overall rating of her physical and mental health.

Table 1: Selected Social Characteristics by Ethnic Group
(Percentages)

| ITEM | ETHNIC GROUP | | | | |
	Central Europeans	Turks	Persians	North Africans	Arabs
	N=(287)	(176)	(160)	(239)	(286)
- Illiterate	0	29	61	60	96
- Husband illiterate	0	25	49	53	66
- Married before age 16	0	5	35	37	30
- 7 or more live births*	0	5	53	59	72
- 5 or more living children	0	14	68	68	76
- 5 or more children currently living at home	0	3	29	36	53
- At least one child under 14 years old	16	30	47	57	56
- Total childbearing span less than 7 years	70	35	13	20	10
- Works outside the home (full or part time, including family business or agriculture)	42	21	29	25	35
- Currently religiously orthodox	21	30	57	85	98

*Percentage based on medical subsamples.

Taken from N. Datan, A. Antonovsky, and B. Maoz, *A Time to Reap: The Middle Age of Women in Five Israeli Subcultures*. Baltimore: The Johns Hopkins University Press, 1981, p. 18.

The fourth and final phase of the study consisted of follow-up psychiatric interviews with 160 subjects, subsamples from each of the five ethnic groups in the survey, who represented the high and low extremes with respect to self-reported psychological well-being. Among other findings, considerable agreement was seen between the woman's self-report and the psychiatrist's diagnosis, although the psychiatrists had no prior knowledge of the woman's report: that is, a woman whose self-report indicated a high measure of psychological well-being was likely to be evaluated by the psychiatrist as well adjusted; and, conversely, women with low self-reports were often independently viewed by the psychiatrist as somewhat depressed.   These findings were interpreted as a measure of support for the validity of the survey responses.

MIDDLE AGE AND MODERNITY

We commenced this study with contradictory views on the relationship between adjustment at middle age and the degree of modernity: the first predicted an inverse linear relationship between adjustment and the degree of modernity, on the basis of the psychiatric literature; the second predicted a direct linear relationship between adjustment and the degree of modernity on the basis of the developmental literature.   The survey findings showed a curvilinear relationship between degree of modernity and self-reported psychological well-being, with the highest reported well-being at the two extremes, among the modern European and traditional Arab subcultures.   This finding has been attributed to the greater cultural stability in these two subcultures: the immigrant European women came to a country where the dominant cultural values were European, while the Muslim Arab villagers, living in a stable traditional setting, saw change gradually penetrate their lives.

The transitional groups, by contrast--the Turks, Persians, and North Africans--had been socialized into traditional settings and transplanted into a modern context, where traditional cues no longer served them, while they were unable to make use of the benefits of modernity, choices among a plurality of roles.   The self-reported psychological well-being was lowest in the group that, by external indicators such as the degree of traditionalism in the life history and the modernity of the present life context, would appear to have experienced the greatest discontinuity: the Persians.

Each subculture viewed climacterium as a combination of gains and losses, but this combination differed by ethnic group: the Europeans saw a possible decline in emotional health; the Near Eastern Jews were concerned over a decline in physical health; and the Muslim Arabs felt there was some decline in the marital relationship.   On the other hand, all groups unanimously welcomed the cessation of fertility, despite large variation in conception control and fertility history, ranging from the Europeans at one extreme, who typically bore one or two children and prevented or aborted unplanned pregnancies to the Arabs at the other extreme, some of whom were continuously pregnant or lactating between menarche and menopause.   That this response is paced by the life cycle and not shaped by prior events in the psychosexual history is suggested by the European women's attitudes toward their actual and ideal family size: two-thirds of the European women reported that they would have wanted to have borne more children but that economic or political circumstances--this group bore children at the time of the establishment of the State of Israel and the attendant war and period of economic austerity--prevented larger families.   Notwithstanding the desire to have borne more children, the European women--like all other groups-- did not now wish to be capable of pregnancy.   We have interpreted this finding as suggestive of a developmental change in adulthood, linked (like many earlier developmental changes) to a maturational change.

INVOLUTIONAL PSYCHOSIS RECONSIDERED

Finally, the multidisciplinary approach to the question of the significance of the changes at middle age permitted us to answer the question that originally stimulated the broader study: that is, is the hospitalization of European women for involutional psychosis a consequence of differential rates of stress in different cultures, different modes of expression of stress, or differential diagnosis?   From the survey, the medical examinations, and the follow-up psychiatric interviews, we were able to provide tentative answers.   There was no support for the first hypothesis, that cultural patterns produced greater stress in the modern culture, manifest at the extreme as involutional depression; on the contrary, as has been shown, self-reported well-being was greatest at the two poles of the traditional-modernity continuum.   There was some support for the second hypothesis: that is, there was a greater incidence of psychosomatic complaints on survey responses among the Persian and North Africans, while the follow-up psychiatric interview showed "psychological" symptomatology among the Europeans and "somatic" symptoms among all other groups.   Finally, there was support for the third hypothesis: clinical depression was found to be rare but appeared in approximately equal rates across cultures in the medical examination and follow-up psychiatric interviews, and diagnosis was considered to have been improved by the use of psychiatrists from the same (or closely related) sub-culture as the respondents.

To sum up, our broad-scale study of normal women showed involutional psychosis to be an extremely infrequent response; we found in general that the response to middle age and to climacterium is shaped by ethnic origin, that the balance of gains and losses is specific to each subculture, that there is no linear relationship between psychological well-being and the degree of modernity, and finally, that the cessation of fertility is welcomed by women in all cultures.

NOTE

This study was an invited contribution to the symposium "Middle-Aged Women: Evolutionary, Ethnographic, and Cross-Cultural Perspectives," organized by J. K. Brown for the 81st annual meeting of the American Anthropological Association, Washington, D.C. December 1982.

The research reported in this chapter was conducted through the Israel Institute of Applied Social Research and supported by the U.S. National Institute of Mental Health (P. L. 480 Agreement 06-276-2).   A detailed treatment of the issues raised in this chapter and a full exposition of the cross-cultural comparisons reported here can be found in *A Time to Reap: The Middle Age of Women in Five Israeli Subcultures* by N. Datan, A. Antonovsky and B. Maoz (Baltimore: The Johns Hopkins University Press, 1981).

12 Midlife in the Midwest:

Canadian Women in Manitoba

Patricia A. Kaufert

In challenging the medical model of menopause, the women's health movement has borrowed from the more positive descriptions of women in their middle years provided by some anthropologists (Kaufert 1982). The objective of this chapter is to set both the medical and anthropological descriptions of what happens to women in midlife against the empirical and perceptual realities of their lives as reported by women themselves. The women come from Manitoba, a province which is geographically--and to some extent socially and economically--the Canadian equivalent to the American Midwest.

THE MEDICAL MODEL OF MENOPAUSE

I am using the phrase "the medical model" as a shorthand reference to the composite of knowledge, concepts, and beliefs about the menopausal woman that are accepted as legitimate by the medical profession and given place within the medical literature. "'Medical knowledge'" as Young has argued, "is not restricted to what is represented in textbooks and journal articles but is a product of a dialectic between knowledge and practice/experience" (Young 1978:107). The latter (i.e., practice/experience) can vary among physicians by such factors as their age, where and when they were trained, their pattern of medical practice and area of specialty, their own personality, and the wider socio-economic framework within which they work (Locke 1982). There are two results. One shows that there is a diversity of practice and opinion rather than the "monolithic" system usually presented as medical knowledge (Blumhagen 1980). The second indicates that "medical knowledge" is a mixed brew of scientific fact (supposedly neutral) and of beliefs and attitudes derived from the ideology of the medical profession and/or of the individual physician.

The heterogeneity of medical practice has been noted by McIntyre (1978) in relation to differences between physicians in the management of pregnancy and has been demonstrated recently by Locke (1982) with reference to the menopause. In a series of interviews with gynecologists and family practitioners, her research uncovered as many "working models" (the equivalent of Helman's [1978] "operational" models), as there were clinicians with menopausal patients. On examination, however, these models are not totally idiosyncratic but draw on a set of recurring themes; it is the manner in which these are selected and combined that creates a model particular to the individual physician. In this chapter I will briefly explore two of these themes: first, the menopause as a physiological loss event and second, the menopause as one in a paired set of psychological events---the loss of fertility concurrent with the loss of the mothering role.

The Menopause as Physiological Loss

In a still widely held model of the female body as reproductive machinery, prone to failure and breakdown (Oakley 1979), the menopause is treated as the naturally occurring mark of its obsolescence and of little medical interest. This view remains medically acceptable and was held by a number of the physicians interviewed by Locke (1982). It is being displaced, however, by a definition of menopause as a pathological event requiring medical management.

The medicalization of menopause is more recent than the medicalization of childbirth and not as widely diffused throughout the medical profession and to the lay public. It is generally accepted that childbirth requires medical supervision, though there is disagreement over the particulars of its management, but many continue to see menopause as a natural event to be individually managed. The specialists in menopause, whether researchers or clinicians, argue against such "laissez-faire" and promote the active management of the menopausal patient. The equivalent message is being spread to women through the women's magazines, which are beginning to give wider coverage to menopause.

The definition of menopause as a pathological event is associated with research linking menopause (and/or hormone therapy for menopause) with the two high-profile areas of medical research, namely cancer and heart disease. Just as the risks faced by some women at childbirth are cited to justify its medicalization, so the "at-risk status" of some menopausal women is used to argue that this period of hormonal transition must also be medically supervised.

The second factor in the medicalization of menopause developed out of the promotion of hormone replacement therapy. By medical logic, given a treatment, there must be a disease to be treated. The menopause became redefined; from a natural happening, it turned into a deficiency disease. Treatment cannot be offered as a "cure," at least not as a cure for infertility. On the other hand, it has been presented as a sovereign remedy against the loss of another aspect of femininity, a woman's sexuality. The converse of the promise is an implied threat that women who refuse hormone replacement therapy will suffer vaginal atrophy and the loss of libido; the end of menstruation becomes the end of sexuality.

In sum, the definition of menopause as a physiological loss event includes more than the loss of reproductive power. Women also lose the special protection that their hormonal characteristics offered against coronary risk factors. Their now useless reproductive organs become increasingly vulnerable to cancer. The source of their sexual response and appeal atrophies and is lost. Physiologically, a woman is bereft.

The Menopause as a Psychological Loss

The theoretical argument behind the definition of menopause as a psychological loss event was made by the Freudians, particularly Deutsch (1945). Her interpretation of the significance of menopause is logically derived from a theory that predicates the meaning of a woman's life on her ability to bear children; to lose this ability is to lose life's meaning. In its strictest form, this Freudian explanation precludes offering more than palliative care to the menopausal patient, who has, in Deutsch's own words, "reached her natural end--her partial death" (1945:459). Writing in the changing climate of the late 1960s and 1970s, Bart (1971) gave a twist to this argument. Using a series of case studies of women under psychiatric care, Bart suggested that negative reaction to menopause occurs not because the patient can no longer bear children, but because of her pathological overidentification with and refusal to surrender the mothering role.   I call this the "empty nest/castrated mother hen" theory of menopausal depression.

Both Bart's theory and that of Deutsch assume that the biological end of fertility coincides with the social end of the mothering role.   In the current literature on the psychology of midlife, women are told that their most "important development task at midlife" is the ability to separate from children as they grow and depart from home (Notman 1980:88).   It is this combination of the loss of fertility with the loss of children that is seen as the key to the psychological symptoms reported by menopausal patients.   The role of the physician is to help the patient accept and adapt to her loss, whether by psychological therapy or by the prescription of antidepressants.

Playing their familiar gadfly role in relation to medical (particularly psychiatric) theories concerning human nature, the medical anthropologists have produced inconvenient evidence with which to challenge the universality of these definitions.   For purposes of this presentation, I will concentrate on what the anthropologists have said concerning the relationship between menopause and sexuality and between menopause and the end of the mothering role.

MENOPAUSE AND THE ANTHROPOLOGISTS

In this section, I will look at two images of the menopausal woman as presented in the anthropological literature, using data from Roy's (1975) work on Bengali women, Bourdieu's (1977) study of the Kabyle, and Poole's (1980) chapter on the Bimin-Kuskusmin.   The first image is of woman as "matron-mother," as in Roy's translation of *ginni-ma*, the term for a Bengali woman who is a mother but beyond the age of childbearing.   By contrast, there is the "menopausal hag," the woman who is no longer fertile, the woman in process of becoming old and ugly, the woman as witch.   Yet there is an alternate face to the hag image. She is the hag defined by Daly (1978) as a figure of "strength, courage and wisdom."   She is the crone, the sibyl, a woman whom men cannot bind by making pregnant--a woman of power.   But whether priestess or crone, she is a woman beyond sexuality.

The Matron-Mother

The matron-mother image has attracted the most attention among feminists. In Roy's (1975) description of the
ginni-ma, she is a woman who is married, has reached menopause, and has children (more particularly, she has sons),
and she is the senior woman in an extended family household. While she lacks formal authority within the family--
this is held by the male members--her support or opposition
can influence and even determine family decision making.
The position of the *ginni-ma* (as with matron-mother type
figures in other traditional societies) is partly based on her
control over the material and labor resources of the domestic
economy, including the productivity of her daughters and
daughters-in-law. The extent of her economic power varies
among societies and from one family to another, depending on
such factors as the division of labor by sex, the value
placed on resources produced and/or controlled by women,
and whether residence patterns subordinate younger women
to the authority of an older woman.

The *ginni-ma* is entitled to respect and deference from
all family members, including her husband, but it is with her
sons that her influence is strongest, persisting even after
they are married. The relationship of a mother to her adult
sons, which provides a source of power and emotional grati-
fication for older women, is characteristic of societies other
than the Bengali. It has been described for Irish women by
Scheper-Hughes (1979), for Andalusian women by Brandes
(1981), for Greek women by Friedl (1967), and for the rural
Japanese family by Bernstein (1976). Anthropologists, perhaps influenced by their own age-group identification and
cultural baggage, tend to present this relationship nega-
tively, either from the perspective of the browbeaten daughter-in-law (Bernstein 1976) or in terms of the psychic dam-
age to the son (Scheper-Hughes 1979). Yet it could also be
seen as the quintessence of the matron-mother role and as a
prime source of emotional security and satisfaction for women
in midlife, whether in Bengali or in other societies.

To summarize, the assumption in the medical model that
menopause coincides with the loss of the mothering role does
not fit what happens to the *ginni-ma*. Rather than the
family group separating and disintegrating, the matron-
mother presides over a household that is growing by the
addition of daughters-in-law and grandchildren. Her family
remains an arena of accomplishment in which she occupies a
position of honor, respect, and, within limits, a degree of
real power. Rather than having to separate, to "de-bond,"
from her sons, she enjoys a relationship that is given cultural primacy over that between husband and wife.

The Menopausal Hag

The role of the *thamgarth*/old woman among the Kabyle (Bourdieu 1977) is similar to that of the Bengali matron-mother in terms of her control over the domestic economy and the respect she enjoys within the household. However, at this point I want to deal not with this aspect of Bourdieu's description, but with his presentation of the other image of the woman at midlife, the woman as menopausal hag. Bourdieu deals with the position of the no-longer-fertile woman not only within the actual, but also within the conceptual, worlds of the Kabyle. His argument is too complex for presentation here. He identifies male with external, public space, and female with internal, domestic space. While she need not be constrained and kept within the household--the internal, domestic space appropriate to the fertile young woman--the postmenopausal woman also cannot be controlled by men by being made pregnant. Bourdieu's description of the *thamgarth* is reminiscent of the descriptions of the menopausal patient in 19th-century medical texts; there is that same combination of disgust, yet fear (cf. Smith-Rosenberg 1974). Bourdieu writes that the *thamgarth* is the "unbridled sterile old woman who no longer has any 'restraint'; she is the old witch, with the cunning and treachery which relate her to the jackal" (1977:126). This is woman reverting to nature; this is also a being whose sexual status is ambiguous. The assumption that she is sexually repugnant denigrates the woman and yet is the source of her independence.

Bourdieu is presenting one aspect of the menopausal hag; the ambiguity of her sexual status places her outside the ordered world of the Kabyle community and makes her a threat to its integrity. The same definition of the postmenopausal woman as a sexually ambiguous figure is used in other societies to create a priestess figure; the hag becomes sacred. Among the Bimin-Kuskusmin (Poole 1981), a post-menopausal woman is chosen for the ritual office of the *waneng aiyem ser*. She presides at the female rituals of menarche and childbirth and at male initiation rites. Symbolically, she is allowed to grow both taro (the crop of men) and sweet potatoes (the crop of women) for she is of neither sex and yet of both. By contrast to the witchlike malevolence of the postmenopausal woman in Kabyle society, this is a benevolent figure, but also an asexual one.

The asexuality of the postmenopausal woman is assumed not only by members in other Islamic societies, but is more widespread (including Bengali society). As I noted earlier, the reaction of the Kabyle male to the postmenopausal woman and sex is not unlike that of the 19th-century physician. The current medical preoccupation with restoring sexuality may seem a more benevolent approach, yet it rests on assumptions that are equally unproven. For there is no evidence indicating how many women would experience the end of their sexuality at menopause unless given estrogen. It is equally unclear how many would regret its passing or would seek to reactivate their sexual lives.

Summary

In summarizing these anthropological accounts of the menopausal woman as mother and as a sexual being, I would add a word of warning. References to the improved position of women in midlife must be interpreted with caution and in context. In each of the three examples discussed, the gains in status, authority, and even physical mobility are all relative to the low status and powerlessness of the same women when younger. They are also dependent on a woman successfully completing the earlier stages of her life according to her group's prescriptions; among the Bimin-Kuskusmin, she must have been a virgin at marriage and fertile within marriage. In all these societies, a woman without sons (more particularly an infertile woman) cannot enjoy the rewards of midlife as honored head of an extended family household.

Furthermore, although these older women may manipulate events and people, they must work within the limits set by a society that is controlled by males. Rosaldo's statement, made about women in general, is particularly apt to women at midlife.

> Some women certainly are strong. But at the same time that women often happily and successfully pursue their ends, and manage quite significantly to constrain men in the process, it seems to me quite clear that women's goals are themselves shaped by the social systems which deny them ready access to the social privilege, authority and esteem enjoyed by the majority of men (1980:395).

Finally, the corollary of the strength and self-assurance women acquire as they age is that they are also resented and feared. Their power over their own sons will ultimately be supplanted by the young wife who bears the son his sons. Their authority within the family is also at the price of the loss of their sexuality. Their symbolic status is both witch and sibyl.

BOTH VIEWS CONSIDERED

Clearly, then, the models of midlife as presented by medicine and the accounts of these anthropologists have little similarity. The immediate explanation lies in the differences between the societies from which each discipline derives its version of the middle years. One based on the midlife of a Bengali matron will read very differently from a model based on the life of a white, middle-class North American woman. But recognition must also be given to differences which stem from the manner in which each discipline customarily creates its models. Even when sharing the same field of investigation, anthropology and medicine differ in the types of relationships that are selected and made explicit, as well as in the types of assumptions which, while integral to the model's form, are left implicit and unquestioned.

It is characteristic of medical science that it requires all physiological and clinical variables to be explicit and clearly defined. On the other hand, assumptions about human nature underlie many medical models. Particularly when women are the patient-subjects, these assumptions tend to be socially naive, and class-, gender-, and ethnocentric. For example, with reference to sexuality and the menopause, the relationships between estrogen deficiency, vaginal atrophy, and estrogen replacement therapy are stated in the terms appropriate to a purely physiological model; however, as discussed earlier, the argument for treatment rests on the assumption that postmenopausal women wish to continue sexual activity and both should and can do so. Aside from the fact that some women may lack a partner, this view of women in middle age reflects attitudes toward sexuality particular to the culture of the North American middle class (Kaufert 1982:159). It also represents a diametric shift from medical opinion in the 19th century (Smith-Rosenberg 1974).

Depending on their theoretical bent, social anthropologists (the term is used in the British manner [cf. Kuper 1973]) tend to build models in which either symbolic or sociopolitical relationships have centrality, but in which physiological ones tend to be left implicit. It is typical that some accounts of women at middle age (e.g., Roy 1975; Bourdieu 1977; Poole 1981) focus on the implications of menopause for a woman's ritual or social status but treat the menopause itself as a given. Yet unlike menarche, when a clear marker event is involved, evidence that a woman is menopausal is more ambiguous in character. Menstruation does end, but this is usually preceded by a number of irregular cycles, and which menses is a woman's last can only be determined in retrospect and after a period of time has elapsed (Kaufert and Syrotuik 1981). Fertility also ends, but not abruptly. It declines gradually as the number of anovulatory cycles increases even as a woman continues to menstruate. Yet she may become pregnant even during the months after her final menses. By paying no attention to the physiological characteristics of the menopause, these anthropological accounts fail to recognize the ambiguities inherent in women's experience as they pass from a "not-menopausal" to a "menopausal" status. Yet how, why, and by whom a woman is defined as menopausal are questions essential to understanding how this physiological process becomes a socially accomplished one.

Other differences between the medical and anthropological versions of midlife stem from the selective nature of model building within each discipline. As noted earlier, these anthropological accounts of midlife tend to ignore women who do not achieve the criteria for a successful middle age, that is, women who are childless, divorced or widowed and who do not belong in an explanation of the change in relationships attendant on becoming the matriarchal figure of the *ginni-ma* or the *thamgarth*. On the other hand, the North American equivalents to such women (that is, women in midlife who are active, independent, and socially, politically, or economically productive) are invisible within the medical model. The woman-as-patient is, as always, dependent, passive, and being menopausal at the end of her useful (i.e., reproductive) life.

Given the characteristics of both the anthropological and the medical versions, the extent to which they are representative of the realities of midlife as experienced by women becomes questionable. There are problems in testing the "goodness-of-fit" of any anthropological model to its empirical base (although clues can sometimes be abstracted from the interstices of an ethnographic report). On the other hand, the midlife of the North American woman is more accessible as a research area. The next section will use data from a Canadian study to explore the extent to which women's own account of their experience accords with the description of midlife contained in the reports of the physician or the social anthropologist.

THE MANITOBA PROJECT

The Manitoba project is a study of women between the ages of 40 and 59. While focused on health , it has collected extensive data on other areas of their lives. There is a tendency among anthropologists to regard large data sets as a vulgarity best suited to sociologists. Yet there are occasions when the lack of basic, general population-based information hampers understanding, whether of an ethnic group or of women in midlife. Despite the categorical nature of the statements made about women in middle age, surprisingly little data have been collected. Such studies as exist tend to deal with women who may be--but probably are not--representative. In a sense, women in middle age are akin to some tribal group whom several anthropologists have studied, but about whom, despite the brilliance of their assorted field reports, we have little systematic knowledge. Yet failing this information, discussion of menopause and its impact takes place in a vacuum, without the possibility of distinguishing speculation from fact.

In response to this situation, the Manitoba project has three stages. Stage 1 is a cross-sectional mail survey designed to establish the basic parameters relative not only to the health of women in middle age, but also to the characteristics of their family structure, their employment status, and their own perceptions of the roles available to them in midlife as wives, mothers, daughters, housewives, and as participants in the work force. Stage 1 is now complete and in the process of analysis.

Stage 2 began last year and is a longitudinal study with six data collection points, which extend over a three-year period and in which the 500 women taking part are a subset of the 2,500 women who completed Stage 1. The objective of the longitudinal study is to collect information not only on changes in physical and psychological health as a response to menopause, but also on changes in family and other roles as parents age and children leave home. Stage 3 will follow more closely the research methods of the anthropologist and will consist of a series of interviews with 100 women, a subset of the subset. These interviews will explore issues in depth and in a way impossible to the formal question-answer format used in Stage 1. In essence, the project has a funnel design: each stage depends on its predecessor, yet also takes the process of information gathering a step further and deeper. Many of the issues raised earlier in the chapter (sexuality, physiological and psychic loss, a woman's sense of self and of her position within a group, whether domestic or communal) can only be explored fully in Stage 3. The data currently available come from Stage 1. This means that the themes that can be pursued here are restricted in number. However, two issues raised by the medical model rest on assumptions that can--and should--be tested against the type of general population data represented in Stage 1 of the Manitoba project. These issues are the relationships between menopause and the loss of fertility, and between menopause and the end of the mothering role.

Stage 1:   Methods

The target population were women between 40 and 59 years of age living in Manitoba.   Using a random sample that was stratified to provide approximately equal representation to Winnipeg and non-Winnipeg women, questionnaires were mailed to those women whose names appeared in either Henderson's Directories for the urban areas or the Voters' Registration Lists for the rural areas.   Following the methods for the mail survey recommended by Dillman (1978), the data collection stage provided 2,500 questionnaires completed and ready for analysis.   After adjustment for errors (such as death or incorrect age identification, or moving out of the province), the overall response rate to the survey was 67 percent.

The socio-demographic profile of the population is set out in Table 1.   The rest of the chapter will deal with the variables relating to the population's reproductive life and to its family structure.

Fertility

In linking together menopausal depression with the loss of fertility, the medical model is presuming that until the moment of their final menses, women have their fertility, want their fertility, and see themselves as potentially fertile. Yet these assumptions are not necessarily compatible with current patterns of reproductive behavior. For example, in the population taking part in this study, only 5 percent of women had continued childbearing after 40 and the majority had had their last child before they reached 35.   Potential, as distinct from actual fertility was also at variance with the medical model; as shown in Table 1, 19 percent of the women had had a hysterectomy. 26 percent had had a tubal liga tion.

Given the assumptions of the medical model, the fertility profile of women coming up to menopause (that is, women who had menstruated during the previous 12 months) was of particular interest.   Slightly less than a third thought that it was still possible that they might become pregnant; others were uncertain.   Among those women convinced that pregnancy was no longer physically possible, almost three-quarters had had a tubal ligation.

The survey contained questions on attitudes toward their reproductive past, including questions on whether they wanted another child after the birth of the last, whether they would like another child in the future, and if they worried about becoming too old to have children (see Table 2).

Table 1: Socio-demographic Characteristics (N=2500)

		Percent
AGE	40-44	28
	45-49	24
	50-54	24
	55-59	24
MARITAL STATUS	Married	85
	Widowed	6
	Divorced/separated	6
	Single	3
PARENTAL STATUS	No children	8
	1-2 children	30
	3-4 children	41
	5 or more children	21
EDUCATIONAL STATUS	Less than secondary	40
	Secondary education	31
	Postsecondary education	29
EMPLOYMENT STATUS	Currently employed	52
	Not currently employed	48
RESIDENT	Winnipeg	48
	Non-Winnipeg	52
MENOPAUSAL STATUS	Has menstruated within the last three months	47
	Has menstruated within last year, but not in the last 3 months (ie., perimenopausal)	4
	Has not menstruated for 12 or more months (ie., post menopausal)	30
	Had a hysterectomy	19

Table 2: Attitudes Toward Past and Future Fertility
among Women with Children (N=2294)

		Percent
After your last child was born	Yes	11
did you intend having more?	No	89
(No answer = 45)		
Looking back, do you wish you	Yes	18
had another child?	No	82
(No answer = 64)		
Would you like to have a child	Yes	2
at some time in the future?	No	96
(No answer = 20)	Don't know	2
Do you worry about being too	A lot	1
old to have children?	A little	3
(No answer = 86)	Not at all	96

In general, women had neither wanted another child at that time nor had they regretted the decision. Furthermore, not being able to have more children was not an aspect in the aging of their bodies that appeared to cause them great distress.

Admittedly, such questions cannot tap the implications of menopause as the symbolic closure of a woman's life as a fertile being. On the other hand, fertility is also a behavioral option and one that the majority of these women have not exercised (or wanted to exercise) for the previous 10 to 15 years. Whatever psychic drama is involved in recognizing that one will not become pregnant again had already been dealt with by the many women who had had a hysterectomy or a tubal ligation.

Children At Home

Seen as compounding the loss of fertility, the medical model attributes depression at midlife to women's reaction to a household without children, to an empty nest. This explanation rests on the assumption that children are leaving home as their mothers are becoming menopausal. By comparison to this image of the child-bereft Western woman, anthropologists present the matron-mother, a figure presiding over an extended family household that includes her grandchildren, her daughters-in-law and her own children. As her child-bearing is presumed to have continued until closer to meno-pause, some of the latter will be relatively young.

Using the data from Stage 1, it is possible to look at the actual patterns of family and household composition among Manitoba women. Very few women had children below the age of 6 (less than 3 percent) and comparatively few had children below the age of 13. Most children were teen-agers (13-17) or adults (18 plus). Only a handful had families in which the children's ages ranged from under 6 to over 18. Based on the data, these Canadian women cannot aspire to the role of matron-mother, the matriarch of an extended family household. Their household groups are small, lacking both grandchildren and married adult sons and daughters; the latter leave home as they go to work, go to school, get married. The former are visitors rather than residents in the home of grandparents.

On the other hand, neither is the empty nest a univ-ersal characteristic of women in this age group. Slightly less than a third of them lived in a household without chil-dren, and 52 percent of the households included children below the age of 18. As would be expected, the likelihood of children having left home increases sharply as one goes from the younger (10 percent of women aged 40-44) to the older women (50 percent of those in the 55-59 age group). Yet although the number of such households increases with age, usually it is not until they are five to ten years beyond final menses that women live in a child-absent household; even then, no more than half are doing so.

The medical model has caught at one dimension of what is happening to women at this stage in their lives. Their roles as mothers are increasingly played vis-à-vis children who are first teenagers, then adults. Domestic groups fluctuate and shrink in size. Yet there is no strict coincidence between menopause and an "empty nest"; neither is it evident that any such synchronization of events would necessarily result in depression.

CONCLUSION

One may simply accept these data as evidence that the medical model is incorrect; it misrepresents the reality of menopause as an event within the lives of women. Alternatively, this failure may itself be seen as a fact requiring explanation according to Ardener's (1975) distinction between dominant and muted models. Ardener argued that a dominant group imposes its version of reality on a subordinate one; the latter's own experience is unheard, for it is muted. In this sense, the relationship between the medical model and women's actual experience at menopause is the relationship between a dominant and a muted version of reality.

The dominant/muted argument can be extended to the anthropological examples discussed earlier in the chapter. The *thamgarth* and the *waneng aiyem ser* are both figures seen from a male perspective on how women's relationship to men changes as they become middle-aged. Despite the brilliance of their analyses, Bourdieu (1977) and Poole (1981) have restricted themselves to the dominant, the male model. By implication, their account may not represent the actual experience of menopause and becoming middle-aged among either Kabyle or Bimin-Kuskusmin women. By contrast, the object of this, and of other chapters in this book, has been to give voice to the muted by allowing women to speak about their own experience of midlife.

NOTE

This study was written when the author was supported by a National Health Research Scholar Award (No. 6607-1213-48) from Health and Welfare, Canada.

REFERENCES

Ardener, S.
  1975   Introduction.   *In* Perceiving Women.   S. Ardener,
  ed. pp. vii-xxiii.   London: Dent.
Bart, Pauline
  1971   Depression in Middle-Aged Women.   *In* Woman in
  Sexist Society.   Vivian Gornick and B. K. Moran, eds.
  pp. 99-117.   New York: Basic Books.
Bernstein, G.
  1976   Women   in   Rural Japan.   *In* Women   in   Changing
  Japan.   Joyce Lebra, Joy Paulson, and Elizabeth Powers,
  eds. pp. 25-50.   Stanford, Calif.:   Stanford University
  Press.
Blumhagen, Dan
  1980   Hypertension: A Folk Illness with a Medical Name.
  Culture, Medicine and Psychiatry 4:197-228.
Bourdieu, Pierre
  1977   Outline of Theory and Practice.   English edition.
  Cambridge: Cambridge University Press.
Brandes, S.
  1981   Like Wounded Stags: Male Sexual Ideologies in an
  Andalusian Town.   *In* Sexual Meanings: The Cultural
  Construction of Gender and Sexuality.   S. Ortner and H.
  Whitehead, eds. pp. 216-239.   Cambridge: Cambridge
  University Press.
Daly, Mary
  1978   Gyn/Ecology: The Metaethics of Radical Feminism.
  Boston: Beacon Press.
Deutsch, Helene
  1945   The Psychology of Women, Vol. 2.   New York:
  Grune and Stratton.
Dillman, Don
  1978   Mail and Telephone Surveys.   New York: John Wiley.
Friedl, Ernestine
  1967   The Position of Women--Appearance and Reality.
  Anthropological Quarterly 40:97-108.
Helman, C.
  1978   Feed A Cold, Starve a Fever--Folk Models of Infec-
  tion in an English Suburban Community.   Culture, Medicine and Psychiatry 2:107-137.
Kaufert, P.
  1982   Myth and Menopause.   Sociology of Health and Illness
  4:141-166.

Kaufert, P., and J. Syrotuik
    1981 Symptom Reporting at the Menopause. Social Science
    and Medicine 15E:173-185.
Kuper, A.
    1973 Anthropologists and Anthropology: The British
    School 1922-72. London: Allen Lane.
Locke, M.
    1982 Models and Practice in Medicine: Menopause as Syn-
    drome or Life Transition. Culture, Medicine and Psy-
    chiatry 6:261-280.
MacIntyre, Sally
    1978 Obstetric Routines in Ante-natal Care. *In* Relation-
    ships Between Doctors and Patients. Alan Davis, ed.
    pp. 76-105. Farnborough, UK: Teakfield.
Notman, M. T.
    1980 Changing Roles for Women at Midlife. *In* Midlife:
    Developmental and Clinical Issues. W. Norman and T.
    Scaramella, eds. pp. 85-109. New York: Brunner/Ma-
    zel.
Oakley, A.
    1979 A Case of Maternity: Paradigms of Women as Mater-
    nity Cases. Signs: Journal of Women in Culture and
    Society 4:607-631.
Poole, F. J. P.
    1981 Transforming "Natural" Woman: Female Ritual Lead-
    ers and Gender Ideology among Bimin-Kuskusmin. *In*
    Sexual Meanings: The Cultural Construction of Gender
    and Sexuality. S. Ortner and H. Whitehead, eds. pp.
    116-165. Cambridge: Cambridge University Press.
Rosaldo, M. Z.
    1980 The Use and Abuse of Anthropology. Signs: Journal
    of Women in Culture and Society 5:389-417.
Roy, M.
    1975 Bengali Women. Chicago: University of Chicago
    Press.
Scheper-Hughes, N.
    1979 Saints, Scholars and Schizophrenics: Mental Illness
    in Rural Ireland. Berkeley: University of California
    Press.
Smith-Rosenberg, C.
    1974 Puberty to Menopause: The Cycle of Femininity in
    Nineteenth Century America. *In* Clio's Consciousness
    Raised. M. Hartman and L. W. Banner, eds. pp.
    23-37. New York: Harper Colophon Books.
Young, A.
    1978 Mode of Production of Medical Knowledge. Medical
    Anthropology 2:97-124.

13　Beyond Nurture:

Developmental Perspectives on the Vital Older Woman

David Gutmann

As a developmental and clinical psychologist, I approach the cross-cultural laboratory with methods and questions quite different from those of anthropologists. Cultural anthropologists use their data to derive laws concerning the relations among the components and functions of a supraindividual entity: culture as such. Anthropologists' subjects are frequently old and they are used as informants not on their own lives, but on aspects of cultural norms and usage. Developmental psychologists like myself are more likely to use our older respondents as informants on themselves--on their own history and circumstances. Nevertheless, we too are *required* to use the cross-cultural laboratory for the final and necessary test of our hypotheses and theories. In fact, *no* developmental hypothesis can be taken seriously until it has shown that the specified maturation has taken place, in predictable form and sequence, across a wide range of societies different from each other and from the culture in which the hypothesis was first conceived. In other words, we confirm a hypothesis of developmental import by demonstrating that some pattern of human growth--whether physical or psychological--is an aspect of *genotypic nature*, peremptory and predictable across widely varying conditions of social nurture. Through use of the cross-cultural, comparative method we randomize the influences of cultural nurture in order to bring out and identify the central thrust toward structural and functional maturation that is imposed by some intrinsic natural design.

This is not to argue a nature-nurture split. Sophisticated developmental theory holds that all adaptive growth of new executive structures requires a reciprocal and sponsoring environment and that the facilitating environment for psychological development is always social (though the versions of the social *other* may range from the mother's breast in infancy to the moral institutions and traditions of society in later life).

Nevertheless, while developmentalists and anthropologists might agree that an organized social life is necessary to development, we disagree as to the role that culture might play in shaping and guiding a developmental sequence. Thus the developmentalist would hold that the early stages of maturation are sui generis and guided by stimuli and programs that reflect evolutionary priorities, whereas the anthropologist is more likely to hold that culture is the independent variable and that the timing, direction, and sequences of development all reflect cultural priorities.[1] As we shall see, this dispute between Nativist and Culturalist understandings becomes particularly sharp when we turn to consider the fate of older women in various societies as documented by the various contributors to this volume.

THE STAGING OF DEVELOPMENT

To underline the source of our differences, and to prepare the ground for the later discussion of the older woman, I will first present my own generic model of development, one that has been greatly influenced by the ideas of Erik Erikson, a leading psychoanalyst.

Anthropologists are mainly interested in the extraindividual collective processes and institutions--rituals of passage, normative models of instruction, etc.--that surround some process of individual growth and they assume that such externalities fully account for the acquisition of new learning or new social statuses. By contrast, our model considers the intraindividual dynamisms that contribute to development and (particularly in the early maturational stages) gives these equal or greater status vis-à-vis extraindividual influence. Thus a full developmental sequence has at least three distinct phases, each keyed to a special form of psychosocial sponsorship and expression. Any significant developmental advance entails the transformation of inchoate strivings into formed, adapted executive capacities. As such, it begins with a *genotypic eruptive* phase (my term) in which "chemical" and biosocial events--e.g., weaning, the advent of siblings, the nutritive acts of a mother, etc.--lead to the emergence of raw, undifferentiated potentials. These diffuse energies are at the outset like the wings of fledgling birds: they have not yet tuned their beat, nor found their proper air.

Put more formally, the genotypic potentials have not yet entered into coordinated behavior or into consciousness, and they are mainly expressed in the relatively stereotyped metaphors of the unconscious, the imagery of dreams, and the preverbal communication of mood and involuntary gesture. At this juncture, behavior may be expressive in the idiosyncratic sense but it has not yet been set in the conventional symbols that make it socially communicative. Indeed, in this phase socially articulated behavior may serve to deny the eruptive potentials, rather than to directly express them: thus adolescents may deny burgeoning sexuality through displays of religious idealism; or older women, as we will see, might deny their emergent aggressivity by extravagant displays of depression and dependency. The contents of the eruptive phase can only be known indirectly and inferentially, through the eliciting of images and associations not under normative, conscious control: responses to projective tests, early memories, free associations to dreams, etc. Needless to say, anthropologists do not usually elicit or analyze such materials; accordingly, they are not likely to recognize the ultimate contribution to social development of this first, incoherent phase.

If the raw potentials of the eruptive phase meet congenial internal (psychological) and external (social) environments, if their first tentative and unfocused expressions are recognized and welcomed by important legitimators such as parents and teachers, then the developmental cycle will move into its second or *reciprocal* phase. At this stage, the social other no longer exists in syncretic unity with primitive drives, as a releaser for instinctual discharge; instead, the other exists in his own right, as a counter player in the developmental drama. This other might be some adult who recognizes the possibilities inherent in the genotypic potentials and brings them into section with the most relevant symbol systems of the culture, so that they may become named and normalized, opened up for exploration and maturation along conventional lines. Again, this crucial period is studied through close observation of private rather than public domains: the often unspoken exchanges of gesture and feeling between parents and children and the private feelings, sensitivities, and fantasies that they bear toward each other (and will reveal only to a trusted investigator). Again, this kind of investigation--of the subjective side of social living--is not undertaken by most anthropologists.

If the role models of the reciprocal phase have done their job properly, mediating between eruptive potentials and their relevant social contexts, then development moves into the final *sculptured*, or phenotypic phase, in which potentials are solidly organized into personal skills and social resources, according to the idiom of a particular society. Thus, it is only in the final phase of a developmental sequence that culture as such becomes crucially relevant in shaping matured outcomes.

In sum, the raw energy that powers development is an aspect of the genotypic phase and has common origins and stereotypic (if unconscious) manifestations across cultures. Culture as such begins to infiltrate the intimate transactions of the reciprocal phase, dictating the persons involved in these exchanges, but not the idiosyncratic and subjective aspects of the relationship between the developing individual and the developmental sponsor. These relationships are shaped not only by role prescriptions, but also by potent transference, reflections of early primary relationships that were even less under normative cultural control. It is only in the terminal, sculptured phase that culture plays a primary role in determining the conventional expressions, the personally useful and socially valued outcomes of the developmental potentials.[2]

COMPARATIVE PERSPECTIVES ON THE OLDER FEMALE

We will bring this multistage model of development to bear on the data from cross-cultural sources, concerning psychological growth and change in older women. But first we must briefly review that data.

The comparative data point to a striking pattern: across a wide range of societies, particularly those characterized by stable, patrilocal extended families, postparental older women move towards a position of matriarchy, sometimes overt and formal, sometimes covert and implicit. This matriarchy, official or unofficial, of later life is so apparent that it has been recorded by many anthropologists. Thus Gold (1960) asked 26 ethnographers, varied as to their theoretical interests, to report on *any* age-related changes in sex role in the varied groups that they had studied. Fourteen reported a shift toward greater female dominance in later life. The remaining 12 reported no change. But in no case was the balance seen to swing, with advancing age, toward greater male authority over the wife.

While the older woman may not always be found in a position of formal dominance, her social stance and behavior is notably ascendant and aggressive. Thus far I have identified, from a variety of ethnographic accounts, five distinct patterns and facilitators of later life matriarchy.

1.   The aging husband gives up interest in secular power, and in the management of the home. Losing his own powers, he becomes religious and links himself, through ritual means, to the power of the gods. The aging wife, often in concert with the oldest son, moves into the socket of power and dominion that the husband has abandoned. This pattern is reported for the traditional Chinese and rural Egyptians, among others.[3]

2.   Another generic family pattern allows the aging wife to gain domestic power through her son. As he attains adult status through marriage, his mother acquires a potential rival in the daughter-in-law, but also a potential servant. If the mother retains some emotional hold over the son during this transitional time when his affections shift to a wife, then she and the son may share dominion over the family, with the mother becoming a senior adviser, an *éminence grise* who works her will through her son. The daughter-in-law then becomes something of a vassal to the mother-in-law, thereby enhancing the senior woman's scope and powers. This pattern is reported for the traditional Japanese and for the traditional Moroccans, among others.

3.   The older women acquire power, particularly in religious circles, following menopause. The ending of her procreative period makes her acceptable in sacred places and rituals on two counts: she is less sexual, less likely to stir men to lustful thoughts when their minds should be on God; and she is no longer a danger to the ritual--she will not pollute the service with her menstrual blood. Accordingly, after menopause, women can join the circle of religious dancers or take on ritual tasks that are forbidden to fertile women. This motif is probably very common, and may be synergistic with other patterns, as noted above. However, we have specific reports for Lebanese Arab villagers and the North Piegan, among others.

4.   Postmenopausal life may bring an endowment of destructive rather than sacred power to the older woman: as she ages, she becomes a witch rather than a priestess. In some instances, this occult transformation is based in family dynamics. Thus, as described in point 2, the older woman does not always establish complete dominion, and there is chronic tension between her and those in her purview--the daughter-in-law or the husband. Under these conditions, the frustrated older woman is often suspected of trying to have her way with the aid of supernatural allies, enlisted through witchcraft practices. This pattern has been noted for the Kikuyu and the Aranda, among others. But whether or not the above family dynamics are involved, the linking of the aging female with eerie power is very widespread.

5. Finally, the last transition, into death, can transform the old woman into a vessel of malign powers: unlike her milder spouse, in death she becomes an evil, retributive spirit, as reported for the Ainu, the Maori, the Tallensi and the Yoruba, among others.

The above list refers mainly to folk-traditional societies; it is in these settings that the older woman's metamorphosis takes place via events and traditions that are explicit, culturally recognized, and even culturally sponsored. However, we have a number of reports from Western societies in which the same social and psychological transformations are noted (even though their manifestations are more subtle, and less stereotyped). Again, the observers of Western societies report the usual outcome--the elevation of the older woman to new (but secular rather than supernatural) realms of influence--though usually without describing the transformative process. Thus later-life matriarchy may be facilitated by certain clear customs and usages of the traditional society, but it does not require them. These transformations occur, apparently with much the same regularity, in secular and nontraditional societies, including those in which elder-matriarchy is not sponsored by shared and rooted customs.

PRIMATOLOGICAL STUDIES OF THE AGING FEMALE

Recent studies of aging among nonhuman primates indicate that the virilization of the older primate female may be general not only across human societies, but across species, as well.[4] Thus Hrdy (1981), who conducted field studies of the langur monkeys and of the very successful macaques (successful in the evolutionary sense: they are distributed across a wide range of varied habitats) finds that, like the majority of younger human mothers, the maternal ape is devoted almost exclusively to the care of the latest infant, the one still clinging to her fur. She is at the same time relatively inoffensive in her dealings with other adults; thus, during the period of intense parenting, she allies herself with dominant males, and trades sexual access for their physical protection. However, in the postparental years, a striking change occurs, which parallels our cross-cultural observations among humans. Hrdy notes that the way in which older monkeys support younger animals "seems to vary with the sex of the animal and the situation of the group. Males generally bow out leaving older females to intervene actively in the fate of their descendants" (1981:75). In effect, female primates have two roles in regard to procreation: they provide physical as well as emotional security, though--consistent with the exclusivity of these roles--they play them out sequentially rather than concurrently. As Hrdy reports: "When a troop of langurs is threatened by dogs or humans, or by encroachments upon its territory by other langurs, it is typically the adult male *or the oldest females* who leave the rest of the troop to charge and slap at the offenders" (1981:73, italics added). Similarly, courageous and persistent defense of younger relatives by older females has been documented for Japanese and rhesus macaques by Partch (1978), who recorded 572 separate instances of protection or defense of infants by postreproductive females, on occasions when breeding females did not take up defense of their own offspring (cited in Hrdy 1981).

Clearly then, postreproductive female primates take up the defender's role that we had thought to be reserved for young and vigorous males. The breeding mothers are almost exclusively providers of emotional security; but, like males, the postreproductive female moves at times of danger not to the protected center of the troop, but to its outer defense line.

MASCULINE VIEW OF THE OLDER WOMAN

Not only anthropologists and primatologists see the older female as masculinized. Though they may, in their public behavior, deny her ascendance, across cultures older men represent the dominant woman in their more private fantasies and projections. I have gathered Thematic Apperception Test (TAT) data from younger and older men in urban areas in the United States and among the Navajo, Mexican Maya, and Druze, using stimuli that elicit covert conceptions of male-female relationships. The results are best summed up by the "heterosexual conflict" card of the standard TAT, which shows a young man half turned away from a young woman who reaches toward him in a restraining or pleading manner. Younger men--urban Americans, Maya, Navajo, or Druze--propose that the young man brushes aside a beseeching or timorous woman and forges out into a dangerous but exciting world of combat, carousal, and mistresses. Thus, for younger men, the sexes are sharply distinguished: the young man pushes toward some extradomestic periphery without much regard for consequences; inhibition and timidity are mainly located in the woman. But to the same stimulus older men propose more anergic, constricted, or "pregenital" themes. In their version the young woman tends to domineer; or the male protagonist retreats back to her consolation and away from a world in which he has known danger and defeat. In either case, initiatives and strength have migrated away from the young man toward the young woman. Finally, for many older men, the male protagonist does not reject the nurturance offered by the young woman, but instead dwells with her in contentment and harmony. Potential trouble comes from outside, not within the dyad, and menaces the young man and woman equally.

These age shifts appear to be developmental rather than secular in nature. Thus they appear with some predictability across a panel of disparate cultures, where the drift of generational, cultural change has been different in each case. Within cultures, these changes in sex-role perceptions show up in longitudinal as well as cross-sectional data--evidence that the original age X theme distributions of responses to this card were produced by psychological changes within individuals, and not by intercohort differences having to do with generational changes in the various cultures. Thus, as they age, men are increasingly prone to assign dominance to the female figure and to see the younger man as her satellite; and this intraindividual change proceeds independently of culture.

This same sex-role turnover is dramatically captured by another card, used only among the Druze, which, for most subjects, elicits concerns around intergenerational and intermale relations and lines of authority. Almost invariably, Druze men below the age of 60 see the card as depicting relations between an executive or advisory older man and usually compliant boys or younger men. However, a number of men over 60 see the older man as a beggar, asking for food or money from a woman, who may or may not indulge him. Again, the tendency to turn a compliant young man into a dominant woman and to turn an authoritative old man into a beggar is not a cohort phenomenon, limited to a particular generation of Druze men. Longitudinal studies with this card reveal that nine Druze, all but one over 60, who saw the older man as an authority at Time 1 see him as a beggar by Time 2.[5]

ENGINES OF LATER GROWTH

In sum, external observers of the older woman, whether these be anthropologists or the women's aging husbands, agree that they change drastically in the later years, showing aggressive and managerial powers that were only latent in their makeup before this postparental advance. In effect they become androgynous, sexually bimodal, a mixture, as many observers have put it, of mother and father. I would argue that these transformations, inasmuch as they fit the model of maturation set forth earlier, are *developmen-*

tal in nature, and betoken a reliable pattern of growth for postparental women across a wide range of "average-expectable" human environments.   Some cultural anthropologists would dispute such a developmental formulation.   They would assert that such changes have an exogenous rather than an endogenous basis and are in each case a result of social opportunities that are made available to older women, in the second half of life.   The office has sought the candidate, rather than the other way around.

Culturalist explanations, which lay stress on causes that are unique to each society, ignore an outcome that is found in all postparental female transitions.   Whether old women become matriarchs or witches, a common factor underlies all these sundry transformations, namely, the general increase in their powers.   Power always bears a double face. In most cases--as when they become matriarchs--older women acquire a new endowment of good power.   In other cases--as when they are reputed to be witches--older women acquire *bad* power.   But in all cases their potencies increase and give evidence of a surgent developmental event.   Thus the transcultural variety in the older woman's role acquisitions registers the disparate effects of the local culture's parochial age norms and social opportunities, as these determine the phenotypic, *sculptured* developmental phase.   By the same token, the generic increase in social and personal *power* registers the effects of the *genotypic*, or *eruptive* phase of development.

The fact that the older woman's postparental, liberated energies have been transmuted and sculpted into a wide array of structures by their impact with the larger social order does not negate either their reality or their developmental origins.   Finally, it is this protean potency of the older woman, notable precisely because it invigorates so many disparate roles, that signals the presence of a unitary endogenous phenomenon, rather than many unrelated parochial and fortuitous social phenomena. [6]

I have contended that the phenotypic virility of the older woman is released when she emerges from the adult period of chronic emergency that we call parenting (Gutmann 1975).   I have proposed that, when her children show that they can maintain their own emotional security, the postparental woman can reclaim the aggression that, earlier on, would have put her children at risk.   In effect, they take back into themselves the aggressive energy lived out vicariously during their parental years, through identification with the prowess and exploits of the husband.   Thus the postparental woman is energized to seek out, to take advantage of, and even to create the powerful roles that fit her expanded energies and new appetites.   She is not merely reactive to expanded social opportunity, but is also proactive in creating new leadership possibilities. Hence, just as the effects of the original "Big Bang" can still be traced in all the varied celestial phenomena of our universe, the energies of the eruptive phase, the energies originally released by the female exit from active parenting, can still be read in all the social activities, malign or beneficial, of the older woman.

ERUPTIVE ENERGIES: A CASE EXAMPLE

The reality of the eruptive phase can be inferred from the common features of the transcultural data--the reported energy that is ubiquitous across the older woman's role acquisitions. But the eruptive stage can also be studied more directly, via instruments that are available to the dynamically oriented psychologist but usually ignored by anthropologists. The Rorschach test, for example, presents unfamiliar, "strange" stimuli, and thereby elicits interpretations metaphoric of the "stranger"--the unsocialized strivings within the personality. As such, the responses to standard psychological tests capture (if one accepts the logic of projection) tracings of the presocial eruptive phase as it shapes the response imagery. In short, the projectives provide "opportunity structures" for the respondent to externalize and review dangerous fantasies and images--the derivatives of surgent energies that have not yet been socially sculptured and normalized. Thus, as we can see in the following case study and Rorschach protocol, the projectives permit us to experience and *study* the derivatives of motives that not only cannot be expressed in public behavior, but that are specifically *denied* through such behavior.

The eruptive aggression of the older woman can lead to rivalry with men, and particularly with the husband; and this change in family politics can bring about a crisis of psychiatric proportions in older women, particularly if the older husband's health or fortunes are low enough to arouse a feeling of guilt in the wife. Thus, in our work at Northwestern Medical School, we find that many women come to psychiatric treatment for the first time in the postparental years, too often with a misdiagnosis of "depression." Such was the case with the 53-year-old Polish-American woman, whose Rorschach record is summarized below.

This patient comes to outpatient treatment in an anxious, weepy state and appears so needy that her novice therapist is reluctant to take her on, fearing that she will be "swallowed up." However, the Rorschach imagery is not consistent with the patient's weak, depressive presentation. Her first response visualizes two bulls in combat: "They're in battle, have hurt each other because there is blood spattering from them; both have collided or have been fighting, have locked horns or tusks." Her fourth response features "an eruption of some kind, with clouds and volcanic acid spewing over the sides." This is followed by "an eagle in flight." But the essential communication is contained in the seventh response, elicited by a stimulus area that normally provokes "phallic" imagery and associations: "It looks like an explosion of something--a coming up of creation. It looks like a butterfly, a beautiful butterfly, but like it broke loose. It's coming out of its cocoon. Out of eruption comes a work of nature. Looks like it would be all rainbow colors, like Niagra Falls. Out of eruption comes a spray of multicolors."

Clearly, this is not the imagery of a truly depressed woman. These are images given by a woman who is both fascinated and terrified by the powerful "masculine" and alien energies--represented by antlered deer, fighting bulls, eagles and volcanoes--that are eruptive within her. These energies could lead on toward a rebirth (the butterfly emerging from a cocoon) in a more "phallic" masculine form; but rebirth necessarily entails the token death of the established, familiar self, as well as the possibility of combat and destruction (the deer that guard their territory; the bulls that collide and fight). Like anthropologists, psychiatrists are prone to view the older woman in externalized terms, and they typically blame this patient's kind of pain on outward and imposed losses: of beauty, of procreative capacity, of the "mothering role," or of the husband. However, when we explore her unconscious fantasies, we find evidence of eruptive energies that are not consistent with such passive victimization and that are at the same time responsible for the symptoms leading to the glibly rendered diagnosis of "depression."

In this instance, the patient was literally poisoned, in the psychological sense, by her own potential strengths. She treated them as though they were foreign invaders and developed psychological antibodies which--just as physical antigens produce fever--in her case produced agitated, weepy depression. Because of her early life in a family of orientation, which taught her to fear aggression, and because of her marriage to a husband who needs a submissive wife, her crescent energies could not move beyond the eruptive phase, and her shackled aggression turned inward, taking the form of self-punishing symptoms. It was only when she found the reciprocator and facilitator, in the person of the psychotherapist, that her aggression could find a more alloplasmic expression and become available for "sculpting" into more personally and socially useful forms. In effect, the therapist took over and performed a self-function that the patient lacked--that of recognizing and welcoming her own assertiveness--and the therapist demonstrated that function, until the patient could take over and exercise the function for herself.

CONCLUSION: DEVELOPMENT OR VICTIMIZATION?

This example from the ranks of the stricken teaches us that late-onset, postparental female psychopathology can have a base in development, rather than depletion and that the causes are often reversible, rather than (as is commonly proposed) irreversible. By supplying the missing facilitator, the practice of psychotherapy can return the patient to the main sequence of female maturation in later life.

Cases like this teach us that the energies driving later-life female development exist apart from and can be studied apart from the social roles and stations into which they are finally articulated. To repeat, the clear and obvious advance of most postparental women across the most varied social settings is a culture-free phenomenon, one that can generate psychopathology as well as useful role adoptions. And while the culture-centered view can help us to understand socially normal outcomes of development, it is not useful in helping us to understand the abnormal outcomes that result when phenotypic energies do not achieve the sculptured phase, and are sidetracked into pathology. In addition, a view of the older woman that ignores her developmental potentials has its own pathogenic effect: when the more hopeful, growth-centered possibilities of the older woman are ignored by social scientists, the "depletion" view, the denigrating view of the older woman as perpetual victim, becomes paramount.

NOTES

[1] Speaking as an outsider, it seems to me that the anthropologist's exclusive focus on cultural variables has a stultifying effect. Anthropology is potentially the most creative and enlightening of the social sciences, and we are all losers when it locks itself ever more firmly into a discipline-centered, defensive parochialism.

² The dialectic relationship between the surgent and the socializing aspects of development shapes two major advances: the formation of self-boundaries and the acquisition of language--both equally vital to individual growth and social continuity. Thus culture may dictate, for the child, the qualities and properties of the social *other,* but the readiness on the child's part to create self-other distinctions, to recognize the social other whatever his properties, constitutes a psychosocial and developmental advance of vast consequence, one that *must* take place in all viable cultures. By the same token, culture dictates the content and syntax of language; but it does not dictate the child's developmentally given readiness to actively *seek out* language and to turn parents into language providers.

³ For additional examples for each of the patterns and for the ethnographic sources, the reader is advised to contact the author.

⁴ Certain crucial similarities among primates allow us to make what are more than accidental interspecies comparisons. Most significantly, human and nonhuman primates have in common the long dependency and vulnerability of infancy and childhood. In both the ape and human cases, the primate infant may have--as we are beginning to discover--some developed communicative and social skills, but it is almost completely lacking in the skills that ensure physical security: it cannot move in any coherent fashion, it cannot remove itself from danger, and it can barely secure its own milk. Among the lower primates, the infant has, at best, the guaranteed capacity to cling, during the first months of life, to its mother's fur. Of necessity then, adult primates-- whether human or otherwise--have in common an intense concern with parenting.

⁵ By the same token, the age distribution of "beggarly man, authoritative woman" themes does not reflect the influence of Druze age-graded prescriptions. The Druze are a fiercely independent people, and it is not proper for a man to beg-- particularly from a woman--at any age.

⁶ Like other behavioral scientists (including developmental psychologists), anthropologists make imperial claims for the cultural variables that they "own"; and they will claim that these are the independent variables that ultimately account for all major patterns of human behavior. By definition, the sculpted phase involves the final fitting in and adaptation of the individual to prior role formats; and the anthropologist who has not observed the connections between the eruptive

and sculptured phases can always claim that the latter outcome was "created" by prior social opportunity rather than by prior, intrinsic development. However, such ad hoc, culture-based interpretations become less plausible and more cumbersome with each fresh observation from another culture and another independent observer.

REFERENCES

Gold, Sue Schlenker
  1960   A Cross-Cultural Comparison of Changes with Aging in Husband-Wife Roles.   Student Journal of Human Development (University of Chicago) 1:11-15.

Gutmann, David
  1975   Parenthood: A Key to the Comparative Study of the Life Cycle.   *In* Life Span Developmental Psychology: Normative Life Crises.   N. Datan and I. Ginsberg, eds. pp. 167-184.   New York: Academic Press.

Hrdy, Sarah
  1981   "Nepotists" and "Altruists": The Behavior of Old Females among Macaques and Langur Monkeys.   *In* Other Ways of Growing Old: Anthropological Perspectives.   P. Amoss and S. Harrell, eds. pp. 59-76.   Stanford, Calif.: Stanford University Press.

Partch, Jennifer
  1978   The Socializing Role of Post-reproductive Rhesus Macaque Females.   Paper presented at the 47th Annual Meeting of the American Association of Physical Anthropologists, Toronto.   (Cited in Hrdy 1981.)

INDEX